RACIAL PROFILING:
ISSUES, DATA AND ANALYSES

RACIAL PROFILING: ISSUES, DATA AND ANALYSES

STEVEN J. MUFFLER
EDITOR

Nova Science Publishers, Inc.
New York

NOTICE TO THE READER

The Publisher has taken reasonable care in the preparation of this book, but makes no expressed or implied warranty of any kind and assumes no responsibility for any errors or omissions. No liability is assumed for incidental or consequential damages in connection with or arising out of information contained in this book. The Publisher shall not be liable for any special, consequential, or exemplary damages resulting, in whole or in part, from the readers' use of, or reliance upon, this material.

Independent verification should be sought for any data, advice or recommendations contained in this book. In addition, no responsibility is assumed by the publisher for any injury and/or damage to persons or property arising from any methods, products, instructions, ideas or otherwise contained in this publication.

This publication is designed to provide accurate and authoritative information with regard to the subject matter cover herein. It is sold with the clear understanding that the Publisher is not engaged in rendering legal or any other professional services. If legal, medical or any other expert assistance is required, the services of a competent person should be sought. FROM A DECLARATION OF PARTICIPANTS JOINTLY ADOPTED BY A COMMITTEE OF THE AMERICAN BAR ASSOCIATION AND A COMMITTEE OF PUBLISHERS.

Library of Congress Cataloging-in-Publication Data
Available upon request

ISBN 1-59454-547-2

Published by Nova Science Publishers, Inc. ✦New York

CONTENTS

PREFACE

In recent years, racial profiling has drawn the attention of state and federal governments. In this book, racial profiling is defined as the practice of targeting individuals for police or security interdiction, detention, or other disparate treatment based primarily on their race, ethnicity, or national origin in the belief that certain minority groups are more likely to engage in unlawful behavior. Assertions that law enforcement personnel at all levels unfairly target certain racial and ethnic groups, particularly but not exclusively for traffic stops and searches, have raised concerns about violations of the Constitution. The major debate on racial profiling centers on whether the practice should be prohibited entirely and whether data on traffic stops and searches should be collected to determine if the practice is occurring. This book gathers presents the major issues, available data, and analyses important to understanding on the most dangerous and divisive practices of our time.

Chapter 1 analyzes the debate and focuses on legislative proposals on racial profiling before Congress. Two bills relating to racial profiling, H.R. 2364 (Title II) and S. 16 (Title V) have been introduced in the 108th Congress and have been referred to their respective committees of jurisdiction. Also, this chapter analyzes legislative proposals in the 107th Congress (H.R. 905, H.R. 1407, H.R. 1778, H.R. 1996, H.R. 2074/S. 989, S. 19, S. 799, and S. 2114). They were varied and included provisions that would have: defined racial profiling, prohibited the practice, required a study of statistical data and/or a report of traffic stops, set data collection standards, established penalties for noncompliance, furnished funding for grants, provided for education and training, and held law enforcement personnel legally accountable for engaging in racial profiling. Both the Senate Subcommittee on the Constitution, Federalism and Property Rights and the House Committee on Government Reform held hearings on racial profiling during the 107th Congress. There has been some recent presidential involvement on the issue of racial profiling. On June 18, 2003, President George W. Bush issued guidelines to bar federal agents from using race or ethnicity in routine investigations. The guidelines, however, exempt investigations of terrorism and other national security concerns. In 2001, the President instructed the Attorney General to review the role of race in the decision of federal law enforcement authorities to conduct stops and searches, to work with Congress on procedures for data collection, and to cooperate with state and local law enforcement to assess the extent and content of those procedures. Two federal agencies, the Bureau of Justice Statistics and the General Accounting Office, have researched and published their findings on aspects of racial profiling. The major recommendations for determining if racial profiling is occurring are to collect data on stops and searches by law enforcement officers and to use technology as an aid in detecting the practice. The collection of data is controversial, leading to questions about what to collect, how to collect it, who is to analyze it, where the data would be housed and for how long, what the collection of statistics would accomplish, and whether its collection is an invasion of privacy.

Racial profiling occurs when a police officer selectively focuses on a person's race, and subsequently follows, harasses, detains or arrests the individual. Broadly construed, racial profiling can be viewed as targeted policing efforts against minority groups. Recent studies in San Diego, New Jersey and other locations have presented evidence to suggest that minorities are disproportionately stopped and searched by police. However, these studies don't tell us how or why the police disproportionately stop minorities; they merely reaffirm what many people have claimed for years. In chapter 2, the authors conducted a field study of police decisions to stop motorists. They went on ride-alongs with officers from various police agencies throughout Southern California. The major finding from this study is that while race is often a factor when police officers initiate stops, other factors are just as important, if not more significant at times, when determining whom the police will stop. The authors concluded that many officers use a "thug profile" rather than just a race profile. The "thug profile" consists of, but is not limited to: type of vehicle, location, clothing, time of day, demeanor and race. Racial profiling is a fact of life in America. It must be addressed. We've all seen the stories about how blacks often have difficulties hailing a taxi cab, renting apartments, getting loans, buying cars, etc. Yet, for some unknown reason, we expect the police to perform their duties within the limits of the law unfettered by the cultural and political biases within which they exist. Ultimately the issue comes down to how we want the police to do their job. If we support proactive policing, then racial profiling will continue to exist. Reactive policing may be the only solution.

The disparate impact of our criminal justice system on racial and ethnic minorities raises serious questions about the way law enforcement officials, prosecutors, courts, and juries go about their jobs as described in chapter 3. Whatever their cause, racial disparities are stark throughout the system. At current levels of incarceration, for example, newborn black males have a greater than 1-in-4 chance of serving prison time, while Latinos have a 1-in-6 chance and whites 1-in-23. The undesirable and illegal consequence results when police officers use race or ethnicity as a deciding factor in focusing suspicion on a particular individual. Because most jurisdictions lack sufficient data on police stops to accurately assess the problem, suspicion and controversy continue to swirl around racial profiling.

Racial profiling sends the dehumanizing message to our citizens that they are judged by the color of their skin and harms the criminal justice system by eviscerating the trust that is necessary if law enforcement is to effectively protect our communities. Chapter 4 focuses on the current administration's policies concerning racial profiling.

"Racial profiling" at its core concerns the invidious use of race or ethnicity as a criterion in conducting stops, searches and other law enforcement investigative procedures. It is premised on the erroneous assumption that any particular individual of one race or ethnicity is more likely to engage in misconduct than any particular individual of another race or ethnicity. As reported in chapter 5, racial profiling in law enforcement is not merely wrong, but also ineffective. Race-based assumptions in law enforcement perpetuate negative racial stereotypes that are harmful to our rich and diverse democracy, and materially impair our efforts to maintain a fair and just society.

For the past 8 years, we have seen a steady decline in the crime rate in nearly every community in America. Even with the advances in crime prevention and law enforcement, however, there are instances in which distrust and tensions between the police and the community are high, and these tensions affect all aspects of the criminal justice system. One of the major causes of this mistrust is the controversial practice of racial profiling. The guarantee to all persons of equal protection under the law is one of the most fundamental principles of our democratic society. Law enforcement officers should not endorse or act upon stereotypes, attitudes, or beliefs that a person's race, ethnicity, or national origin increases that person's general propensity to act unlawfully. There is no tradeoff between effective law enforcement and protection of the civil rights of all Americans; we can and must have both. One of the ways that law enforcement agencies are addressing concerns and allegations regarding discriminatory policing is through data collection. By collecting information on the nature, character, and demographics of police enforcement practices, we enhance our ability to assess the appropriate application of the authority and broad discretion entrusted to law enforcement. In June 1999, when President Clinton and U.S. Attorney General Reno convened the conference *Strengthening Police-Community Relationships*, only a few jurisdictions—including San Diego, San Jose, and the state of North Carolina—had voluntarily agreed to collect traffic-stop data. When a followup meeting on racial profiling and data collection was held this past February, more than 100 jurisdictions indicated that they had plans to collect data on traffic or pedestrian stops. To encourage voluntary data collection, the U.S. Department of Justice set about developing a resource guide on this subject. Chapter 6 provides an overview of the nature of racial profiling; a description of data collection and its purpose; current activities in California, New Jersey, North Carolina, and Great Britain; and recommendations for the future. Our hope is that this resource guide will assist jurisdictions in developing and implementing their own data collection systems. Our ultimate goals are to restore trust in the police and to ensure that all citizens are treated equally by law enforcement officers.

Chapter 7 found no comprehensive, nationwide source of information that could be used to determine whether race has been a key factor in motorist stops. The available research is currently limited to five quantitative analyses that contain methodological limitations; they have not provided conclusive empirical data from a social science standpoint to determine the extent to which racial profiling may occur. However, the cumulative results of the analyses indicate that in relation to the populations to which they were compared, African American motorists in particular, and minority motorists in general, were proportionately more likely than whites to be stopped on the roadways studied. Data on the relative proportion of minorities stopped on a roadway, however, is only part of the information needed from a social science perspective to assess the degree to which racial profiling may occur.

In: Racial Profiling: Issues, Data and Analyses
Editor: Steven J. Muffler, pp. 1-23

Chapter 1

RACIAL PROFILING: ISSUES AND FEDERAL LEGISLATIVE PROPOSALS AND OPTIONS[*]

Garrine P. Laney

ABSTRACT

In recent years, racial profiling has drawn the attention of state and federal governments. In this article, racial profiling is defined as the practice of targeting individuals for police or security interdiction, detention, or other disparate treatment based primarily on their race or ethnicity, in the belief that certain minority groups are more likely to engage in unlawful behavior. Assertions that law enforcement personnel at all levels unfairly target certain racial and ethnic groups, particularly but not exclusively for traffic stops and searches, have raised concerns about violations of the Constitution. Major debate on racial profiling centers on whether the practice should be prohibited entirely and whether data on traffic stops and searches should be collected to determine if the practice is occurring.

This chapter analyzes the debate and focuses on legislative proposals on racial profiling before Congress. Two bills relating to racial profiling, H.R. 2364 (Title II) and S. 16 (Title V) have been introduced in the 108th Congress and have been referred to their respective committees of jurisdiction. Also, this chapter analyzes legislative proposals in the 107th Congress (H.R. 905, H.R. 1407, H.R. 1778, H.R. 1996, H.R. 2074/S. 989, S. 19, S. 799, and S. 2114). They were varied and included provisions that would have: defined racial profiling, prohibited the practice, required a study of statistical data and/or a report of traffic stops, set data collection standards, established penalties for noncompliance, furnished funding for grants, provided for education and training, and held law enforcement personnel legally accountable for engaging in racial profiling. Both the Senate Subcommittee on the Constitution, Federalism and Property Rights and the House Committee on Government Reform held hearings on racial profiling during the 107th Congress.

---

[*] Excerpted from CRS Report RL32231 dated February 17, 2004.

There has been some recent presidential involvement on the issue of racial profiling. On June 18, 2003, President George W. Bush issued guidelines to bar federal agents from using race or ethnicity in routine investigations. The guidelines, however, exempt investigations of terrorism and other national security concerns. In 2001, the President instructed the Attorney General to review the role of race in the decision of federal law enforcement authorities to conduct stops and searches, to work with Congress on procedures for data collection, and to cooperate with state and local law enforcement to assess the extent and content of those procedures. Two federal agencies, the Bureau of Justice Statistics and the General Accounting Office, have researched and published their findings on aspects of racial profiling.

The major recommendations for determining if racial profiling is occurring are to collect data on stops and searches by law enforcement officers and to use technology as an aid in detecting the practice. The collection of data is controversial, leading to questions about what to collect, how to collect it, who is to analyze it, where the data would be housed and for how long, what the collection of statistics would accomplish, and whether its collection is an invasion of privacy.

BACKGROUND

There are many definitions of racial profiling. For this report, racial profiling is defined as the practice of targeting individuals for police or security interdiction, detention or other disparate treatment based primarily on their race or ethnicity in the belief that certain minority groups are more likely to engage in unlawful behavior.[1] For years, members of African-American and Hispanic communities have complained that they were victims of profiling. The circumstances under which profiling may occur vary. For example, allegations of racial profiling have been aimed at security personnel of department stores who suspect African American shoppers of stealing. Traditionally, however, accusations of racial profiling have resulted from encounters at traffic stops and have been directed at local and state police. The impetus for police traffic stops and searches may be the perception that members of certain minority groups are more likely to be engaged in the illicit drug trade. In searching for illicit drugs, U.S. Customs agents and Border Patrol officers have been charged with racial profiling as well.[2] With the racial and ethnic makeup of the nation changing and after the terrorist attacks of September 11, 2001, other groups, such as Arab Americans, Muslims, and Asian Americans, have joined the call for an end to racial profiling.

Anecdotal accounts of racial profiling have been the basis for most complaints against the practice. Individuals reportedly have been subjected to racial profiling while walking, shopping and driving. Sometimes black individuals are stopped and questioned by police if, in the perception of the police, these individuals are walking in the "wrong" neighborhood; i.e., a white neighborhood or upper-middle class neighborhood.[3] Other points of contact with law enforcement personnel that lead to allegations of racial profiling are airports and border points of entry. More often, however, charges of racial profiling occur when a person is driving a vehicle and the driver or passengers of a car, based on the judgment of law enforcement personnel, do not apparently "fit" the type of vehicle they occupy; that is, they may be, for instance, a young black male in an expensive car.

Both S. 16 (Title V) and H.R. 2364 (Title II) have been introduced in the 108th Congress and contain provisions relating to racial profiling.[4] S. 16 (Daschle), an omnibus civil rights bill, includes provisions that would express a sense of the Senate that Congress enact legislation banning racial profiling and requiring law enforcement at the federal, state, and local levels to prevent the practice. H.R. 2364 (Engel), among other provisions, would amend provisions of the Immigration and Nationality Act by establishing a Visa Fairness Commission to collect data on racial profiling by American embassies and U.S. border and immigration inspectors.

Because a number of bills that were introduced in the 107th Congress offered a variety of approaches to addressing racial profiling, this report provides a detailed analysis of them. Some of these legislative proposals were directed specifically at certain federal agencies, others at state law enforcement officials. This report examines racial profiling and legislative proposals that affect law enforcement efforts.[5]

POLICY QUESTIONS

Racial profiling is a complex and controversial issue. In addressing the matter of racial profiling, whether practiced at the state and local levels or in federal agencies to combat illicit drug activity or terrorism, Congress is faced with a number of questions. Some of these questions are listed here, followed by a more detailed section on "Arguments on Racial Profiling."

How Should Profiling Be Defined?

There are many definitions of profiling, with federal agencies, states, local jurisdictions, and citizens all offering their own definitions; some are more comprehensive than others. Racial profiling may be defined as all law enforcement activities that are initiated solely on the basis of race, while another definition may focus only on the context of vehicle stops. The term racial profiling can overemphasize race, leaving out ethnicity, gender or other considerations as factors that influence law enforcement action.

Is Racial Profiling a Common or an Exceptional Practice?

Studies that have attempted to measure the extent of racial profiling have been for the most part methodologically flawed. While some studies have shown that minorities are disproportionately subjected to traffic stops and searches, a General Accounting Office (GAO) report concluded that the studies did not distinguish between the seriousness of traffic violations nor did the analyses provide information on which traffic violations, if any, were more likely to result in a stop.[6] GAO suggests that analyses examine whether different groups may have been at different levels of risk for being stopped because their rates and/or severity of violating traffic laws differed. In other words, some racial/ethnic groups may commit more traffic violations such as speeding, tailgating, or having faulty equipment than other groups.

Should Data on Stops and Searches Be Collected?

Supporters of data collection maintain that it can help determine if racial profiling is occurring, can assist law enforcement agencies in becoming more effective in identifying problems, and can indicate to the community a level of commitment to unbiased policing. Opponents of data collection believe that it is not cost effective. In addition, they warn that it can harm relations between police and the community because despite the limitations of data collection, there may be a public perception that conclusions drawn from analyses of these data are valid. Sometimes, law enforcement personnel and departments are unfairly disparaged based on data collection studies. Some feel the nature and extent of racial profiling cannot be determined by using social science methods.

Who Should Be Held Accountable When Racial Profiling is Practiced and How?

Some feel that ultimately, the head of an agency or department is responsible for establishing policies and procedures, not staff. In this view, the top administrator must set the cultural tone of the agency in word and action. Checks and balances and a review system can be established to ensure that laws, policies, and procedures relating to racial profiling are carried out at all levels in an acceptable fashion. They suggest that those who violate established rules of operation should be provided training, should be monitored in the future, and if they continue to disregard official policy and procedure, then they should be discharged from service.

Others believe that to eliminate racial profiling, there should be more severe consequences for individuals who practice it, as well as their supervisors. They want law enforcement agents and managers subject to civil suit. Opponents of lawsuits believe this is not a good way to solve the problem. They predict it will exacerbate tensions between police and minority communities and will cause valuable resources to be used defending law enforcement rather than battling crime.

Should Technology Be Used as a Tool in Eliminating Racial Profiling?

It is generally accepted that technology can play an important role in identifying and eliminating racial profiling. Concerns, however, have been expressed about the sole reliance on technological devices to record traffic stop and passenger search occurrences. Some argue that the use of audio/video technological devices invades the privacy of citizens.

What Data Should be Collected?

Elements suggested for documentation in data collection include race; ethnicity; location of the traffic stop; reasons for the stop; searches conducted, if any; consent of vehicle occupants to the search; identification and confiscation of contraband; and action taken by law enforcement such as an arrest or issuance of a ticket. In addition, at issue is uniform data collection on traffic stops. Some feel it is sufficient to collect data only on certain law enforcement actions, e.g. arrests and issuance of tickets. Others argue that in order to accurately assess racial profiling, data on all traffic stops must be recorded.

Who Will Analyze the Data Collected?

The same data can yield very different interpretations depending upon who analyzes it. Some suggest that the collected data be analyzed not by affected law enforcement departments or agencies but by an outside group or persons with recognized training in statistics design and data analysis. In this view, objective analysts would more likely be associated with a college or university or an independent social science research firm.

How Should Collected Data be Used?

Some question the need and appropriateness for the mass collection of racial and ethnic data. Their data collection concerns are citizen privacy, access to the material, protection of the identity of individuals and law enforcement agents, and maintenance, storage, and final disposition of the data.

Who Will Provide Funds for the Cost of Purchasing, Maintaining, and Storing Technological Equipment and Data Collected?

Video technological devices are expensive. They are costly to purchase, require maintenance, and need to be stored. Who will bear the cost of acquiring and maintaining this equipment?

Is Federal Racial Profiling Legislation Needed?

Many argue that racial profiling is largely a state and local problem and believe there is no good reason for ordering federal law enforcement agencies to record the race and origin of everybody they question, search, or arrest. They point to the current activity on racial profiling at both the state and local levels as an adequate response to the problem, to the extent that there is a problem.[7] Some believe that law enforcement personnel are more than capable of correcting racial profiling and want to do so. Further, they claim that not enough is known about the issue for Congress to offer broad solutions that affect states and localities. Others question whether, even at the federal level, legislation is needed to eliminate racial profiling in the executive branch, maintaining that if a federal agency is engaging in the practice, agency administrators can handle the problem by ordering an investigation and taking corrective action as needed.

Supporters of federal action respond by pointing out that there are many approaches to correcting racial profiling and that this creates a problem when comparative studies of different jurisdictions and agencies are made to determine the nationwide extent of the practice. GAO reported difficulty in determining whether race had been a primary factor in motorist stops because the studies it examined had methodological limitations that subjected conclusions drawn from this data to serious challenge. Trying to compare studies was like comparing apples and nuts because of problems with data components. Others argue that states and localities use different strategies and policies to address racial profiling. Consequently, an individual's protection against this "unconstitutional practice" varies depending upon the jurisdiction in which the stop or profiling incident happens. According to this argument, provisions of the Constitution should uniformly protect citizens against racial profiling in all areas of the United States and federal legislation would ensure that this occurs. Further, federal legislation requiring uniform data collection standards could offer a comprehensive response to racial profiling and would allow a more valid comparison of studies of racial profiling in different jurisdictions or agencies to be conducted.[8]

ARGUMENTS ON RACIAL PROFILING

Law enforcement has been accused of practicing racial profiling in the pursuit of two major goals — to prevent illicit drug activity and to stop terrorists. In the debate on the appropriateness of profiling, some make a distinction between the two. According to polls conducted since 1999, the vast majority of Americans disapprove of racial profiling when traffic stops are involved.[9] When questioned about racial profiling to identify terrorists, however, their response was quite different. A majority of Americans polled approved of racial profiling to intercept terrorists. Because the terrorist attackers of September 11, 2001 were identified as Arabs, many have asked for increased scrutiny of them. A majority of Americans polled favored "requiring Arabs, including those who are U.S. citizens, to undergo special, more intensive security checks before boarding U.S. airplanes." Nearly 50% of persons responding to one poll reportedly would support "requiring Arabs, including those who are U.S. citizens, to carry a special I.D."[10] According to another national poll of June 2002, conducted by Opinion Dynamics, 54 percent of respondents approved of "using racial profiling to screen Arab-male airline passengers," while 34 percent disapproved of the practice. A more recent national poll, conducted between October 21 and November 25, 2002 by Cornell University, indicated that 68 percent of respondents supported racial profiling as a tool to fight terrorism.[11] Some argue that an increased scrutiny of Arabs is justified because the public safety issue should be the major factor in deciding whether to profile any group. According to this view, when practiced "politely and respectfully," racial profiling may be a vital component of efforts to prevent mass murder, as occurred with the terrorist attacks;[12] thus, the advantages of using racial profiling might outweigh the disadvantages.

Identifying an Arab by physical traits, however, is troublesome. Of the estimated 3 million Arab Americans in the United States, 63% were born in this country. Their appearance can vary from blond hair, white skin, and blue eyes to dark hair, dark skin, and brown eyes. Although they are often perceived as Muslims, the majority of Arab Americans are reportedly Christian. Of the estimated 6 million Muslims in the United States, the largest group is African American, not Arab according to *The Economist* magazine.[13]

Concern about terrorism also has prompted calls for profiling persons entering this country from a specific geographic region of the world, i.e., persons whose national origin is the Middle East. Proponents of this practice argue that the lack of technological means to detect bombs and long delays caused by searching the luggage of passengers make effective screening nearly impossible. Also, it is argued that were a policy of profiling by national origin in place on September 11, 2001, all 19 of the terrorists might have been intercepted. Those who oppose this strategy point out that Muslims and people of Middle Eastern descent have migrated to countries around the world. Terrorists of Middle Eastern background could come from Germany, France, or any country outside of the Middle Eastern region. In addition, the largest population of Muslims (about 200 million) lives in Indonesia. They suggest that, in searching for terrorists, the emphasis should be on suspicious behavior.[14]

Some believe that racial profiling has been shown to be ineffective when used to identify persons involved in illicit drug activities. In support of their argument, they offer an *Orlando Sentinel* investigation of vehicle stops on an interstate highway in Florida. While nearly 70% of motorists stopped were black or Hispanic, only 5% of the drivers on that highway were minorities. Of the 1,000 stops police made, nine resulted in a traffic ticket. As another example, they point to the New York Attorney General's report that found stop-and-frisk tactics on minorities were less likely to lead to arrests than stops of whites.[15] Critics of using racial profiling to combat illicit drugs argue that despite rising rates of arrest and incarceration and record drug seizures, drugs are more available than ever. They also point to the difficulty in visibly discerning race or ethnicity.[16]

Many civil rights advocates charge that racial profiling violates individuals' constitutional rights, specifically, the Fourth (protects against unreasonable searches and seizures), Fifth (protects against discrimination by federal law enforcement officers that is based on race, ethnicity, or national origin) and the Fourteenth Amendment (provides security and equal protection of the laws).[17]

Spokesmen for various law enforcement groups have commented on the practice of racial profiling. Recognizing the central and difficult position that law enforcement officers occupy in balancing individual rights and public safety in basic enforcement, the International Association of Chiefs of Police (IACP) states that if officers are perceived as biased in their actions, it can foster mistrust and suspicion among some members of the public. According to the IACP, those persons who mistrust law enforcement officers often believe that police officers violate rather than protect their civil rights. IACP states that although this perception is inaccurate, it damages efforts to reduce crime because law enforcement agencies need community support to solve crimes. Therefore, to build confidence in law enforcement, the IACP opposes "biased enforcement practices."[18]

The National Organization of Black Law Enforcement Executives (NOBLE), another law enforcement group, opposes racial profiling whether it is used to fight illicit drugs or terrorism on the grounds that it threatens our democratic way of life. Pointing to historical abuses that have occurred under the umbrella of national security (for example, the internment of Japanese-Americans in World War II), a spokesman for NOBLE rejects justification of the practice on those grounds. Arguing further that people, not a race or ethnicity, commit crime, he questions linking an entire group of people to crime based on the behavior of a few of that race or ethnicity. He uses the following example: Blacks are responsible for 80% of reported crime in a town, but that doesn't mean that 80% of blacks commit crime. More likely, 5% of the town's black population is responsible for the high crime rate. In addition, he states that fear is the driving force behind demands for ethnic and racial profiling, whether it is fear of crime and violence or fear of another terrorist attack, and that "[b]ias, prejudice and racism only add fuel to the fire of fear."[19] NOBLE believes that over the past few years law enforcement has lost the respect and confidence of the public and that the heroic response of public safety officers to the terrorist attacks offers a second chance to restore that trust and achieve national unity. Therefore, it maintains that we should learn from our historical mistakes and be creative in addressing national challenges.

The Fraternal Order of Police (FOP) opposes the practice of stopping someone based solely on race because it is wrong to believe a person is a criminal based on the color of his or her skin. According to a spokesman for FOP, "racism is never a legitimate law enforcement tool."[20] He also states that, "Statistically, minorities have a greater chance of being crime victims because crimes occur more frequently in areas with a large minority population. Good policing means going after criminals and patrolling areas where crimes are committed. This is good police work — not racism."[21]

COLLECTION OF TRAFFIC STOP DATA

Collecting data that might help in evaluating the relationship between race and traffic stops by law enforcement officers has been offered as the primary way of determining whether racial profiling is practiced. But analyzing data on the nature, character, and demographics of law enforcement practices to determine racial profiling is very complex. A major problem with data collection is how to analyze data once collected, since there are no national data-collection standards or guidelines. There is no agreement on what racial profiling is or how to measure it. For instance, if blacks comprise 15% of a city's population but 20% of the traffic stops, is that evidence of racial profiling; what if traffic stops for them were 30%? Should the number of searches conducted at traffic stops be recorded? Not only what information is collected but where it is collected is relevant. Should residential populations or driving populations be used? Are the population data used current; census data may be 10 years old and may poorly reflect the changing populations in urban areas with increased mobility and immigration. Data collected in an urban area, with a dense, poor minority population with few car owners, will likely result in very different findings than data collected on an interstate highway where the driving population is likely to be more diverse.

The same data can result in divergent interpretations. The challenge, according to Harvard Law School professor Margo Schlanger, is that legally it is very difficult to use statistics to determine a police officer's motivation. Officers can respond to statistics revealing that a high percentage of blacks is indeed stopped and searched by saying that there are just more blacks who do suspicious things. Statistics alone cannot prove intentional discrimination.[22]

When first proposed, the International Association of Chiefs of Police and the Grand Lodge Fraternal Order of Police opposed the collection of data. Three police chiefs charged the methodology was flawed that was used in an ACLU report which found their departments practiced racial profiling.[23] Some groups deny that racial profiling occurs, stating that police are using professional crime-stopping methods. Others express concerns that the traffic-stop data proposals would burden already overworked police forces and would run counter to police training efforts to teach officers not to consider race.[24] Another argument of opponents is that resources might be better used fighting racially biased policing and the perceptions thereof rather than collecting data.[25] In 1999, the executive director of the Fraternal Order of Police said, "It [collecting data] shortcuts meaningful dialogue between the police and the community. If anything, it exacerbates the gulf."[26]

Some oppose the federal government's mass collection of racial and ethnic data "without good reason"[27] on the grounds that it is an invasion of privacy. Proponents of this view state that when police stop people because of racial or ethnic characteristics and not what they have done, it is both wrong and bad police work. To them, the objective of wanting to do something about racial profiling is too vague to merit intrusion in "our shrinking zone of privacy."[28] They also question the ultimate use of these data.

By 2000, however, the International Association of Chiefs of Police had joined other groups, such as NOBLE, in support of legislation requiring collection of traffic-stop data. NOBLE supports data collection citing the following reasons: to build trust between law enforcement and minority communities; to identify and stop inappropriate police conduct; to improve police productivity by enabling police to use the most effective stop-and-search practices by assessing and studying the types of stops, time spent on them, and the results of such stops; to reenforce to officers that racial profiling is not consistent with effective policing and with equal protection under the law; to identify practices that some officers may be using subconsciously; and to assist law enforcement departments in developing strategic ways to use the power at their disposal.[29]

Yet many police remain uncomfortable with data collection. They fear that "statistics fuel allegations of racism without offering clear solutions."[30] Recognizing the complexity of data collection and the potential to abuse interpretation of statistics, the International Association of Chiefs of Police issued another statement in 2001 qualifying its endorsement of data collection. The Association will only support data collection legislation "that ensures that an impartial and scientifically sound methodology will be used for evaluating collected data."[31]

While some governmental agencies and private groups have collected data that suggest minorities are disproportionately the subject of routine traffic stops, many law enforcement organizations challenge these findings. To demonstrate how law enforcement results can be misinterpreted, FOP representative Steven Young cited an experience of the Arlington County, Virginia Police Department. In response to demands from the black community for increased enforcement against drug dealers in Arlington County, the police instituted aggressive motor-vehicle checks and other actions to make dealers uncomfortable in the neighborhood. Their efforts, however, resulted in increased arrests of minorities and, ironically, left the police department vulnerable to accusations of disproportionately arresting minorities. He argued that "To use statistical data without an adequately sophisticated benchmark for analysis is bad policy."[32]

Efforts to rely on comprehensive data, rather than anecdotal accounts, to determine if racial profiling occurs in federal, state, or local law enforcement have proved troubling, primarily because the lack of *uniform data components* makes the validity of comparing different studies questionable. Both of two federally sponsored studies conducted by the Bureau of Justice Statistics (BJS) of the Department of Justice (DOJ) and the United States General Accounting Office (GAO) found limitations in data components.

BUREAU OF JUSTICE STATISTICS STUDY

In 1999, the Bureau of Justice Statistics conducted a national survey of 19.3 million people, aged 16 and older. The survey examined how often and under what circumstances contact and traffic stops between police and U.S. residents occurred. Key data elements included the number of licensed drivers, vehicle stops and searches, and race or ethnicity. In the survey, police searched the driver, the vehicle or both for drugs, alcohol, stolen property or other evidence of criminal wrongdoing. Published in February 2001, the survey indicated that blacks were disproportionately likely to be stopped at least once by police. On the other hand, Hispanics were less likely to be stopped by police (**Table 1**). Both black and Hispanic drivers/vehicles, Yet many police remain uncomfortable with data collection. They fear that "statistics fuel allegations of racism without offering clear solutions."[30] Recognizing the complexity of data collection and the potential to abuse interpretation of statistics, the International Association of Chiefs of Police issued another statement in 2001 qualifying its endorsement of data collection. The Association will only support data collection legislation "that ensures that an impartial and scientifically sound methodology will be used for evaluating collected data."[31]

While some governmental agencies and private groups have collected data that suggest minorities are disproportionately the subject of routine traffic stops, many law enforcement organizations challenge these findings. To demonstrate how law enforcement results can be misinterpreted, FOP representative Steven Young cited an experience of the Arlington County, Virginia Police Department. In response to demands from the black community for increased enforcement against drug dealers in Arlington County, the police instituted aggressive motor-vehicle checks and other actions to make dealers uncomfortable in the neighborhood. Their efforts, however, resulted in increased arrests of minorities and, ironically, left the police department vulnerable to accusations of disproportionately arresting minorities. He argued that "To use statistical data without an adequately sophisticated benchmark for analysis is bad policy."[32]

**Table 1. Percentage of Licensed Drivers by Race/Ethnicity
Who Were Stopped at Least Once: Survey Results**

Race/ethnicity	Number with driver's license	Percent of licensed drivers	Percent of licensed drivers stopped at least once
Black	18,134,397	9.8	11.6
White	142,767,917	76.8	77.0
Hispanic	18,298,101	9.8	8.4
Other races	6,708,204	3.6	3.0
Total	186,322,014	100.0	100.0

Source: U.S. Department of Justice, Bureau of Justice Statistics, Contacts between Police and the Public, Findings from the 1999 National Survey, by Patrick A. Langan, et al., (Washington: Feb. 2001), p. 13.

Efforts to rely on comprehensive data, rather than anecdotal accounts, to determine if racial profiling occurs in federal, state, or local law enforcement have proved troubling, primarily because the lack of *uniform data components* makes the validity of comparing different studies questionable. Both of two federally sponsored studies conducted by the Bureau of Justice Statistics (BJS) of the Department of Justice (DOJ) and the United States General Accounting Office (GAO) found limitations in data components.

BUREAU OF JUSTICE STATISTICS STUDY

In 1999, the Bureau of Justice Statistics conducted a national survey of 19.3 million people, aged 16 and older. The survey examined how often and under what circumstances contact and traffic stops between police and U.S. residents occurred. Key data elements included the number of licensed drivers, vehicle stops and searches, and race or ethnicity. In the survey, police searched the driver, the vehicle or both for drugs, alcohol, stolen property or other evidence of criminal wrongdoing. Published in February 2001, the survey indicated that blacks were disproportionately likely to be stopped at least once by police. On the other hand, Hispanics were less likely to be stopped by police (**Table 1**). Both black and Hispanic drivers/vehicles, however, were disproportionately searched by police relative to their numbers of licensed drivers. White drivers/vehicles had a greater chance of escaping a search (**Table 2**).[33]

Table 2. Percentage of Selected Licensed Drivers by Race/Ethnicity Who Were Searched: Survey Results

Race/ethnicity	Percent licensed drivers stopped at least once	Percent drivers/vehicles searched
Black	11.6%	19.4%
Hispanic	8.4%	14.4%
White	77%	63.2%

Source: U.S. Department of Justice, Bureau of Justice Statistics, Contacts between Police and the Public, Findings from the 1999 National Survey, by Patrick A. Langan, et al., (Washington: Feb. 2001), p. 18.

Although survey results indicated that in 1999 the chance of blacks being stopped at least once was slightly higher than that of whites, these differences do not necessarily mean that law enforcement officers used racial profiling. The survey only provided data on how often people were stopped; it did not address the question of whether blacks were more likely than whites to violate traffic laws. To determine if racial profiling occurs, the survey needed to show both that, all other things being equal, blacks were no more likely than whites to break traffic laws and that law enforcement agents stopped blacks at a higher rate than whites.[34]

GENERAL ACCOUNTING OFFICE REPORT

In response to a congressional request, GAO sought analyses of racial profiling of motorists, as well as federal, state, and local data on motorist stops. On March 13, 2000, GAO reported that it found no comprehensive source of information that could be used to determine if race had been a primary factor in motorist stops. A problem associated with traffic data analysis is the small number of locations studied. Only five quantitative analyses were available and, according to GAO, they were methodologically flawed. GAO stated that these analyses failed to provide conclusive empirical data from a social science standpoint[35] to determine the extent to which racial profiling may have occurred. That is, while the analyses included data on the relative proportion of minorities stopped on a roadway, GAO believes that is only part of the information needed to assess the extent of racial profiling that may have occurred.

The best of the studies that GAO analyzed determined the race of motorists at risk of being stopped and collected information on the number of travelers and traffic violations on specific roads, but even this study did not distinguish between the gravity of different traffic violations. These analyses did not provide information on which traffic violations, if any, were more likely to result in a stop. GAO suggests that analyses fully examine the question of whether different groups may have been at different levels of risk for being stopped because they differed in their rates and/or the severity of traffic law violations. That is, were some groups more likely than others to commit certain traffic violations, such as speeding, tailgating, failing to give a signal when changing lanes, driving without a license or without proper vehicle registration, and equipment violations? Such a consideration might determine if minority groups are stopped at the same rate that they violate traffic laws, and if so, might suggest that group members were stopped for particular traffic violations rather than for race or ethnicity.[36] Despite these limitations, GAO found that in the studies it reviewed, African-American and other minority motorists "were proportionately more likely than whites to be stopped on the roadways studied."[37]

EXECUTIVE ACTION

In recent years, the issue of racial profiling has attracted the attention of both the Clinton and Bush Administrations. In 1999, the Clinton Administration determined that a systematic collection of statistics on traffic stops that tracked the race, ethnicity, and gender of individuals stopped or searched by law enforcement was needed to establish where problems exist and to develop solutions. Therefore, on June 9, 1999, President Clinton issued a memorandum to the Secretary of the Treasury, the Attorney General, and the Secretary of the Interior instructing them to design and implement such a plan within 120 days. They were to provide the President with information on departmental training programs, policies, and practices on using race, ethnicity, and gender in law enforcement activities. After a year, each department was to submit to the Attorney General a summary of the information collected, including complaints lodged by civilians claiming bias by law enforcement based on race, ethnicity, or gender; how complaints were investigated and resolved; and the results of any investigations. In consultation with agency heads, the Attorney General was to report to the

President on an evaluation of the field tests, a plan to broaden the data collection system, and a recommendation on providing the fair administration of law enforcement to all.

In response to the directive, Richard J. Gallo, president of the Federal Law Enforcement Officers Association, stated that, "[f]ederal agencies do not do traffic stops."[38] Clearly, some federal agencies, such as the Bureau of Alcohol, Tobacco and Firearms of the Department of the Treasury and the Federal Bureau of Investigation of DOJ, do address criminal conspiracies and are concerned with long-term investigations rather than spot enforcement. Aware that most police work is performed by state and local agencies, and not the federal government, President Clinton also urged state and local law enforcement agencies to collect data and analyze the results to determine if racial profiling was occurring.[39]

The Bush Administration has not released reports on statistics on traffic stops that were completed during the Clinton Administration. On February 27, 2001, President George W. Bush issued a memorandum to the Attorney General directing him to review the role of race in the decision of federal law enforcement authorities to conduct stops, searches, and other investigative procedures. Further, the President instructed the Attorney General to develop, in concert with Congress, procedures for collecting any relevant data from federal law enforcement agencies and, in cooperation with state and local law enforcement, to assess the extent and nature of those procedures.[40]

Recently, in response to the President's directive on racial profiling, DOJ issued a policy-guidance that bars all federal law enforcement agents from using race or ethnicity in routine investigations. The guidelines, however, exempt investigations that involve terrorism or other national security concerns.[41]

LEGISLATIVE PROPOSALS AND OPTIONS

108th Congress

Two bills, S. 16 and H.R. 2364, have been introduced into the 108th Congress with provisions on racial profiling. Title V of S. 16 would express a sense of the Senate that Congress enact legislation to ban racial profiling and require law enforcement to take steps to prevent the practice at the federal, state and local levels. Title II of H.R. 2364 would establish a Visa Fairness Commission which, in concert with the Director of the Bureau of Citizenship and Immigration Services, would gather empirical data on economic and racial profiling by Consular Affairs Offices in American embassies and by U.S. Customs and immigration inspectors at points of entry into the United States. S. 16 was referred to the Senate Committee on Finance on January 1, 2003; H.R. 2364 was referred to the House Committee on the Judiciary on June 5, 2003.

107th Congress

Multiple proposals for addressing racial profiling were introduced in the 107th Congress, but with the exception of S. 989, no further action was taken on them. The Senate Subcommittee on the Constitution, Federalism, and Property Rights held a hearing on S. 989, the End Racial Profiling Act of 2001, but no further action was taken on it. The bills contained provisions that would have: defined racial profiling, prohibited the practice, established standards that would have included a report on racial profiling, required collection of data, required a study of statistical data, provided for civil suits, provided for a complaint process, required training, and protected the privacy of individuals. Because of the variety and comprehensiveness of legislation on racial profiling that was proposed in the 107th Congress, following are selected provisions and the bills that contained them. (For a tabular presentation of this information, see **Table 3**.)

Definition

The four racial profiling bills that specifically would have defined the term were H.R. 1907, *Racial Profiling Prohibition Act of 2001*; H.R. 2074/S. 989, *End Racial Profiling Act of 2001*; and S. 799, *Reasonable Search Standards Act*. All of these bills would have prohibited a law enforcement officer from relying solely on race, national, or ethnic origin of drivers or passengers in deciding which individuals to subject to routine investigatory activities. Only S. 799 would have added the sexual orientation of an individual to this list of prohibited factors.

Prohibition of Racial Profiling

The following bills contained provisions that specifically would have prohibited a law enforcement agent or law enforcement agency from practicing racial profiling: H.R. 965, H.R. 1907, H.R. 1996, H.R. 2074/S. 989, and S. 799. Both H.R. 965 and H.R. 1907 would have required a state to adopt and enforce standards that would have prohibited state law enforcement officers from using racial profiling to enforce state laws on federal-aid-highways.

Provisions of H.R. 1996 and S. 799 would have been directed at the United States Customs Service inspectors or other officials. These bills would have prohibited pat down searches, intrusive nonroutine searches, or similar investigative actions based solely on the actual or perceived race, religion, gender, national origin, or sexual orientation of the traveler. S. 799 would have required Customs Service personnel to document why a person was suspected of carrying prohibited contraband, unless a person was believed to have been armed.

Grants

Under S. 19 and H.R. 1778, the Attorney General would have been authorized to provide grants *directly* to law enforcement agencies. To complete a study of stops for traffic violations, the Attorney General, under provisions of S. 19, would have been able to offer grants to law enforcement agencies to collect and submit data on:

- the alleged traffic infraction;
- identifying characteristics of the driver who was stopped; ! the number of occupants in the vehicle; ! the duration of the stop;
- whether a search was conducted, and if so, whether the driver consented to it; ! whether the driver was engaged in criminal behavior that justified the search; ! whether any items were seized, including money or contraband; ! whether a warning or citation was made;

- whether an arrest was made and why; and
- whether immigration status was questioned or an inquiry was made to the Immigration and Naturalization Service.

The Attorney General would have designated what agency would have received this data. H.R. 1778 contained data collection provisions similar to S. 19 except that it would have required the data to include whether any occupant of the vehicle was turned over to immigration officials.

Both bills would have required the Attorney General, after performing an initial analysis of existing traffic-stops data on racial profiling, to use the above data provided by law enforcement agencies to conduct a nationwide study of police stops for traffic violations. Not later than 120 days after enactment of this legislation, the Attorney General would have been required to report to Congress and to inform the public of the initial analysis of racial profiling data. On completion of this analysis, the Attorney General then would have been required to gather data on traffic stops from a nationwide sample of jurisdictions, including jurisdictions identified in the initial analysis. Not later than two years after enactment of this act, the Attorney General again would have reported to Congress on the results of the nationwide study. A copy of the report also would have been published in the *Federal Register*.

Another method of providing grants, which was proposed in H.R. 2074/S. 989, would have authorized the Attorney General to use funding under *existing* grant programs (such as the Community Oriented Policing Services Program and the Edward Byrne Memorial State and Local Law Enforcement Assistance program)[42] to make grants to states and federal law enforcement agencies. Bill provisions also would have authorized the Attorney General to make grants to states and other entities to develop best practice systems that ensure justice would be administered in a racially neutral way. These grants specifically would have supported:

- training to prevent racial profiling;
- acquiring technology to both collect data on routine investigatory activities to determine if racial profiling is occurring and to verify the accuracy of data collection, including in-car video cameras and portable computer systems; ! developing and acquiring early warning systems that enable the officers engaged in or likely to engage in racial profiling or other misconduct to be identified; ! establishing procedures for receiving and responding responsibly to complaints of misconduct by law enforcement officers; and ! installing management systems that would hold supervisors accountable for the actions of their subordinates.

State and Federal Policy Requirements to Eliminate Racial Profiling

Under provisions of H.R. 2074/S. 989 any state or governmental unit that applied for funding under a covered federal program would have had to certify that program participants had effective policies and procedures to eliminate racial profiling and to stop practices that encouraged racial profiling. Policies and procedures that would have been established for state and federal law enforcement agencies would have included:

–   prohibiting racial profiling;
–   collecting data on routine investigatory activities so that a determination can be made
    if law enforcement officers are practicing racial profiling, and submitting that data to
    the Attorney General; ! establishing independent procedures for receiving,
    investigating, and responding responsibly to complaints of racial profiling; !
    disciplining law enforcement officers who practice racial profiling; and ! ending the
    practice of racial profiling by using other policies or procedures that the Attorney
    General deems necessary.

Under provisions of another bill, H.R. 1907, any state or governmental unit seeking
funding would also have had to have policies and procedures that included a record of the
name and identification number of the law enforcement officer making the stop,
characteristics of the car passengers including race, national origin, ethnic origin, the alleged
traffic violation, whether a search was conducted and, if so, the legal basis for it, the results of
the search, and whether a warning, citation, or arrest occurred as a result of the stop.

Noncompliance

Under provisions of H.R. 2074/S. 989, if the Attorney General determined that a state
was not complying with provisions to eliminate racial profiling, the Attorney General could
have withheld all or part of certain federal grants until compliance was established. The bill
would have provided opportunities for a private party to report a grantee that violated anti-
racial profiling provisions.

Measures such as H.R. 965 and H.R. 1907 would have used federal funds for highways,
under the Interstate System and the National Highway System, to ensure that provisions
prohibiting racial profiling were adopted and that standards were enforced. A maximum of
10% of funds apportioned to a state could have been withheld for noncompliance. A state's
funds would have been held for three fiscal years before lapsing.

Accountability

To receive funding under a covered grant, H.R. 2074/S. 989 would have required a
federal, state or governmental unit to have procedures for disciplining law enforcement agents
who use racial profiling, although the specific disciplinary procedures were not outlined in the
bill.

Standards

Several bills would have required either the Attorney General or the Commissioner of the
U.S. Customs Service to submit a report summarizing data collected on routine investigatory
activities. Bills also would have required federal agencies and states to establish standards for
the collection of data and to review the effectiveness of procedures used to end the practice of
racial profiling.

Collection of Data. Some legislative proposals were directed at federal agencies and
others at states in requiring racial profiling data collection. Both H.R. 1996 and S. 799 would
have required the Commissioner of U.S. Customs to conduct, annually, a study on detentions
and searches of persons by the agency's personnel, during the preceding calendar year, that

would have included the race, gender, and citizenship of travelers searched, the type of search conducted and the results of the search.

H.R. 2074/S. 989 would have required the Attorney General to establish standards for the collection of data no later than six months after passage of the Act, including standards for setting benchmarks against which collected data could be measured. Specifically, the data collected would have included stops, searches, seizures, and arrests, to determine if law enforcement agencies were practicing racial profiling and to monitor the effectiveness of policies and procedures established to eliminate the practice.

Both S. 19 and H.R. 1778 would have required the Attorney General to collect nationwide data on:

- the alleged traffic infraction that led to the stop;
- the race, gender, ethnicity, and approximate age of the driver; ! the number of occupants in the vehicle; ! whether passengers were questioned on their immigration status; ! whether passengers were asked for immigration documents; ! whether an inquiry to the Immigration and Naturalization Service was made on car passengers; ! whether the vehicle was searched and if permission was requested for the search; ! whether a warning or citation was issued; ! whether anyone was arrested; ! any alleged criminal behavior by the driver that justified the search; ! any items seized, including contraband or money; and ! the duration of the stop.

H.R. 1778 also would have required a comparison of the number of stops made within 25 miles of the United States-Mexican border with the number of stops made within 25 miles of the United States-Canadian border.

In order to have federal funds fully apportioned to a state for use on federal-aid highways, H.R. 1907 would have required the state to maintain and allow public inspection of statistical information on every motor vehicle stop made by a law enforcement agent on a federal-aid highway.

Reports. H.R. 2074/S. 989 provided that not later than two years after the enactment of the act and then annually, the Attorney General would have had to submit a report to Congress on racial profiling by federal, state, and local law enforcement agencies that would have summarized data collected on routine investigatory activities. Also, the report would have included information on the status of racial profiling policies and procedures implemented by federal and state law enforcement agencies.

H.R. 1996 and S. 799, would have required similar information from the U.S. Customs Service, as noted earlier. In addition, the Commissioner of Customs would have been required to submit a report to Congress by March 31 of each year on the results of the study conducted the preceding calendar year.

Civil Suits

Only H.R. 2074/S. 989 would have permitted a victim of racial profiling to seek injunctive relief from the practice by filing a civil suit against the government employing a law enforcement agent practicing racial profiling, an agent of such a unit, and any supervisor of the agent. The suit could have been filed in either a state court or in a District Court of the United States. If routine investigatory activities of law enforcement officers in a jurisdiction had a disparate impact on racial or ethnic minorities, that would have been prima facie evidence of racial profiling. Further, if the plaintiff prevailed in the lawsuit, the plaintiff could have received reasonable reimbursement for attorney and expert fees.

Complaints

H.R. 2074/S. 989 would have provided funding for best practices development grants to support establishment of independent procedures at both the state and federal levels for receiving, investigating, and responding to complaints of racial profiling by law enforcement officers. Bill provisions would have provided funding to establish a system for disciplining law enforcement agents who practice racial profiling and, at the state level, their supervisors, but did not state what the disciplinary measures should be.

Education and Training

Bills that would have provided for training for law enforcement agents at the federal and/or state levels, were H.R. 1996, H.R. 2074/S. 989, S. 799, and S. 2114. H.R. 1996 would have required Customs Service inspectors and officials to have periodic training on procedures for detaining and searching travelers without the use of racial profiling. S. 799 would have required a review of why Customs Service personnel conducted certain searches, the results of the searches conducted, and the effectiveness of the searches in detecting contraband. H.R. 2074/S. 989 would have required that law enforcement officers receive training both to prevent racial profiling and to improve their interaction with the public. S. 2114 would have authorized the Attorney General to establish, in consultation with law enforcement agencies and civil rights groups, education and awareness programs on racial profiling and the negative effects of the practice on individuals and law enforcement. The purposes of the programs would have been to encourage state and local law enforcement agencies to stop racial profiling and to assist them in developing and maintaining adequate policies and procedures to do so. This bill would have provided for evaluation of best practices of programs.

Privacy

Bills containing provisions that would have protected the identity of any individual or law enforcement officer involved in a traffic stop include H.R. 1778, and H.R. 2074/S. 989. S. 19 and H.R. 1907 would have provided for the protection only of the identity of the driver of a car stopped.

CONGRESSIONAL HEARINGS

108th Congress

To date, no hearing has been held on racial profiling in the 108th Congress.

107th Congress

Senate Subcommittee on the Constitution, Federalism, and Property Rights

The Senate Subcommittee on the Constitution, Federalism and Property Rights of the Judiciary Committee, on August 1, 2001, held a hearing on S. 989, the End Racial Profiling Act of 2001. Some witnesses, for example David Harris, Law Professor, University of Toledo College of Law, testified in support of the bill's provisions that would have required a DOJ study of traffic stops, would have required data collection and training, and would have offered grants to law enforcement agencies. To them, these just continued state and local law enforcement cooperative efforts to enhance public safety. Other witnesses, including Reuben M. Greenberg, Chief of Police, Charleston, South Carolina Police Department, expressed concerns about certain provisions of the bill. They questioned whether the legislation would interfere in an area that states and localities are currently and legitimately addressing. Some opposed mandatory data collection and provisions that would deny funds to states and localities that do not comply with federal mandates. Representing the Grand Lodge Fraternal Order of Police, Steve Young opposed provisions that would have used statistical data against law enforcement officers and agencies in court. Young believed that the bill, rather than repairing the bonds of trust and respect between law enforcement and minority communities, would widen them because it presumed that racist tactics are commonly used by police departments. According to him, the definition of racial profiling was too broad because unless there was an eyewitness or a specific description of a suspect's race or ethnicity, a law enforcement officer could never use race as a factor in an investigation.[43]

House Committee on Government Reform

On July 19, 2001, the House Government Reform Committee held a hearing that focused on technology as a tool to eliminate racial profiling.[44] Witnesses identified advantages and disadvantages of using the two major visual technologies — analog and digital — in traffic stops. These surveillance systems are often mounted in the grill, on the dash or on the roof of a car, with a recorder placed in the trunk. Similar to the home VHS video cassette recorder, the analog video simply records an image on tape and the tapes are kept for a certain period of time and then either discarded or reused. With digital technology, the recorded image is converted into a digital file and recorded on either tape, flash memory cards, hard drives, CD ROMs or DVD discs. The advantages of video technologies are: they provide an objective documentation of events that the camera can see and hear; the material can be reviewed by supervisors and researchers; and they can influence in a positive way the behavior of a citizen and law enforcement officer. Video tapes also can be used as a teaching tool for law enforcement officers.

A disadvantage of using video technologies is that if relied upon solely to detect racial profiling, the device usually sees less than the officer can. Cameras may not show what precipitated the stop before filming began. The purchase price ($3,000-$5,000 per video camera) and maintenance of equipment are expensive. Maintenance is expensive because of the number of tapes used (typically, six patrol cars use over 500 tapes each month), of storage facilities that would be needed, and of the review of videos that a supervisor would have to conduct. Many systems are improperly installed and poorly maintained, resulting in poor audio and image quality. Most installations allow the operator to re-record which could result in tampering. Finally, privacy concerns are raised in using technological devices.

Former Commissioner of the U.S. Customs Service, Raymond Kelly, testified about the effective use that Customs made of technology in addressing charges of racial profiling.[45] According to him, technological devices reduced considerably the number of intrusive body searches that many travelers were subjected to at ports of entry into the United States and increased the amount of contraband discovered.

Table 3. Racial Profiling Bills Introduced in 107th Congress: Selected Provisions

Bill	Definition	Standards	Prohibition	Data Collection	Data Specification	Complaints	Training	Grants	Civil Suits	Accountability	Penalties
H.R. 965 (Norton)	—	X	X	—	—	—	—	—	—	—	X
H.R. 1907 (Norton)	X	X	X	X	X	—	—	—	—	—	—
H.R. 1778 (Jackson-Lee)	—	—	—	X	X	X	—	X	—	—	—
H.R. 1996 (Lewis)	—	X	X	X	X	—	—	—	—	—	—
H.R. 2074 (Conyers)	X	X	X	X	X	X	X	X	X	X	X
S. 19 (Daschle)	—	X	—	X	X	X	—	X	—	—	—
S. 799 (Durbin)	X	X	X	X	X	—	X	—	—	—	—
S. 989 (Feingold)	X	X	X	X	X	X	X	X	X	X	X
S. 2114 (Voinovich)	—	—	—	—	—	—	X	—	—	—	—

Source: This table summarizes provisions of the above identified racial profiling bills. For further details of provisions of these bills, see full text.

Note: — denotes "no provisions found"; X denotes "would have provided for."

ENDNOTES

[1] Charles Dale, Legislative Attorney, CRS, American Law Division, provided this definition. See CRS Report RL31130, *Racial Profiling: Legal and Constitutional Issues*, by Charles V. Dale.

[2] U.S. Customs Service, Personal Search Review Commission, *Report on Personal Searches by the United States Customs Service*, June 21, 2000, p. 1; Lori Montgomery, *Seattle Times*, "Under Suspicion Law-Enforcement Agencies Do Some Soul-Searching over Racial Profiling," July 1, 2001, p. A3.

[3] Katheryn K. Russell, *Boston College Law Review*, "'Driving While Black': Corollary Phenomena and Collateral Consequences," vol. 40, pp. 721-724.

[4] Racial profiling is sometimes referred to as "profiling" and "ethnic profiling."

[5] For a fuller discussion of the action of *state legislatures* on racial profiling, see CRS Report RL31950, *Racial Profiling and Traffic Stops in the States: Selected Issues and Legislative Approaches*, by Sula P. Richardson. For literature on racial profiling, see CRS Report RS20954, *Racial Profiling: Bibliography-in-Brief*, by Tangela G. Roe. For legal issues, see

CRS Report RL31130, *Racial Profiling: Legal and Constitutional Issues*, by Charles V. Dale.

[6] U.S. General Accounting Office, *Racial Profiling, Limited Data Available on Motorist Stops*, GAO Report GGD-00-41, Mar. 2000.

[7] See CRS Report RL31950, *Racial Profiling and Traffic Stops in the States: Selected Issues and Legislative Approaches*, by Sula P. Richardson.

[8] For constitutional arguments, see CRS Report RL31130, *Racial Profiling*.

[9] Neil Kurlander, "How to Track Traffic Stop Data," *Law Enforcement Technology*, July 2000, p. 148; *Gallup Poll* on racial profiling, released Dec. 9, 1999. See also, ACLU, "New Poll Shows Public Overwhelmingly Disapproves of Racial Profiling," Dec. 9, 1999. Gia Fenoglio, et al., "How Life Could Change, A Look at Some 30 Proposals to Combat Terrorism. Are They Worth the Trade-Offs?," *National Journal*, Sept. 22, 2001, p. 2912 .

[10] Henry Weinstein, et al., "Racial Profiling Gains Support As Search Tactic," *The Los Angeles Times*, Sept. 24, 2001, p. 1; see also, Nicole Davis, "The Slippery Slope of Racial Profiling," *Color Lines Magazine*, Mar. 10, 2003.

[11] Dan Higgins, "Freedom Losing Its Grip," *Ithaca Journal*, January 23, 2003, p. 1.

[12] Stuart Taylor, Jr., "The Case for Using Racial Profiling at Airports," *National Journal*, Sept. 22, 2001, p. 2877.

[13] *The Economist,* "Arab-Americans, Suddenly Visible," Sept. 22, 2001, p. 31; Evan P. Schultz, "Whatever It Takes?," *Legal Times*, Oct. 1, 2001, p. 50.

[14] Stuart Taylor, Jr., "All About Security, Passport Profiling is Necessary, Not Evil,"*Legal Times*, Nov. 5, 2001, p. 52.

[15] U.S. Congress, Senate, Committee on the Judiciary, Subcommittee on the Constitution, Federalism, and Property Rights, *S. 989: The End Racial Profiling Act of 2001*, hearings, 107th Cong. 2nd sess., Aug. 1, 2001 (Washington: GPO, 2001), p. 114.

[16] David Borden, Executive Director, Drug Reform Coordination Network, "Profiling and the Drug War."

[17] For a legal analysis of the issue of racial profiling see CRS Report RL31130, *Racial Profiling: Legal and Constitutional Issues*, by Charles V. Dale.

[18] Bruce D. Glasscock, President, International Association of Chiefs of Police, remarks at the 2nd National Symposium on Racial Profiling, Northwestern University — Center for Public Safety, Rosemont, Illinois, Oct. 1, 2001, pp 17-20.

[19] Captain Ronald L. Davis, Keynote address, 2nd National Symposium on Racial Profiling, Northwestern University — Center for Public Safety, Rosemont, Illinois, Oct. 2, 2001, pp. 5-6.

[20] Steve Young, National Vice President, Fraternal Order of Police, Testimony before the U.S. Senate Committee on the Judiciary, Subcommittee on the Constitution, Federalism and Property Rights, *S. 989, The End Racial Profiling Act of 2001,* 107th Cong., 2nd sess., Aug. 1, 2001 (Washington: GPO, 2002), p. 35.

[21] Ibid.

[22] Justin Pritchard, "More Police Study Racial Profiling, But What Are They Looking For?" Associated Press State and Local Wire, Jan. 13, 2001; Deborah Ramirez, McDevitt, and Amy Farrell, *A Resource Guide on Racial Profiling Data Collection Systems, Promising Practices and Lessons Learned*, U.S. Department of Justice, Nov. 2000.

[23] Finn Bullers, "Three Chiefs Criticize ACLU's Traffic Study," *Kansas City Star*, Jan. 13, 2001, p. B1.

[24] Keith W. Strandberg, "Racial Profiling," *Law Enforcement Technology*, June 1999, p. 64.

[25] Lorie Fridell and Robert Lunney, et al., *Racially Biased Policing, A Principled Response*, Police Executive Research Forum, Washington, D.C., 2001, pp. 117-119.

[26] Naftali Bendavid, "Collect Racial Data, Feds Told," *Sun-Sentinel* (Fort Lauderdale), June 10, 1999, p. 3A; Finn Bullers, "Three Police Chiefs Criticize ACLU's Traffic Study; Race-Profiling Report Was Flawed, They Say," *The Kansas City Star*, Jan. 13, 2001, p. B1.

[27] *Ventura County Star* (Ventura County, California), Editorial: "One More Intrusion," June 24, 1999, p. B06.

[28] Ibid.

[29] National Organization of Black Law Enforcement Executives, "A Noble Perspective: Racial Profiling — A Symptom of Bias-Based Policing (Next Steps — Creating Blindfolds to Justice)," May 3, 2001, p. 7.

[30] Lori Montgomery, "Under Suspicion Law-Enforcement Agencies Do Some Soul-Searching Over Racial Profiling," *Seattle Times*, July 1, 2001, p. A3.

[31] Fridell, *Racially Biased Policing, A Principled Response*, p. 116.

[32] Steve Young, National Vice President, Fraternal Order of Police, Testimony before the U.S. Senate Committee on the Judiciary, Subcommittee on the Constitution, Federalism and Property Rights, *S. 989, The End Racial Profiling Act of 2001,* 107th Cong., 2nd sess., Aug. 1, 2001 (Washington: GPO, 2002), p. 35.

[33] Survey findings passed a significance test at .05-level. Patrick Langan, Statistician, Department of Justice, Bureau of Statistics, telephone conversation with, February 3, 2004.

[34] U.S. Department of Justice, Bureau of Justice Statistics, *Contacts between Police and the Public, Findings from the 1999 National Survey,* by Patrick Langan, et al., BJS Statisticians, (Washington: Feb. 2001), p. 12.

[35] According to GAO, a basic social science research principle is that studies rule out plausible alternative explanations for findings. GAO found that available research on racial profiling of motorists did not sufficiently rule out factors other than race to account for differences in stops. See U.S. General Accounting Office, *Racial Profiling, Limited Data Available on Motorist Stops*, GAO Report GGD-00-41 (Washington: Mar. 2000), pp. 18-20.

[36] Ibid., pp. 1-3.

[37] Ibid.

[38] Steven Holmes, "Clinton Orders Investigation on Possible Racial Profiling," *New York Times*, June 10, 1999, p. A22.

[39] Patrick Strawbridge, "President Seeks Data on Profiling, Federal Agencies Are Told to Provide Race and Gender Statistics on Everyone They Stop," *Omaha World-Herald*, June 10, 1999, p. 1; Steven A. Holmes, "Clinton Orders Investigation on Possible Racial Profiling," *The New York Times*, June 10, 1999, p. 22.

[40] No report on these efforts has yet been released.

[41] U.S. Department of Justice, "Justice Department Issues Policy Guidance to Ban Racial Profiling, *Fact Sheet*, June 17, 2003; U.S. Department of Justice, "Racial Profiling," *Fact Sheet,"* June 17, 2003; Eric Lichtblau, "Bush Issues Federal Ban on Racial Profiling, But Exempts Security Inquiries," *New York Times*, June 18, 2003, pp. A1, A14.

[42] See CRS Report 97-265, *Crime Control Assistance Through the Byrne Programs* by Garrine P. Laney, CRS Report RS20539 *Federal Crime Control Assistance to State and*

Local Governments, by Joanne O'Bryant, and CRS Report 97-196, *Community Oriented Policing Services: An Overview*, by Joanne O'Bryant.

[43] Testimony of Steve Young, National Vice President of the Grand Lodge, Fraternal Order of Police, in the U.S. Senate Subcommittee on the Constitution, Federalism and Property Rights, *S. 989, the End Racial Profiling Act of 2001*, [In] U.S. Congress, Senate Committee on the Judiciary, Subcommittee on the Constitution, Federalism and Property Rights, hearings on S.989, the End Racial Profiling Act of 2001, 107th Cong., 1st sess., Aug. 1, 2001, pp. 33-35.

[44] U.S. Congress, House Committee on Government Reform, *The Benefits of Audio-Visual Technology in Addressing Racial Profiling*, hearing, 107th Cong., 1st sess., July 19, 2001 (Washington: GPO), 186 pp.

[45] Ibid., pp. 136-140.

In: Racial Profiling: Issues, Data and Analyses
Editor: Steven J. Muffler, pp. 25-29

Chapter 2

A CLOSER LOOK AT RACIAL PROFILING[*]

Steve Cooper[†]
California State University, Fullerton
Fullerton, CA 92831

ABSTRACT

Racial profiling occurs when a police officer selectively focuses on a person's race, and subsequently follows, harasses, detains or arrests the individual. Broadly construed, racial profiling can be viewed as targeted policing efforts against minority groups. Recent studies in San Diego, New Jersey and other locations have presented evidence to suggest that minorities are disproportionately stopped and searched by police. However, these studies don't tell us how or why the police disproportionately stop minorities; they merely reaffirm what many people have claimed for years. During 2000, I conducted a field study of police decisions to stop motorists. I went on ride-alongs with officers from various police agencies throughout Southern California. The major finding from this study is that while race is often a factor when police officers initiate stops, other factors are just as important, if not more significant at times, when determining whom the police will stop. I concluded that many officers use a "thug profile" rather than just a race profile. The "thug profile" consists of, but is not limited to: type of vehicle, location, clothing, time of day, demeanor and race. Racial profiling is a fact of life in America. It must be addressed. We've all seen the stories about how blacks often have difficulties hailing a taxi cab, renting apartments, getting loans, buying cars, etc. Yet, for some unknown reason, we expect the police to perform their duties within the limits of the law unfettered by the cultural and political biases within which they exist. Ultimately the

---

[*] Excerpted from http://www.facsnet.org/tools/nbgs/p_thru_%20z/pq/profile.php3

[†] Steve Cooper is a professor and program coordinator of Criminal Justice at American Military University and lecturer at California State University, Fullerton, and Chapman University. During fall 2000, Cooper taught what is considered to be the first university level course entirely devoted to the topic of racial profiling. He is the author and editor of two forthcoming books on racial profiling. He can be contacted at professorcooper@charter.net

issue comes down to how we want the police to do their job. If we support proactive policing, then racial profiling will continue to exist. Reactive policing may be the only solution.

WHAT IS RACIAL PROFILING?

Narrowly defined, racial profiling occurs when a police officer selectively focuses on a person's race, and subsequently follows, harasses, detains or arrests the individual. Broadly construed, racial profiling can be viewed as targeted policing efforts against minority groups. In laymen's terms, racial profiling has become the catch-all phrase to describe any form of racial injustice, such as "shopping while black." I suggest the term be limited in its application to the narrowest definition.

Due to intense public scrutiny and public policy considerations, accurate usage of the term is paramount if we are to better understand the nuances of racially motivated traffic stops. Placing every form of racism and injustice under the auspices of racial profiling thwarts efforts to bring about its demise and shifts focus away from the real issue. Moreover, if we label every form of racial injustice as racial profiling, then we are creating the impression that the problem is larger than it really is and threaten to jeopardize already tenuous police-community relations.

BREAKING DOWN THE ISSUE

Recent studies in San Diego, New Jersey and other locations have presented evidence to suggest that minorities are disproportionately stopped and searched by police. However, these studies don't tell us how or why the police disproportionately stop minorities; they merely reaffirm what many people have claimed for years.

Most of these studies have been quantitative. Common practice is to use statistical analyses to explore the relationship between the number of traffic stops for each ethnic group compared with Census track data or records from the department of motor vehicles in order to determine the disparate impact, if any, of race on traffic stops. While this type of research is necessary to establish baseline data, racial profiling is a phenomenon that must be studied in conjunction with the question of why a person of color is stopped.

Harassment of a minority group will not be solved as a result of these large quantitative studies. For example, 15 black men were killed by Cincinnati police officers in recent years, but no whites were killed during that period. Also, such analyses probably wouldn't discover the fact that Timothy Thomas was stopped by Cincinnati police 11 times by 10 different officers during an eight-week period before they shot and killed him April 7, 2001. Thomas received 21 citations during those stops from Feb. 29 to May 4, 2000. The slaying of Thomas, the fourth black person killed in Cincinnati by police since November 2000, led to massive civil unrest and rioting.

Even if such studies do reveal these statistical anomalies, the researchers may disregard such instances as just statistical blips. These studies will not reveal the patterns leading up to an arrest, nor will they allow us to carefully examine the intricacies inherent with racial profiling cases.

There are other challenges associated with understanding racial profiling through mere data collection. Take, for example, a young black man who is stopped by a police officer for an illegal lane change in an area known for narcotic trafficking. This type of enforcement practice is often referred to as a "pretext stop" when the officer's actual motivation for pulling the car over was to see if he could further investigate for drugs or weapons. During the traffic stop the officer observes a small quantity of drugs and subsequently arrests the driver for possession of narcotics. Most likely, the suspect will not be cited for an illegal lane change. In many jurisdictions, officers will only charge the person with the most serious offense; therefore, the traffic violation will be disregarded. Researchers will have a difficult time determining if this person was "racially profiled" for purposes of their statistical analysis since no traffic citation was issued.

FIELD RESEARCH

During 2000, I conducted a field study of police decisions to stop motorists. I went on ride-alongs with officers from various police agencies throughout Southern California. Having worked in law enforcement, I had several preconceived notions about how and why traffic stops are conducted and this ethnography afforded me an opportunity to challenge, and reaffirm, many of my assumptions.

The major finding from this study is that while race is often a factor when police officers initiate stops, other factors are just as important, if not more significant at times, when determining whom the police will stop. I concluded that many officers use a "thug profile" rather than just a race profile. The "thug profile" consists of, but is not limited to: type of vehicle, location, clothing, time of day, demeanor and race. The predictors are not mutually exclusive, although they can be at times, but an individual's chance of being stopped by the police rises as the number of variables present increases. This explanation is the sine qua non of the drug courier profile: A young black man who is driving an expensive vehicle late at night in an area known to be associated with drugs stands a very good chance of being stopped by the police.

Even though race may only be one factor that an officer takes into account when deciding whether to initiate a traffic stop, a salient explanation of racial profiling would suggest that the ethnicity of an individual can trigger the profile.

Police Chief Jim Charley of Chester, Pa., succinctly conveyed this notion when he said, "I believe a legitimate traffic stop can be made on the basis of viewing a black individual in a white neighborhood in a fancy car, wearing a multitude of gold chains, wearing sunglasses." His first indicator of potential criminality was the race of the individual, but the other factors (gold chains, white neighborhood, etc.) also appear to be influential variables.

REPORTING ON RACIAL PROFILING

We have begun to move past the sensationalism of racial profiling in reporting and are now challenged with taking a closer look at the intricacies surrounding this topic. Some of the issues for reporters to consider include the following:

– *Racial profiling may explain disproportionate minority offenders.* Whites commit the majority of offenses in America. But minorities tend to be overrepresented in rates of offending. While critics may cite this disproportionality as a justification for race-based traffic stops, racial profiling may actually serve as the catalyst for the disparity in rates of offending for blacks and Hispanics. This is especially true with regard to drug-related arrests. All indicators suggest that blacks and whites use drugs at approximately the same rate, yet blacks are arrested on drug charges at much higher rates than whites.

– *The aggregate consequences of racial profiling.* Racial profiling has played a role in the alarming numbers of minorities who are in the criminal justice system. The aggregate consequences of racial profiling — arrest and conviction statistics — for blacks and other minorities are startling. The Sentencing Project and others have documented that as many as one in three, and even as high as one in two black men in certain areas of the country are under some form of criminal justice control (i.e., parole, probation or prison). Also, data from the California Post-Secondary Education Commission and the California Department of Corrections for 1994 reveal that for every black man enrolled in a four-year degree program in California, there were five black men under some form of criminal justice control. Extending this analysis in 2001, I found what I refer to as the "one-tenth reality." For approximately every one black man graduating with a bachelor's degree from a public college or university in California, about 10 black men are sentenced to prison with a felony conviction (the rates are slightly less for Hispanic men), whereas for every one white man who is sentenced to prison with a felony conviction, about 1.1 white men will graduate from a public college or university in California.

– *"In-house" vs. "third-party" data collection.* The results of studies conducted by departments that collect and publish their own data on traffic stops should be closely scrutinized. Many policing experts have recognized the San Diego Police Department as a leader for innovative policing strategies and addressing challenges sooner rather than later. In response to rising complaints across the country with regard to racial profiling, the San Diego Police Department used third-party consultants to conduct the study rather than doing it "in-house." Using outside researchers is generally regarded as more scientifically sound than having people within the organization collect and analyze the data.

– *Where there's smoke there's fire.* A red flag appears when police departments aren't willing to provide data or other public information. In May 2001 the Washington, D.C., police chief announced that several inappropriate e-mails were sent between his officers. The department's initial response was to handle the matter internally. It has now been reported that these e-mails may indicate a proclivity toward racial profiling. On the other hand, the San Diego Police Department may have to worry less about racial profiling claims than other similar agencies because it has taken the initiative to address the issue. Even if a lawsuit were filed against the San Diego Police Department based on allegations of racial profiling, any directives under a consent decree would most likely already be in place (i.e., holding focus groups, creating an advisory board, collecting data, etc.).

– *Other ways of looking at the issue.* Statistics on traffic stops have limitations. People thinking outside the box have conducted several innovative studies. For example, a few years ago the TV news magazine "20/20," had white and black men drive around Los Angeles in the same type of car, documenting the harassment the blacks endured by police and the lack of attention officers paid to the whites. Diop Kamau, a former police officer turned advocate for police change, studies racial profiling and police abuse in a unique manner. He and his investigators use hidden video cameras to document how blacks are treated when they seek to file a complaint against a police officer. Last year, criminologist Charles Crawford found in a recent study on vehicle noise violations that African-Americans were more likely than whites to be cited and/or arrested. Racial profiling is not limited to local police departments. Some military and federal police, as well as private and in-house security officers, correctional, probation and parole officers may also have occasion to racially profile.

– *Some black officers racially profile.* Some minority officers may be just as harsh on blacks and other minorities. They may feel pressure from peers and supervisors to treat black and Hispanic suspects as tough, if not tougher, than white offenders if they choose to assimilate into the department and be accepted within the police subculture.

– *Racial profiling by police crosses ethnic boundaries.* Some officers that patrol predominately minority communities pay "special attention" to whites that travel through their jurisdiction. A white man driving in a predominately black community late at night may be investigated just as vigorously as any minority citizen.

CONCLUDING THOUGHTS

Racial profiling is a fact of life in America. It must be addressed. We've all seen the stories about how blacks often have difficulties hailing a taxi cab, renting apartments, getting loans, buying cars, etc. Yet, for some unknown reason, we expect the police to perform their duties within the limits of the law unfettered by the cultural and political biases within which they exist. Ultimately the issue comes down to how we want the police to do their job. If we support proactive policing, then racial profiling will continue to exist. Reactive policing may be the only solution.

In: Racial Profiling: Issues, Data and Analyses
Editor: Steven J. Muffler, pp. 31-39

ISBN 1-59454-547-2
© 2006 Nova Science Publishers, Inc.

Chapter 3

RACIAL PROFILING[*]

Merrick J. Bobb, Nicolas H. Miller, Ronald L. Davis and Oren Root

Police Assessment Resource Center
Biltmore Court
520 South Grand Avenue, Suite 1070
Los Angeles, California 90071

ABSTRACT

The disparate impact of our criminal justice system on racial and ethnic minorities raises serious questions about the way law enforcement officials, prosecutors, courts, and juries go about their jobs. Whatever their cause, racial disparities are stark throughout the system. At current levels of incarceration, for example, newborn black males have a greater than 1-in-4 chance of serving prison time, while Latinos have a 1-in-6 chance and whites 1-in-23. The undesirable and illegal consequence results when police officers use race or ethnicity as a deciding factor in focusing suspicion on a particular individual. Because most jurisdictions lack sufficient data on police stops to accurately assess the problem, suspicion and controversy continue to swirl around racial profiling.

The disparate impact of our criminal justice system on racial and ethnic minorities raises serious questions about the way law enforcement officials, prosecutors, courts, and juries go about their jobs.[1] Whatever their cause, racial disparities are stark throughout the system. At current levels of incarceration, for example, newborn black males have a greater than 1-in-4 chance of serving prison time, while Latinos have a 1-in-6 chance and whites 1-in-23. While all racial disparity in the justice system merits further scrutiny, a particular aspect of the problem – racial profiling – has attracted considerable public attention in recent years. The term "racial profiling" has been used loosely and lacks a universally accepted definition, but

---

[*] Excerpted from http://www.parc.info/pubs/pdf/racial_profiling.pdf

it most commonly refers to police practices in which traffic and pedestrian stops, and the ensuing searches of cars or individuals, are shown to have a discriminatory impact. The undesirable and illegal consequence results when police officers use race or ethnicity as a deciding factor in focusing suspicion on a particular individual. Because most jurisdictions lack sufficient data on police stops to accurately assess the problem, suspicion and controversy continue to swirl around racial profiling.

In discussing the issue, it is important to distinguish between disparate impact and discriminatory impact. They are not the same, and it is unwarranted to leap from one to the other. A finding of a disparate racial or ethnic impact in traffic and pedestrian stops calls for further study and reflection, but there can be valid reasons for the disparities that do not derive from race-based discrimination, much less racial animus, and not every police action that considers the race of a suspect is racial profiling. It is not racial profiling, for example, for police to take into account that the victim of a crime described the assailant as "African-American" or "Hispanic." Nor is it racial profiling when the conduct of a black or Latino individual provides a legally sufficient basis for a stop or detention without regard to race or ethnicity. On the other hand, it *is* racial profiling when mere stereotypes (a black man driving a BMW is a mismatch) or loose generalizations (a black man does not belong in this predominately white neighborhood) are used to justify a stop. And it *is* racial profiling when broad statistical correlations are used as a basis of focusing suspicion on a given individual; *i.e.,* more Latino than white teenagers are arrested for street drug crimes, therefore that specific Latino teenager in this high drug crime area should be checked out. More generally, enforcement of certain laws may produce a disparate impact overall: The proportion of blacks or Latinos stopped by law enforcement – or ticketed, arrested, frisked, or searched – may turn out to be higher than it is reasonable to expect given the mix in the population. And there may be no convincing explanation for the disparity apart from race or ethnicity. That kind of law enforcement activity produces a high level of "false positives" that falls more heavily on racial and ethnic minorities. The more general the criteria used to isolate individuals, the greater the likelihood that people will be targeted repeatedly or erroneously: the same black man is stopped again and again on his way home from work late at night; the correlation between a busted tail light and illegal drugs in a given car is so weak that many innocent people will be stopped. Any police decision to detain an individual who is not visibly engaged in a crime may stir feelings of indignity and resentment. But it is even more corrosive and potentially explosive when the person believes he has been stopped solely because of his race or ethnicity, or because race or ethnicity is part of an over-generalized dragnet. Hence, the term "driving while black or brown." So-called "pretext stops" add to the complexity of the racial profiling issue. In the case of traffic stops, for example, it is virtually impossible to drive any length of time without committing a traffic or vehicle code violation of some kind. The police, therefore, have a choice about whom to pull over. Whatever the underlying intent of the police officer, it does not violate the Fourth Amendment protection against unreasonable searches and seizures when the officer uses the "pretext" of a traffic or vehicle code violation to stop a motorist as long as probable cause exists to believe those laws have been violated. *Whren v. United States*, 517 U.S. 806 (1996). We would venture, however, that the traffic law "pretexts" used to stop a car rarely match the underlying suspicion of criminal activity motivating the police to want to check the car out. A drug interdiction program using busted tail lights and minor traffic violations as "pretexts" for a stop will likely yield too few drug violators to justify the proliferation of stops and the displeasure or animus engendered in the drivers. It is especially problematical when the "pretext" is so common – illegal lane changes or rolling stops, for example – that the police officer can choose with relative impunity whom to stop based on any factor, legal or illegal, including race or ethnicity. This does not, of course, mean that there must always be a one-to-one correlation between persons stopped by the police and persons found to have committed a crime. Nor does it mean that a weapon or contraband must be found every time there is legal justification for a frisk or pat-down. Nor does it mean that randomized, non-discriminatory stops should be condemned merely because of overbreadth problems. An example of the latter is a sobriety checkpoint – where scores of people, all of whom happen to be passing by the checkpoint, are stopped and inconvenienced without individualized suspicion. Where the basis for the stop is truly randomized and non-discretionary – every third car, for example – few will argue that the checkpoint is unlawful or wrong, even if the basis for a stop results in considerable overbreadth and few persons are found to be inebriated. Perhaps such stops can be rationalized on the grounds that drunk drivers pose an immediate danger to others.[2] The elimination of that danger is the predominant goal of the police; the checkpoint is not being used as a pretext to stop persons who may have committed other crimes. Tacit consent by those stopped, therefore, might be easier to obtain or assume: We agree you may stop us briefly for our own personal safety in order to take drunk drivers off the very road we are traveling because we know that the stop won't be used to conduct a fishing expedition for possible criminal activity and that we will be on our way as soon as you see we're not drunk.

Similarly, in the wake of the events of September 11, 2001, there is manifestly greater public tolerance of airport checkpoints and more intrusive and frequent searches of baggage and passengers.

The rationale for public acceptance is similar to that described above for sobriety checkpoints. But unlike sobriety checkpoints, airport checks are a more complex combination of universal searches (everyone goes through the metal detector), random, non-discretionary searches (every fourth or fifth passenger stopped immediately prior to boarding for a particularized search of hand-luggage), particularized suspicion (bag going through the x-ray machine contains an object that looks suspicious), and profile -based stops (young male traveling alone with a one-way ticket paid for in cash). Because of the heightened danger associated with a terrorist act and the irreparable injuries occasioned thereby, as in a sobriety checkpoint, there may be a tacit agreement by travelers that they can be stopped briefly so that the very airplane they will be traveling upon can be made less vulnerable to a terrorist act. Everyone swept into the dragnet benefits directly in terms of a safer flight. The airport check is not being used as a pretext or fishing expedition for criminal activity other than terrorism. Although many are swept into the dragnet and at best an infinitesimal few will be found to pose the danger for which they are stopped or searched, the horrendous consequences and massive loss of life from an undetected terrorist act is seen as justifying the inconvenience. It seems safe to say that for many people, the greater the potential harm, the greater the tolerance, at least momentarily, for dragnet-like stops with the barest minimal nexus between the person stopped and the potential culprit sought. We are fortunate that the occasions where such programs have seemed necessary, if only fleetingly, have been few.

These instances of airport searches should be clearly distinguished, however, from airport searches in which race or ethnicity is a factor in deciding whom to single out for a stop or search or to prevent from boarding. In the immediate aftermath of September 11, there was some public debate whether specific profiling of Arab-Americans or persons with a Middle

Eastern appearance should be tolerated or even encouraged. There have been instances at airports where such persons have not been permitted to fly. Although the fear or panic that makes such profiling seem rational might seem at first blush to be understandable, we do not endorse such profiling. The nexus between the characteristic – looks Arab-American or Middle Eastern – and the potential culprit (a terrorist) is so attenuated as to be ephemeral, at best. Hence, the overbreadth of the searches will be extremely high without a corresponding benefit in improved air safety. And there will not be the same tacit acceptance of the inconvenience because those stopped will accurately see the stops as discriminatory and highly discretionary; not random.

Other hard cases to rationalize are when the motivation for a dragnet-like approach is general crime suppression rather than an attempt to solve a specific crime or to eliminate an immediate threat to public safety like the drunk driver. Assume that a given neighborhood, predominantly black, is experiencing an uptick in gun-related crime with a predominance of black victims and black perpetrators. The police perceive that the area has become saturated with guns. They decide, therefore, to deploy a massive force in the neighborhood, to stop and search lots of cars, and to stop and frisk lots of individuals with the goal of seizing as many guns and making as many arrests for illegal possession of concealed weapons as possible. And if other contraband – drugs, for example – is found, arrests also will be made. Additionally, the police embark on a program of rigid enforcement of a wide variety of laws relating to relatively trivial offenses that are often overlooked or not worth the effort to process – breaking a window, drinking beer from an open container on the corner, jumping turnstiles on the subway. People detained for these offenses are then searched for contraband or weapons and arrested for those more serious offenses if the search produces a "hit." At the station house they are questioned about other, more serious criminal activity of which they may be aware. The result of all this police activity it is that in this predominantly black neighborhood, blacks – particularly young black males – are "tossed" and arrested in substantial numbers without the police necessarily running afoul of the Fourth Amendment. Thus, even if each individual arrest seems to be properly grounded in probable cause and each stop grounded in reasonable, individualized suspicion – however pretextual or flimsy – it nonetheless happens that black male pedestrians and drivers are rousted repeatedly and unceremoniously and perceive themselves singled out by race. The number of "false positives" not only creates widespread inconvenience, it appears to validate a suspicion that people are being stopped because they are black. Unlike the example of the sobriety checkpoint, there is not tacit consent on the part of those stopped. At the same time, however, when taken together, the massive police presence, the increased likelihood of being caught with a gun and arrested, and the number of guns seized produce the intended effect: gun-related crime plummets. In this example, the minor offenses and the pretextual stops are essentially surrogates for stronger, more individualized suspicion. The correlations between stops and arrests may be weak, but in the end the goal is achieved. Whether the residents of the neighborhood in question accept the crime suppression program is another question, and one that is hard to gauge. And the views of the residents may not be uniform: The storekeeper who has been held up repeatedly at gun point will feel differently than the mother whose son is repeatedly "rousted" by the police when he is out at night.

But one thing is clear: When a police stop of an innocent black or Latino results in serious injury or death – as in the case of the Amadou Diallo shooting in New York – whatever goodwill the police may have banked will evaporate. There will be little tolerance of, and forgiveness for, serious police error, even if it is the result of negligence or recklessness rather than intentional misconduct. Generalized beliefs that the criminal justice system impacts disproportionately on minorities will be focused with laser-like intensity on the specific controversial incident. And the impact on policy is likely to be that officers will face greater hostility, anger, and risk of injury. Even so, these may not be the hardest cases of all. In the absence of a search for a particular criminal or a targeted crime suppression effort, it becomes an even more complex societal problem when the cumulative results of uncoordinated, discrete, individual decisions by police officers about whom to stop and whom to search fall, over time, more heavily on racial and ethnic minorities. Even if almost all police officers make decisions about whom to stop without intentionally acting in a discriminatory way, it is still possible, over time, to produce disparate results from the actions of the few who do use race improperly and the stops that occur because of the unintentional stereotyping that is so prevalent in our society. What to do about this is a knotty question. But a good starting point is to collect the data that show what is actually happening on the streets.

For example, the Attorney General of the state of New York determined, after a review of some 175,000 stops documenting the race of persons stopped by the police in New York City, that blacks were stopped six times more often than whites. NYPD keeps statistics by race. *The New York City Police Department's "Stop & Frisk" Practices ("NYPD Stop and Frisk Practices"), Office of New York State Attorney General Eliot Spitzer, Civil Rights Bureau (December 1, 1999), pp. 88 et seq. The report can be found on the Internet at* http://www.oag.state.ny.us/press/reports/stop_frisk/stop_frisk.html . Whereas blacks constituted one-fourth of New York City's residents, they accounted for half of the individuals stopped. *Id.* Not all stops led to an arrest, however. The Attorney General then sought to discover if similar racial disparities existed when only stops that had resulted in arrests were examined. They did:

There were more "false positives" among blacks than among whites. The NYPD stopped 9.5 blacks to Less than ten percent of the searches resulted in seizures of contraband or property. Id., Preliminary Observations, paragraph 4, p. 11. The San Diego report stressed its preliminary nature and emphasized that it did not purport to explain why the disparities occurred. "Numerous hypotheses could be offered, ranging from intentional police discrimination to unintentional stereotyping to the unintended consequences of police deployment practices to actual differences in gang involvement by race/ethnicity, and so on." Id., at p. 8. The authors urged further analysis to get at the real answers. Id. Because the implications of these studies are difficult to assess and, if looked at only cursorily, potentially inflammatory, it is not surprising that some leaders in law enforcement question the wisdom of compiling statistics for similar studies.[7] Yet despite the risk that the answers might be uncomfortable, many cities and 13 states require some form of data collection, and a number of them have drafted detailed collection procedures. The Sacramento (CA) Police Department has a particularly thorough policy that requires officers to answer 17 specific questions for each stop.[8] We strongly recommend that departments collect data on stops, while recognizing that there are both risks and rewards in doing so. If the data reveal patterns similar to those in New York or San Diego, a police department leaves itself open to arguments that it is simply creating bad publicity for itself, for use by persons with a political or ideological axe to grind or seeking a shocking headline. It may be leaving itself open to outright charges of racial bias. The contrary view, which we submit is the better one, is that lack of knowledge is a dangerous thing and that a willful lack of knowledge is more dangerous still. If the police do not collect and analyze data, it is certain that plaintiffs' experts will. Facts are only facts; what they mean is often in dispute. As noted earlier, it is too simplistic to leap to conclusions of racial animus or bias, or illegality, solely because differential patterns emerge on racial or ethnic grounds. Concededly, the public may do so, and police departments will necessarily, have to deal with this perception. Second, forewarned is forearmed: If the a police department discovers that its officers are lax or less than precise in assessing probable cause or reasonable suspicion to stop or to search, better to know it and institute remedial training than face the risk of ongoing liability. Third, the tracking of the data and the their inclusion in an early warning system will allow the police department to spot patterns or identify particular officers whose conduct may require attention, counseling, or re-training.

It's not unusual to hear the thoroughly discredited argument that collecting data is "only putting evidence in the plaintiff's hands." It's true that the more that has to explained away in a lawsuit against the department, the harder the job of the defense counsel. And in the short run, an individual case might be dismissed or settled at less expense without the data. But such arguments are ultimately specious, and in the long run the department is poorly served by the lawyer who opposes collecting data. Police departments with their head in the sand do not win lawsuits. Their opponents, armed with data, do. More importantly, they lack the information to manage risk. In the business of law enforcement, people do the same things in the same ways day in and day out, year in and year out. New training and techniques may introduce variations, but the basic job – patrolling, responding to calls, making stops, questioning people, performing searches, making arrests, being on the lookout – does not change. Accordingly, law enforcement is a business that is particularly vulnerable to multiple claims based upon similar conduct. It is vulnerable because if one officer is engaging in a risky pattern that may give rise to litigation, it's likely that many, many officers are doing the same thing. By the same token, if the risk can be analyzed and managed, the results can drop risk substantially. Likewise, if race and ethnicity are improperly entering into decisions about whom to stop or search, the way to avoid liability is to respond sensibly to problems that need to be addressed. Collecting data is the first step. It is important to focus on the impact of data collection on the police officers who will be called upon to record the information. Even if, as in San Diego, it takes no more than 20 seconds to complete a form or, as in Sacramento, the form is set up so that it can be rapidly filled out and fed into a scanner, the departments clearly are asking officers to do something additional. The officers likely will see data collection as an unwelcome burden. But there is more to their grumbling than that.

Line police officers also ask what's in it for them. Is data collection simply another way of appeasing the segment of the public that is already angry at the police? Or a way to create more opportunities to sue police officers? Will officers have to start acting defensively, keeping track of whom they stop? If, by the end of the month, the percentage of blacks that they have stopped is more than the proportion of blacks in the overall population, should they start pulling over more whites to bring the percentage down? Or will they simply quit making stops? These arguments and attitudes do not seem to abate until the police department's management lets it be known that it will tolerate neither officers who fail to do their sworn duty nor unfair and baseless attempts by the public to smear the reputation of good officers. When a police officer being asked to record data on stops wants to know, "What's in it for me?" the answer should be: Everything. If you do your job well and professionally and adhere strictly to legal and constitutional requirements, you will find that the department will strongly back you when times get rough and similarly will reward you when it is time to do so. Police leadership must both "talk and walk" this message. Some police officers are already too quick to see themselves as victims or to interpret events to match their freewheeling, corrosive cynicism about management. It is vitally important, in an area as inflammatory as data collection and race, that management stack the tinder carefully, lest unintended victims get scorched.

ENDNOTES

[1] We want to thank Chris Stone, Janet Mandelstam, and Jennifer Trone of the Vera Institute of Justice for their insights and suggestions for this article. In particular, we thank Janet Mandelstam for her wonderful editing assistance.

Whatever their cause, racial disparities are stark throughout the criminal justice system. A recent Justice Department study showed that 70 percent of the defendants facing the death penalty are black or Latino. As of the end of 1998, approximately 43 percent of all persons on Death Row in the United States were African-American men. Capital Punishment 1998, United States Department of Justice, Bureau of Justice Statistics (December 1999) (revised January 6, 2000) NCJ 179012. Black males comprise 49 percent of persons in prison. Correctional Populations in the United States 1997, United States Department of Justice, Bureau of Justice Statistics (November 2000). Black males comprise 42 percent of persons in local jails Id. Nine percent of all black adults over the age of 18 are in prison, jail, probation or parole, as contrasted to two percent of all white adults. Id. At current levels of incarceration, newborn black males in this country have greater than a 1 in 4 chance of going to prison during their lifetimes, while Latinos have a 1 in 6 chance, and white males a 1 in 23 chance of serving prison time. Lifetime Likelihood of Going to State or Federal Prison, United States Department of Justice, Bureau of Justice Statistics (March 1997) NCJ160092.

[2] The Supreme Court recently reiterated this rationale in *City of Indianapolis v. Edmond*, ___ U.S. ____ (2000).

[3] Studies in New Jersey of stops on the New Jersey Turnpike reached similar results: 13.5 percent of the individuals using the New Jersey Turnpike were African-American, and African-Americans comprised 15 percent of the drivers who sped on that Turnpike. Blacks, however, constituted 35 percent of the drivers stopped on the Turnpike and 73.2 percent of those arrested. Report of Dr. John Lamberth, Plaintiff's Expert, Revised Statistical Analysis.

[4] A second report, dated May 8, 2001, reconfirming the results of the first study, was recently published at the same San Diego Police Department website.

[5] The San Diego PD collects for every vehicle stop:
  – Date and time of the stop;
  – Division where the stop occurred;
  – Primary reason for the stop (moving violation; equipment violation; radio
  – call/ citizen contact; officer observation/knowledge; supplemental information on the suspect, etc.);
  – Driver's sex and age;
  – Driver's race;

- Action taken (citation, written warning, verbal warning, field interrogation, other);
- Whether the driver was arrested;
- Whether the driver was searched, and if so:
  a   Type of search (vehicle, driver, passengers);
  b   Basis for search (visible contraband, contraband odor, canine alert, consent search; 4th Amendment waiver, search incident to arrest, inventory search prior to impound, observed evidence related to criminal activity, other);
  c   Whether a Consent Search Form was obtained;
  d   Whether contraband was found;
  e   Whether property was seized.

[6] If stopped, Latinos had a 10.6 percent chance of being searched; blacks a 10.2 percent chance; Asians and Pacific Islanders, a 3.4 percent chance, and whites, a 3.0 percent chance. If inventory searches of impounded vehicles were not counted, blacks had a 5.8 percent chance of being searched; Latinos, 2.8 percent; Asians/Pacific Islanders, 2.0 percent; whites, 1.5 percent. If stopped, blacks had a 3.0 percent chance of being arrested; Latinos, 2.7 percent; whites, 1.3 percent; Asian/Pacific Islander, 0.9 percent. Id.

[7] Respected academics, including Professor Sam Walker of the University of Nebraska at Omaha, have also raised questions about how to interpret the data the appropriate benchmark to do so. Walker, Samuel (2000)(draft). "Searching for the Denominator: Problems with Police Traffic Stop Data and an Early Warning System Solution." The challenge is to identify the right base against which to measure the disparate impact of traffic stops on minorities. It is relatively easy to do so on a controlled access Interstate highway; it is tougher- although doable- in a large metropolitan area. The US Department of Justice is in the forefront in attempts to do so.

[8] The Sacramento SPD employs a Scantron form which has 17 different variables for the officer to fill in. The form is set up so that it can be filled out quickly after each stop by darkening an appropriate box in each category. The 17 categories and related choices are:
- Time of stop, with choices for am or pm and the hour and minute of the stop;
- Date of stop, with choices for date, month, and year;
- Reason for stop; with choices for:
  - Hazardous violation of the Vehicle Code
  - Violation of the Penal Code
  - Violation of a city ordinance
  - Call for service
  - Preexisting knowledge or information
  - Equipment or registration violation
  - Special detail (i.e., DUI checkpoint; narcotic suppression detail)
  - Other
- Race and gender of the driver
- Driver's date of birth
- Driver's license no. and state
- Yes or no to whether the driver was asked to exit the car
- The number of passengers
- Was a search done, with choices for the driver, passenger, or the vehicle or no.

- Search authority, with choices for consent, Terry cursory (reasonable grounds to believe that the person
- may be armed and dangerous), incident to arrest, parole/probation, or tow inventory.
- What was discovered or seized, with choices for weapons, drugs, cash, the vehicle, alcohol, other property,
- or nothing
- The result of the stop, with choices for citation, arrest, etc.
- The stop location, by precinct
- The vehicle license plate and state
- The duration of the stop in total minutes
- The officer's badge number and the badge number of a secondary officer, if applicable
- Whether the radio car was equipped with a video camera or not.

In: Racial Profiling: Issues, Data and Analyses
Editor: Steven J. Muffler, pp. 41-46

ISBN 1-59454-547-2
© 2006 Nova Science Publishers, Inc.

Chapter 4

RACIAL PROFILING FACT SHEET[*]

U.S. Department of Justice
Washington, DC

"It's wrong, and we will end it in America. In so doing, we will not hinder the work of our nation's brave police officers. They protect us every day -- often at great risk. But by stopping the abuses of a few, we will add to the public confidence our police officers earn and deserve."

President George W. Bush, Feb. 27, 2001

"This administration... has been opposed to racial profiling and has done more to indicate its opposition than ever in history. The President said it's wrong and we'll end it in America, and I subscribe to that. Using race... as a proxy for potential criminal behavior is unconstitutional, and it undermines law enforcement by undermining the confidence that people can have in law enforcement."

Attorney General John Ashcroft, Feb. 28, 2002

DEFINING THE PROBLEM:
Racial Profiling Is Wrong and Will Not Be Tolerated

Racial profiling sends the dehumanizing message to our citizens that they are judged by the color of their skin and harms the criminal justice system by eviscerating the trust that is necessary if law enforcement is to effectively protect our communities.

- *America Has a Moral Obligation to Prohibit Racial Profiling.* Race-based assumptions in law enforcement perpetuate negative racial stereotypes that are harmful to our diverse democracy, and materially impair our efforts to maintain a fair and just society. As Attorney General John Ashcroft said, racial profiling creates a "lose-lose" situation because it destroys the potential for underlying trust that "should

---

[*] Excerpted from http://www.usdoj.gov/opa/pr/2003/June/racial_profiling_fact_sheet.pdf

support the administration of justice as a societal objective, not just as a law enforcement objective."

— *The Overwhelming Majority of Federal Law Enforcement Officers Perform Their Jobs with Dedication, Fairness and Honor, But Any Instance of Racial Profiling by a Few Damages Our Criminal Justice System.* The vast majority of federal law enforcement officers are hard-working public servants who perform a dangerous job with dedication, fairness and honor. However, when law enforcement practices are perceived to be biased or unfair, the general public, and especially minority communities, are less willing to trust and confide in officers, report crimes, be witnesses at trials, or serve on juries.

— *Racial Profiling Is Discrimination, and It Taints the Entire Criminal Justice System.* Racial profiling rests on the erroneous assumption that any particular individual of one race or ethnicity is more likely to engage in misconduct than any particular individual of other races or ethnicities.

TAKING STEPS TO BAN RACIAL PROFILING:
Due to the Seriousness of Racial Profiling, the Justice Department Has Developed Guidelines to Make Clear that It Is Prohibited in Federal Law Enforcement

√ *President Bush Has Directed that Racial Profiling Be Formally Banned.* In his February 27, 2001, Address to a Joint Session of Congress, President George W. Bush declared that racial profiling is "wrong and we will end it in America." He directed the Attorney General to review the use by federal law enforcement authorities of race as a factor in conducting stops, searches and other law enforcement investigative procedures. The Attorney General, in turn, instructed the Civil Rights Division to develop guidance for federal officials to ensure an end to racial profiling in federal law enforcement.

√ *The Bush Administration Is the First to Take Action to Ban Racial Profiling in Federal Law Enforcement.* The guidance has been sent to all federal law enforcement agencies and is effective immediately. Federal agencies will review their policies and procedures to ensure compliance.

√ *The Guidance Requires More Restrictions on the Use of Race by Federal Law Enforcement than Does the Constitution.* The guidance in many cases imposes *more* restrictions on the use of race and ethnicity in federal law enforcement than the Constitution requires. This guidance prohibits racial profiling in federal law enforcement practices without hindering the important work of our nation's public safety officials, particularly the intensified anti-terrorism efforts precipitated by the attacks of September 11, 2001.

√ *Prohibiting Racial Profiling in Routine or Spontaneous Activities in Domestic Law Enforcement:* In making routine or spontaneous law enforcement decisions, such as ordinary traffic stops, federal law enforcement officers may *not* use race or ethnicity to any degree, except that officers may rely on race and ethnicity if a specific suspect description exists. This prohibition applies even where the use of race or ethnicity might otherwise be lawful.

- *Routine Patrol Duties Must Be Carried Out Without Consideration of Race.* Federal law enforcement agencies and officers sometimes engage in law enforcement activities, such as traffic and foot patrols, that generally do not involve either the ongoing investigation of specific criminal activities or the prevention of catastrophic events or harm to the national security. Rather, their activities are typified by spontaneous action in response to the activities of individuals whom they happen to encounter in the course of their patrols and about whom they have no information other than their observations. These general enforcement responsibilities should be carried out without *any* consideration of race or ethnicity.

  - *Example*: While parked by the side of the highway, a federal officer notices that nearly all vehicles on the road are exceeding the posted speed limit. Although each such vehicle is committing an infraction that would legally justify a stop, the officer may not use race or ethnicity as a factor in deciding which motorists to pull over. Likewise, the officer may not use race or ethnicity in deciding which detained motorists to ask to consent to a search of their vehicles.

- *Stereotyping Certain Races as Having a Greater Propensity to Commit Crimes Is Absolutely Prohibited.* Some have argued that overall discrepancies in crime rates among racial groups could justify using race as a factor in general traffic enforcement activities and would produce a greater number of arrests for non-traffic offenses (*e.g.*, narcotics trafficking). We emphatically reject this view. It is patently unacceptable and thus prohibited under this guidance for federal law enforcement officers to engage in racial profiling.

- *Acting on Specific Suspect Identification Does Not Constitute Impermissible Stereotyping.* The situation is different when a federal officer acts on the personal identifying characteristics of potential suspects, including age, sex, ethnicity or race. Common sense dictates that when a victim or witness describes the assailant as being of a particular race, authorities may properly limit their search for suspects to persons of that race. In such circumstances, the federal officer is not acting based on a generalized assumption about persons of different races; rather, the officer is helping locate a specific individual previously identified as involved in crime.

  - *Example:* While parked by the side of the highway, a federal officer receives an "All Points Bulletin" to be on the look-out for a fleeing bank robbery suspect, a man of a particular race and particular hair color in his 30s driving a blue automobile. The officer may use this description, including the race of the particular suspect, in deciding which speeding motorists to pull over.

√ *Prohibiting Racial Profiling in Federal Law Enforcement Activities Related to Specific Investigations*: In conducting activities in connection with a specific investigation, federal law enforcement officers may consider race and ethnicity only to the extent that there is trustworthy information, relevant to the locality or time frame, that links persons of a particular race or ethnicity to an identified criminal incident, scheme, or organization. This standard applies even where the use of race or ethnicity might otherwise be lawful.

- *Acting on Specific Information Does Not Constitute Impermissible Stereotyping.* Often federal officers have specific information, based on trustworthy sources, to "be on the lookout" for specific individuals identified at least in part by race or ethnicity. In such circumstances, the officer is not acting based on a generalized assumption about persons of different races; rather, the officer is helping locate specific individuals previously identified as involved in crime.

  • *Example:* In connection with a new initiative to increase drug arrests, federal authorities begin aggressively enforcing speeding, traffic, and other public area laws in a neighborhood predominantly occupied by people of a single race. The choice of neighborhood was not based on the number of 911 calls, number of arrests, or other pertinent reporting data specific to that area, but only on the general assumption that more drug-related crime occurs in that neighborhood because of its racial composition. This effort would be *improper* because it is based on generalized stereotypes.

  • *Example:* The victim of an assault at a local university describes her assailant as a young male of a particular race with a cut on his right hand. The investigation focuses on whether any students at the university fit the victim's description. Here investigators are properly relying on a description given by the victim, part of which included the assailant's race. Although the ensuing investigation affects students of a particular race, that investigation is not undertaken with a discriminatory purpose. Thus use of race as a factor in the investigation, in this instance, is permissible.

- *Reliance Upon Generalized Stereotypes Continues to Be Absolutely Forbidden.* Use of race or ethnicity is permitted only when the federal officer is pursuing a specific lead concerning the identifying characteristics of persons involved in an *identified* criminal activity. The rationale underlying this concept carefully limits its reach. In order to qualify as a legitimate investigative lead, the following must be true:

  • The information must be relevant to the locality or time frame of the criminal activity;

  • The information must be trustworthy; and,

  • The information concerning identifying characteristics must be tied to a particular criminal incident, a particular criminal scheme, or a particular criminal organization.

  • *Example:* The FBI is investigating the murder of a known gang member and has information that the shooter is a member of a rival gang. The FBI knows that the members of the rival gang are exclusively members of a certain ethnicity. This information, however, is not suspect-specific because there is no description of the particular assailant. But because authorities have reliable, locally relevant information linking a rival group with a distinctive ethnic character to the murder, federal law enforcement officers could properly consider ethnicity in conjunction with other appropriate factors in the course of conducting their investigation. Agents could properly decide to focus on persons dressed in a manner consistent with gang activity, but ignore persons dressed in that manner who do not appear to be members of that particular ethnicity.

- *Example*: While investigating a car theft ring that dismantles cars and ships the parts for sale in other states, the FBI is informed by local authorities that it is common knowledge locally that most car thefts in that area are committed by individuals of a particular race. In this example, although the source (local police) is trustworthy, and the information potentially verifiable with reference to arrest statistics, there is no particular incident- or scheme- specific information linking individuals of that race to the particular interstate ring the FBI is investigating. Thus, agents could not use ethnicity as a factor in making law enforcement decisions in this investigation.

TAKING STEPS TO BALANCE NATIONAL SECURITY CONCERNS
The Justice Department's Policy Guidance Ensures that Federal Law Enforcement Continues to Have the Tools Needed to Identify Terrorist Threats and Stop Potential Catastrophic Attacks

- *Federal Law Enforcement Will Continue Terrorist Identification.* Since the terrorist attacks on September 11, 2001, the President has emphasized that federal law enforcement personnel must use every legitimate tool to prevent future attacks, protect our nation's borders, and deter those who would cause devastating harm to our country and its people through the use of biological or chemical weapons, other weapons of mass destruction, suicide hijackings, or any other means.
  - Therefore, the racial profiling guidance recognizes that race and ethnicity may be used in terrorist identification, but only to the extent permitted by the nation's laws and the Constitution. The policy guidance emphasizes that, even in the national security context, the constitutional restriction on use of generalized stereotypes remains.
- *Federal Law Enforcement Must Adhere to Limitations Imposed by the Constitution.* In investigating or preventing threats to national security or other catastrophic events (including the performance of duties related to air transportation security), or in enforcing laws protecting the integrity of the nation's borders, federal law enforcement officers may not consider race or ethnicity except to the extent permitted by the Constitution and laws of the United States.
  - *The Constitution Prohibits Consideration of Race or Ethnicity in Law Enforcement Decisions in All But the Most Exceptional Instances.* Given the incalculably high stakes involved in such investigations, federal law enforcement officers who are protecting national security or preventing catastrophic events (as well as airport security screeners) may consider race, ethnicity, alienage, and other relevant factors. Constitutional provisions limiting government action on the basis of race are wide-ranging and provide substantial protections at every step of the investigative and judicial process. Accordingly, this policy will honor the rule of law and promote vigorous protection of our national security.

– *Federal Law Enforcement Must Guard Against Uncertain Threats of Terrorism.* Because terrorist organizations might aim to engage in unexpected acts of catastrophic violence in any available part of the country (indeed, in multiple places simultaneously, if possible), there can be no expectation that the information must be specific to a particular locale or even to a particular identified scheme.

– *Even in the National Security Context, Reliance Upon Generalized Stereotypes Is Restricted by the Constitution.* For example, at the security entrance to a federal courthouse, a man who appears to be of a particular ethnicity properly submits his briefcase for x-ray screening and passes through the metal detector. The inspection of the briefcase reveals nothing amiss. The man does not activate the metal detector, and there is nothing suspicious about his activities or appearance. Absent any threat warning or other particular reason to suspect that those of the man's apparent ethnicity pose a heightened danger to the courthouse, the federal security screener may not order the man to undergo a further inspection solely because of his apparent ethnicity.

 – *Example*: U.S. intelligence sources report that Middle Eastern terrorists are planning to use commercial jetliners as weapons by hijacking them at an airport in California during the next week. Before allowing men appearing to be of Middle Eastern origin to board commercial airplanes in California airports during the next week, Transportation Security Administration personnel, and other federal and state authorities, may subject them to heightened scrutiny.

 – *Example*: The FBI receives reliable information that persons affiliated with a foreign ethnic insurgent group intend to use suicide bombers to assassinate that country's president and his entire entourage during an official visit to the United States. Federal law enforcement may appropriately focus investigative attention on identifying members of that ethnic insurgent group who may be present and active in the United States and who, based on other available information, might conceivably be involved in planning some such attack during the state visit.

In: Racial Profiling: Issues, Data and Analyses
Editor: Steven J. Muffler, pp. 47-56

ISBN 1-59454-547-2
© 2006 Nova Science Publishers, Inc.

Chapter 5

GUIDANCE REGARDING THE USE OF RACE BY FEDERAL LAW ENFORCEMENT AGENCIES[*]

U.S. Department of Justice
Civil Rights Division, Washington, DC

INTRODUCTION AND EXECUTIVE SUMMARY

In his February 27, 2001, Address to a Joint Session of Congress, President George W. Bush declared that racial profiling is "wrong and we will end it in America." He directed the Attorney General to review the use by Federal law enforcement authorities of race as a factor in conducting stops, searches and other law enforcement investigative procedures. The Attorney General, in turn, instructed the Civil Rights Division to develop guidance for Federal officials to ensure an end to racial profiling in law enforcement.

"Racial profiling" at its core concerns the invidious use of race or ethnicity as a criterion in conducting stops, searches and other law enforcement investigative procedures. It is premised on the erroneous assumption that any particular individual of one race or ethnicity is more likely to engage in misconduct than any particular individual of another race or ethnicity.

Racial profiling in law enforcement is not merely wrong, but also ineffective. Race-based assumptions in law enforcement perpetuate negative racial stereotypes that are harmful to our rich and diverse democracy, and materially impair our efforts to maintain a fair and just society.[1]

The use of race as the basis for law enforcement decision-making clearly has a terrible cost, both to the individuals who suffer invidious discrimination and to the Nation, whose goal of "liberty and justice for all" recedes with every act of such discrimination. For this reason, this guidance in many cases imposes more restrictions on the consideration of race and ethnicity in Federal law enforcement than the Constitution requires.[2] This guidance prohibits racial profiling in law enforcement practices without hindering the important work

---

[*] Excerpted from http://www.usdoj.gov/crt/split/documents/guidance_on_race.htm

of our Nation's public safety officials, particularly the intensified anti-terrorism efforts precipitated by the events of September 11, 2001.

Traditional Law Enforcement Activities

Two standards in combination should guide use by Federal law enforcement authorities of race or ethnicity in law enforcement activities:

- In making routine or spontaneous law enforcement decisions, such as ordinary traffic stops, Federal law enforcement officers may not use race or ethnicity to any degree, except that officers may rely on race and ethnicity in a specific suspect description. This prohibition applies even where the use of race or ethnicity might otherwise be lawful.
- In conducting activities in connection with a specific investigation, Federal law enforcement officers may consider race and ethnicity only to the extent that there is trustworthy information, relevant to the locality or time frame, that links persons of a particular race or ethnicity to an identified criminal incident, scheme, or organization. This standard applies even where the use of race or ethnicity might otherwise be lawful.

National Security and Border Integrity

The above standards do not affect current Federal policy with respect to law enforcement activities and other efforts to defend and safeguard against threats to national security or the integrity of the Nation's borders,[3] to which the following applies:

- In investigating or preventing threats to national security or other catastrophic events (including the performance of duties related to air transportation security), or in enforcing laws protecting the integrity of the Nation's borders, Federal law enforcement officers may not consider race or ethnicity except to the extent permitted by the Constitution and laws of the United States.

Any questions arising under these standards should be directed to the Department of Justice.

THE CONSTITUTIONAL FRAMEWORK

"[T]he Constitution prohibits selective enforcement of the law based on considerations such as race." *Whren v. United States*, 517 U.S. 806, 813 (1996). Thus, for example, the decision of federal prosecutors "whether to prosecute may not be based on 'an unjustifiable standard such as race, religion, or other arbitrary classification.'"[4] *United States v. Armstrong*, 517 U.S. 456, 464 (1996) (quoting *Oyler v. Boles*, 368 U.S. 448, 456 (1962)). The same is true of Federal law enforcement officers. Federal courts repeatedly have held that any general policy of "utiliz[ing] impermissible racial classifications in determining whom to stop, detain, and search" would violate the Equal Protection Clause. *Chavez v. Illinois State Police*, 251 F.3d 612, 635 (7th Cir. 2001). As the Sixth Circuit has explained, "[i]f law enforcement adopts a policy, employs a practice, or in a given situation takes steps to initiate an investigation of a citizen based solelyupon that citizen's race, without more, then a violation of the Equal Protection Clause has occurred." *United States v. Avery*, 137 F.3d 343, 355 (6th Cir. 1997). "A person cannot become the target of a police investigation solely on the basis of skin color. Such selective law enforcement is forbidden." *Id.* at 354.

As the Supreme Court has held, this constitutional prohibition against selective enforcement of the law based on race "draw[s] on 'ordinary equal protection standards.'"*Armstrong*, 517 U.S. at 465 (quoting *Wayte v. United States*, 470 U.S. 598, 608 (1985)). Thus, impermissible selective enforcement based on race occurs when the challenged policy has "'a discriminatory effect and . . . was motivated by a discriminatory purpose.'"*Id.* (quoting *Wayte*, 470 U.S. at 608).[5] Put simply, "to the extent that race is used as a proxy" for criminality, "a racial stereotype requiring strict scrutiny is in operation." *Cf. Bush v. Vera*, 517 U.S. at 968 (plurality).

I. Guidance for Federal Officials Engaged in Law Enforcement Activities

A. Routine or Spontaneous Activities in Domestic Law Enforcement

In making routine or spontaneous law enforcement decisions, such as ordinary traffic stops, Federal law enforcement officers may not use race or ethnicity to any degree, except that officers may rely on race and ethnicity in a specific suspect description. This prohibition applies even where the use of race or ethnicity might otherwise be lawful.

Federal law enforcement agencies and officers sometimes engage in law enforcement activities, such as traffic and foot patrols, that generally do not involve either the ongoing investigation of specific criminal activities or the prevention of catastrophic events or harm to the national security. Rather, their activities are typified by spontaneous action in response to the activities of individuals whom they happen to encounter in the course of their patrols and about whom they have no information other than their observations. These general enforcement responsibilities should be carried out without *any* consideration of race or ethnicity.

— *Example:* While parked by the side of the George Washington Parkway, a Park Police Officer notices that nearly all vehicles on the road are exceeding the posted speed limit. Although each such vehicle is committing an infraction that would legally justify a stop, the officer may not use race or ethnicity as a factor in deciding which motorists to pull over. Likewise, the officer may not use race or ethnicity in deciding which detained motorists to ask to consent to a search of their vehicles.

Some have argued that overall discrepancies in certain crime rates among racial groups could justify using race as a factor in general traffic enforcement activities and would produce a greater number of arrests for non-traffic offenses (*e.g.*, narcotics trafficking). We emphatically reject this view. The President has made clear his concern that racial profiling is morally wrong and inconsistent with our core values and principles of fairness and justice. Even if there were overall statistical evidence of differential rates of commission of certain offenses among particular races, the affirmative use of such generalized notions by federal law enforcement officers in routine, spontaneous law enforcement activities is tantamount to stereotyping. It casts a pall of suspicion over every member of certain racial and ethnic groups without regard to the specific circumstances of a particular investigation or crime, and it offends the dignity of the individual improperly targeted. Whatever the motivation, it is patently unacceptable and thus prohibited under this guidance for Federal law enforcement officers to act on the belief that race or ethnicity signals a higher risk of criminality. This is the core of "racial profiling" and it must not occur.

The situation is different when an officer has specific information, based on trustworthy sources, to "be on the lookout" for specific individuals identified at least in part by race or ethnicity. In such circumstances, the officer is not acting based on a generalized assumption about persons of different races; rather, the officer is helping locate specific individuals previously identified as involved in crime.

- *Example*: While parked by the side of the George Washington Parkway, a Park Police Officer receives an "All Points Bulletin" to be on the look-out for a fleeing bank robbery suspect, a man of a particular race and particular hair color in his 30s driving a blue automobile. The Officer may use this description, including the race of the particular suspect, in deciding which speeding motorists to pull over.

B. Law Enforcement Activities Related to Specific Investigations

In conducting activities in connection with a specific investigation, Federal law enforcement officers may consider race and ethnicity only to the extent that there is trustworthy information, relevant to the locality or time frame, that links persons of a particular race or ethnicity to an identified criminal incident, scheme, or organization. This standard applies even where the use of race or ethnicity might otherwise be lawful.

As noted above, there are circumstances in which law enforcement activities relating to particular identified criminal incidents, schemes or enterprises may involve consideration of personal identifying characteristics of potential suspects, including age, sex, ethnicity or race. Common sense dictates that when a victim describes the assailant as being of a particular race, authorities may properly limit their search for suspects to persons of that race. Similarly, in conducting an ongoing investigation into a specific criminal organization whose membership has been identified as being overwhelmingly of one ethnicity, law enforcement should not be expected to disregard such facts in pursuing investigative leads into the organization's activities.

Reliance upon generalized stereotypes is absolutely forbidden. Rather, use of race or ethnicity is permitted only when the officer is pursuing a specific lead concerning the identifying characteristics of persons involved in an *identified* criminal activity. The rationale underlying this concept carefully limits its reach. In order to qualify as a legitimate investigative lead, the following must be true:

- The information must be relevant to the locality or time frame of the criminal activity;

– The information must be trustworthy;

– The information concerning identifying characteristics must be tied to a particular criminal incident, a particular criminal scheme, or a particular criminal organization.

The following policy statements more fully explain these principles.

1. *Authorities May Never Rely on Generalized Stereotypes, But May Rely Only on Specific Race- or Ethnicity-Based Information*
   This standard categorically bars the use of generalized assumptions based on race.

   – *Example:* In the course of investigating an auto theft in a federal park, law enforcement authorities could not properly choose to target individuals of a particular race as suspects, based on a generalized assumption that those individuals are more likely to commit crimes.

   This bar extends to the use of race-neutral pretexts as an excuse to target minorities. Federal law enforcement may not use such pretexts. This prohibition extends to the use of other, facially race-neutral factors as a proxy for overtly targeting persons of a certain race or ethnicity. This concern arises most frequently when aggressive law enforcement efforts are focused on "high crime areas." The issue is ultimately one of motivation and evidence; certain seemingly race-based efforts, if properly supported by reliable, empirical data, are in fact race-neutral.

   – *Example:* In connection with a new initiative to increase drug arrests, local authorities begin aggressively enforcing speeding, traffic, and other public area laws in a neighborhood predominantly occupied by people of a single race. The choice of neighborhood was not based on the number of 911 calls, number of arrests, or other pertinent reporting data specific to that area, but only on the general assumption that more drug-related crime occurs in that neighborhood because of its racial composition. This effort would be improper because it is based on generalized stereotypes.

   – *Example:* Authorities seeking to increase drug arrests use tracking software to plot out where, if anywhere, drug arrests are concentrated in a particular city, and discover that the clear majority of drug arrests occur in particular precincts that happen to be neighborhoods predominantly occupied by people of a single race. So long as they are not motivated by racial animus, authorities can properly decide to enforce all laws aggressively in that area, including less serious quality of life ordinances, as a means of increasing drug-related arrests. *See, e.g., United States v. Montero-Camargo,* 208 F.3d 1122, 1138 (9th Cir. 2000) ("We must be particularly careful to ensure that a 'high crime" area factor is not used with respect to entire neighborhoods or communities in which members of minority groups regularly go about their daily business, but is limited to specific, circumscribed locations where particular crimes occur with unusual regularity.").

   By contrast, where authorities are investigating a crime and have received *specific information* that the suspect is of a certain race (*e.g.,* direct observations by the victim or other witnesses), authorities may reasonably use that information, even if it is the only descriptive information available. In such an instance, it is the victim or other witness making the racial classification, and federal authorities may use reliable incident-specific identifying information to apprehend criminal suspects. Agencies and departments, however, must use caution in the rare instance in which a suspect's race is the only available information. Although the use of that information may not be unconstitutional, broad targeting of discrete racial or ethnic groups always raises serious fairness concerns.

- *Example:* The victim of an assault at a local university describes her assailant as a young male of a particular race with a cut on his right hand. The investigation focuses on whether any students at the university fit the victim's description. Here investigators are properly relying on a description given by the victim, part of which included the assailant's race. Although the ensuing investigation affects students of a particular race, that investigation is not undertaken with a discriminatory purpose. Thus use of race as a factor in the investigation, in this instance, is permissible.

2. *The Information Must be Relevant to the Locality or Time Frame*

Any information concerning the race of persons who may be involved in specific criminal activities must be locally or temporally relevant.

- *Example:* DEA issues an intelligence report that indicates that a drug ring whose members are known to be predominantly of a particular race or ethnicity is trafficking drugs in Charleston, SC. An agent operating in Los Angeles reads this intelligence report. In the absence of information establishing that this intelligence is also applicable in Southern California, the agent may not use ethnicity as a factor in making local law enforcement decisions about individuals who are of the particular race or ethnicity that is predominant in the Charleston drug ring.

3. *The Information Must be Trustworthy*

Where the information concerning potential criminal activity is unreliable or is too generalized and unspecific, use of racial descriptions is prohibited.

- *Example:* ATF special agents receive an uncorroborated anonymous tip that a male of a particular race will purchase an illegal firearm at a Greyhound bus terminal in a racially diverse North Philadelphia neighborhood. Although agents surveilling the location are free to monitor the movements of whomever they choose, the agents are prohibited from using the tip information, without more, to target any males of that race in the bus terminal. *Cf. Morgan v. Woessner*, 997 F.2d 1244, 1254 (9th Cir. 1993) (finding no reasonable basis for suspicion where tip "made all black men suspect"). The information is neither sufficiently reliable nor sufficiently specific.

4. *Race- or Ethnicity-Based Information Must Always be Specific to Particular Suspects or Incidents, or Ongoing Criminal Activities, Schemes, or Enterprises*

These standards contemplate the appropriate use of both "suspect-specific" and "incident-specific" information. As noted above, where a crime has occurred and authorities have eyewitness accounts including the race, ethnicity, or other distinguishing characteristics of the perpetrator, that information may be used. Federal authorities may also use reliable, locally relevant information linking persons of a certain race or ethnicity to a particular incident, unlawful scheme, or ongoing criminal enterprise--even absent a description of any particular individual suspect. In certain cases, the circumstances surrounding an incident or ongoing criminal activity will point strongly to a perpetrator of a certain race, even though authorities lack an eyewitness account

- *Example:* The FBI is investigating the murder of a known gang member and has information that the shooter is a member of a rival gang. The FBI knows that the members of the rival gang are exclusively members of a certain ethnicity. This information, however, is not suspect-specific because there is no description of the particular assailant. But because authorities have reliable, locally relevant information linking a rival group with a distinctive ethnic character to the murder, Federal law enforcement officers could properly consider ethnicity in conjunction with other appropriate factors in the course of conducting their investigation. Agents could properly decide to focus on persons dressed in a manner consistent with gang activity, but ignore persons dressed in that manner who do not appear to be members of that particular ethnicity.

It is critical, however, that there be reliable information that ties persons of a particular description to a specific criminal incident, ongoing criminal activity, or particular criminal organization. Otherwise, any use of race runs the risk of descending into reliance upon prohibited generalized stereotypes.

- *Example:* While investigating a car theft ring that dismantles cars and ships the parts for sale in other states, the FBI is informed by local authorities that it is common knowledge locally that most car thefts in that area are committed by individuals of a particular race. In this example, although the source (local police) is trustworthy, and the information potentially verifiable with reference to arrest statistics, there is no particular incident- or scheme- specific information linking individuals of that race to the particular interstate ring the FBI is investigating. Thus, without more, agents could not use ethnicity as a factor in making law enforcement decisions in this investigation.

Note that these standards allow the use of reliable identifying information about planned future crimes. Where federal authorities receive a credible tip from a reliable informant regarding a planned crime that has not yet occurred, authorities may use this information under the same restrictions applying to information obtained regarding a past incident. A prohibition on the use of reliable prospective information would severely hamper law enforcement efforts by essentially compelling authorities to wait for crimes to occur, instead of taking pro-active measures to prevent crimes from happening.

- *Example:* While investigating a specific drug trafficking operation, DEA special agents learn that a particular methamphetamine distribution ring is manufacturing the drug in California, and plans to have couriers pick up shipments at the Sacramento, California airport and drive the drugs back to Oklahoma for distribution. The agents also receive trustworthy information that the distribution ring has specifically chosen to hire older couples of a particular race to act as the couriers. DEA agents may properly target older couples of that particular race driving vehicles with indicia such as Oklahoma plates near the Sacramento airport.

II. Guidance for Federal Officials Engaged in Law Enforcement Activities Involving Threats to National Security or the Integrity of the Nation's Borders

In investigating or preventing threats to national security or other catastrophic events (including the performance of duties related to air transportation security), or in enforcing laws protecting the integrity of the Nation's borders, Federal law enforcement officers may not consider race or ethnicity except to the extent permitted by the Constitution and laws of the United States.

Since the terrorist attacks on September 11, 2001, the President has emphasized that federal law enforcement personnel must use every legitimate tool to prevent future attacks, protect our Nation's borders, and deter those who would cause devastating harm to our Nation and its people through the use of biological or chemical weapons, other weapons of mass destruction, suicide hijackings, or any other means. "It is 'obvious and unarguable' that no governmental interest is more compelling than the security of the Nation." *Haig v. Agee*, 453 U.S. 280, 307 (1981) (quoting *Aptheker v. Secretary of State*, 378 U.S. 500, 509 (1964)).

The Constitution prohibits consideration of race or ethnicity in law enforcement decisions in all but the most exceptional instances. Given the incalculably high stakes involved in such investigations, however, Federal law enforcement officers who are protecting national security or preventing catastrophic events (as well as airport security screeners) may consider race, ethnicity, and other relevant factors to the extent permitted by our laws and the Constitution. Similarly, because enforcement of the laws protecting the Nation's borders may necessarily involve a consideration of a person's alienage in certain circumstances, the use of race or ethnicity in such circumstances is properly governed by existing statutory and constitutional standards. *See, e.g., United States v. Brignoni-Ponce*, 422 U.S. 873, 886-87 (1975).[6] This policy will honor the rule of law and promote vigorous protection of our national security.

As the Supreme Court has stated, all racial classifications by a governmental actor are subject to the "strictest judicial scrutiny."*Adarand Constructors, Inc. v. Peña*, 515 U.S. 200, 224-25 (1995). The application of strict scrutiny is of necessity a fact-intensive process. *Id.* at 236. Thus, the legality of particular, race-sensitive actions taken by Federal law enforcement officials in the context of national security and border integrity will depend to a large extent on the circumstances at hand. In absolutely no event, however, may Federal officials assert a national security or border integrity rationale as a mere pretext for invidious discrimination. Indeed, the very purpose of the strict scrutiny test is to "smoke out" illegitimate use of race, *Adarand*, 515 U.S. at 226 (quoting *Richmond v. J.A. Croson Co.*, 488 U.S. 469, 493 (1989)), and law enforcement strategies not actually premised on *bona fide* national security or border integrity interests therefore will not stand.

In sum, constitutional provisions limiting government action on the basis of race are wide-ranging and provide substantial protections at every step of the investigative and judicial process. Accordingly, and as illustrated below, when addressing matters of national security, border integrity, or the possible catastrophic loss of life, existing legal and constitutional standards are an appropriate guide for Federal law enforcement officers.

- *Example:* The FBI receives reliable information that persons affiliated with a foreign ethnic insurgent group intend to use suicide bombers to assassinate that country's president and his entire entourage during an official visit to the United States. Federal law enforcement may appropriately focus investigative attention on identifying members of that ethnic insurgent group who may be present and active in the United States and who, based on other available information, might conceivably be involved in planning some such attack during the state visit.
- *Example:* U.S. intelligence sources report that terrorists from a particular ethnic group are planning to use commercial jetliners as weapons by hijacking them at an airport in California during the next week. Before allowing men of that ethnic group to board commercial airplanes in California airports during the next week, Transportation Security Administration personnel, and other federal and state authorities, may subject them to heightened scrutiny.

Because terrorist organizations might aim to engage in unexpected acts of catastrophic violence in any available part of the country (indeed, in multiple places simultaneously, if possible), there can be no expectation that the information must be specific to a particular locale or even to a particular identified scheme.

Of course, as in the example below, reliance solely upon generalized stereotypes is forbidden.

- *Example:* At the security entrance to a Federal courthouse, a man who appears to be of a particular ethnicity properly submits his briefcase for x-ray screening and passes through the metal detector. The inspection of the briefcase reveals nothing amiss, the man does not activate the metal detector, and there is nothing suspicious about his activities or appearance. In the absence of any threat warning, the federal security screener may not order the man to undergo a further inspection solely because he appears to be of a particular ethnicity.

ENDNOTES

1. *See United States v. Montero-Camargo*, 208 F.3d 1122, 1135 (9th Cir. 2000) ("Stops based on race or ethnic appearance send the underlying message to all our citizens that those who are not white are judged by the color of their skin alone.").

2. This guidance is intended only to improve the internal management of the executive branch. It is not intended to, and does not, create any right, benefit, trust, or responsibility, whether substantive or procedural, enforceable at law or equity by a party against the United States, its departments, agencies, instrumentalities, entities, officers, employees, or agents, or any person, nor does it create any right of review in an administrative, judicial or any other proceeding.

3. This guidance document does not apply to U.S. military, intelligence, protective or diplomatic activities conducted consistent with the Constitution and applicable Federal law.

4. These same principles do not necessarily apply to classifications based on alienage. For example, Congress, in the exercise of its broad powers over immigration, has enacted a number of provisions that apply only to aliens, and enforcement of such provisions properly entails consideration of a person's alien status.

5. Invidious discrimination is not necessarily present whenever there is a "disproportion" between the racial composition of the pool of persons prosecuted and the general public at large; rather, the focus must be the pool of "*similarly situated* individuals of a different race [who] were not prosecuted."*Armstrong*, 517 U.S. at 465 (emphasis added). "[R]acial disproportions in the level of prosecutions for a particular crime may be unobjectionable if they merely reflect racial disproportions in the commission of that crime."*Bush v. Vera*, 517 U.S. 952, 968 (1996) (plurality).

6. Moreover, as in the traditional law enforcement context described in the second standard, *supra,* officials involved in homeland security may take into account specific, credible information about the descriptive characteristics of persons who are affiliated with identified organizations that are actively engaged in threatening the national security.

In: Racial Profiling: Issues, Data and Analyses
Editor: Steven J. Muffler, pp. 57-108

Chapter 6

A RESOURCE GUIDE ON RACIAL PROFILING DATA COLLECTION SYSTEMS: PROMISING PRACTICES AND LESSONS LEARNED[*]

Deborah Ramirez,[†] Jack McDevitt and Amy Farrell

Northeastern University,
Boston, MA

FOREWORD

For the past 8 years, we have seen a steady decline in the crime rate in nearly every community in America. Even with the advances in crime prevention and law enforcement, however, there are instances in which distrust and tensions between the police and the community are high, and these tensions affect all aspects of the criminal justice system. One of the major causes of this mistrust is the controversial practice of racial profiling.

The guarantee to all persons of equal protection under the law is one of the most fundamental principles of our democratic society. Law enforcement officers should not endorse or act upon stereotypes, attitudes, or beliefs that a person's race, ethnicity, or national origin increases that person's general propensity to act unlawfully. There is no tradeoff between effective law enforcement and protection of the civil rights of all Americans; we can and must have both.

One of the ways that law enforcement agencies are addressing concerns and allegations regarding discriminatory policing is through data collection. By collecting information on the nature, character, and demographics of police enforcement practices, we enhance our ability

---

[*] This document was prepared by Northwestern University, supported with funding from the U.S. Department of Justice. The opinions, findings, and conclusions or recommendations expressed in this document are those of the authors and do not necessarily represent the official position or policies of the U.S. Department of Justice. Excerpted from http://www.ncjrs.gov/pdffiles1/bja/184768.pdf

[†] E-mail: d.ramirez@nunet.neu.edu Fax: 617–373–5056, Tel: 617–373–4629

to assess the appropriate application of the authority and broad discretion entrusted to law enforcement.

In June 1999, when President Clinton and U.S. Attorney General Reno convened the conference *Strengthening Police-Community Relationships*, only a few jurisdictions—including San Diego, San Jose, and the state of North Carolina—had voluntarily agreed to collect traffic-stop data. When a followup meeting on racial profiling and data collection was held this past February, more than 100 jurisdictions indicated that they had plans to collect data on traffic or pedestrian stops.

To encourage voluntary data collection, the U.S. Department of Justice set about developing a resource guide on this subject. The result is this publication, *A Resource Guide on Racial Profiling Data Collection Systems*, prepared by staff of Northeastern University. This document provides an overview of the nature of racial profiling; a description of data collection and its purpose; current activities in California, New Jersey, North Carolina, and Great Britain; and recommendations for the future.

Our hope is that this resource guide will assist jurisdictions in developing and implementing their own data collection systems. Our ultimate goals are to restore trust in the police and to ensure that all citizens are treated equally by law enforcement officers.

Nancy E. Gist
Director, Bureau of Justice Assistance U.S. Department of Justice

INTRODUCTION

On June 9–10, 1999, President Bill Clinton, Attorney General Janet Reno, civil rights leaders, police, and other government leaders participated in the *Strengthening Police-Community Relationships* conference in Washington, D.C. During the conference, President Clinton called racial profiling a "morally indefensible, deeply corrosive practice" and further stated that "racial profiling is in fact the opposite of good police work, where actions are based on hard facts, not stereotypes. It is wrong, it is destructive, and it must stop."[1] As a result of increased national concern over racial profiling, the President directed federal agencies to begin gathering data on the race and ethnicity of persons stopped for future analysis.

At a later session of the same conference, participants discussed the design and implementation of racial profiling data collection systems. That discussion featured presentations by state and local jurisdictions where efforts were already under way to collect data on the race, ethnicity, and gender of the individuals police stop. This guide is an outgrowth of that breakout session. As its title suggests, the guide is designed to provide law enforcement, state and local elected officials, civil rights leaders, community organizations, and other local stakeholders with strategies and practices for gathering and analyzing data about police stops. By providing information about the nature, characteristics, and demographics of police enforcement patterns, these data collection efforts have the potential for shifting the rhetoric surrounding racial profiling from accusations, anecdotal stories, and stereotypes to a more rational discussion about the appropriate allocation of police resources.

Well-planned and comprehensive data collection efforts can serve as a catalyst for nurturing and shaping this type of community and police discussion.

This guide is a blueprint that police and communities can use to develop data collection systems. It offers practical information about implementing these systems and analyzing the data. The guide is not intended to serve as a comprehensive and thorough inventory of all existing data collection systems. It focuses on providing detailed descriptions of data collection efforts in a few selected sites: San Jose, California, which has designed a simple letter-code system allowing information to be collected verbally (via radio) or by computer; San Diego, California, which utilizes an online data collection system; North Carolina, the first state to collect data on traffic stops pursuant to state legislation; Great Britain, which uses a paper-based system to collect information on both traffic and pedestrian stops and searches; and New Jersey, which is collecting information on traffic-stops pursuant to a consent decree with the U.S. Department of Justice (DOJ). These sites were first identified by DOJ in preparation for the conference and represent various population sizes and geographic locations.

Site visits were later made to obtain further information about each site's data collection process.

Since the conference, there has been a flurry of activity in this area and hundreds of jurisdictions have begun to initiate data collection efforts. For example, Connecticut, Kansas, Missouri, and Washington have passed state legislation requiring state police and/or local police agencies to record and make public the racial and ethnic pattern of their traffic-stops. In California, approximately 75 agencies, including the California Highway Patrol, have begun to implement data collection systems. Florida Governor Jeb Bush directed the Florida Highway Patrol to begin collecting traffic-stop data in 2000. In August 1999, Houston's police department began to collect data on its traffic and pedestrian stops. Moreover, several other cities and towns have voluntarily agreed to implement data collection systems, including San Francisco, California; Tallahassee, Florida; Dearborn, Michigan; and Richmond, Virginia. In addition, some states have begun to implement statewide systems, including Michigan and Washington. Pursuant to federal consent decrees and settlements, Montgomery County, Maryland; Steubenville, Ohio; and Pittsburgh, Pennsylvania, have also implemented data collection systems. As part of settlements with the American Civil Liberties Union (ACLU), the Maryland State Police (MSP) and the Philadelphia Police Department have also begun to collect data.

This resource guide is organized into four main sections:

- An introduction to the nature of the problem of racial profiling.
- A general description of data collection and its limitations.
- Study-site descriptions and analysis.
- Recommendations and future goals.

The "selected site" approach of this resource guide is intended to encourage and guide police and communities as they begin to take action to evaluate allegations of racial profiling and to help police and communities learn from one another's experiences and successes. To facilitate this exchange of ideas, contact information is provided for each site described in this guide. To promote the continued exchange of facts, forms, and new data collection systems, one recommendation of this guide is to create a Web site for sharing information about racial profiling and data collection.

THE NATURE OF THE PROBLEM OF RACIAL PROFILING

The problem of racial profiling is complex and multifaceted. Dedicated police officers and professional police practices have contributed to making our communities safer. The majority of police officers are hard-working public servants who perform a dangerous job with dedication and honor; however, the perception that some police officers are engaging in racial profiling has created resentment and distrust of the police, particularly in communities of color. These communities applaud the benefits of community policing in reducing crime, but they also believe that truly effective policing will only be achieved when police both protect their neighborhoods from crime and respect the civil liberties of all residents. When law enforcement practices are perceived to be biased, unfair, or disrespectful, communities of color are less willing to trust and confide in police officers, report crimes, participate in problem-solving activities, be witnesses at trials, or serve on juries.

Defining Racial Profiling

When seeking to determine whether allegations of racial profiling are accurate, any analysis concerning the nature and scope of the problem depends on the definition of racial profiling used. For this guide, racial profiling is defined as any police-initiated action that relies on the race, ethnicity, or national origin rather than the behavior of an individual or information that leads the police to a particular individual who has been identified as being, or having been, engaged in criminal activity.

There is almost uniform consensus on two corollary principles that follow from adopting this definition of racial profiling: police may not use racial or ethnic stereotypes as factors in selecting whom to stop-and-search, and police may use race or ethnicity to determine whether a person matches a specific description of a particular suspect.[2]

Developing consensus on whether race can be used when police are addressing a crime committed by a group of individuals who share racial or ethnic characteristics is more difficult. Of course, when police know that a particular individual is a member of a criminal organization, police may legitimately use that information as a factor in the totality of the circumstances that may indicate ongoing criminal activity. For example, many criminal organizations are composed of persons with similar ethnic, racial, or national origin characteristics. Under the definition used in this guide, however, if police use a person's race, ethnicity, or national origin in determining whether a specific individual is a member of a criminal organization, they have engaged in racial profiling.

Nature and Extent of Perceptions of Racial Profiling

In the late 1990s, the American news media exploded with coverage of the problem of racial profiling. Indeed, the allegations have become so common that the community of color has labeled the phenomenon with the derisive term "driving while black" or "driving while brown." Front-page news stories and editorials in both the national and local press began to illustrate the individual and social costs of racial profiling.

National surveys have confirmed that most Americans, regardless of race, believe that racial profiling is a significant social problem. According to a Gallup Poll released on December 9, 1999, more than half of Americans polled believed that police actively engage in the practice of racial profiling and, more significantly, 81 percent of them said they disapprove of the practice.[3] In a national sample of adults, 59 percent said that racial profiling is widespread.[4] When the responses to the survey question were broken down by race, 56 percent of Whites and 77 percent of Blacks responded that racial profiling was pervasive. Additionally, the Gallup survey asked respondents how often they perceived having been stopped by the police based on their race alone. Six percent of Whites and 42 percent of Blacks responded that they had been stopped by the police because of their race, and 72 percent of Black men between ages 18 and 34 believed they had been stopped because of their race.

Recent survey data also confirm a strong connection between perceptions of race-based stops by police and animosity toward local and state law enforcement. In addition to gathering data on individual perceptions of stops by the police, the 1999 Gallup Poll asked respondents how favorably they viewed the police. Eighty-five percent of White respondents had a favorable response toward local police and 87 percent of White respondents had a favorable response to state police. Black respondents, overall, had a less favorable opinion of both state and local police, with just 58 percent having a favorable opinion of the local police and 64 percent having a favorable response to the state police. Fifty-three percent of Black men between ages 18 and 34 said they had been treated unfairly by local police.

Similarly, a 12-city survey conducted by DOJ in 1998 demonstrated that, although most people in the African American community felt satisfied with police services in their neighborhoods, their level of dissatisfaction was approximately twice that of the White community.[5] This wide schism in all 12 cities surveyed indicates the need for law enforcement to work harder to restore the confidence of communities of color in the critical work being done by law enforcement. Police departments that fail to address the perception of racially discriminatory policing within minority neighborhoods may find their law enforcement efforts undermined.

Evidence of Racial Profiling

Anecdotal and empirical evidence confirm national perceptions about the pervasiveness of racial profiling. To better understand the issues associated with identifying racial profiling in police stops, concerns about police discretion have been broken into two stages: an officer's decision to stop a vehicle or person and the actions of the officer during the stop. The second issue may include a number of questions: Are passengers and drivers ordered to step out of the car? Is the suspect treated with respect? Are police questioning the occupants about subjects unrelated to the traffic-stop violation? Were drug-sniffing dogs summoned to the scene? Did the officer request permission to search the car and its contents? How long did the encounter last? The answers to these and other questions are critical for understanding the complexities and nuances of racial profiling. Evidence from anecdotal accounts and statistical studies has begun to address these important issues.

Anecdotal Evidence

Personal anecdotes and stories help illustrate the experiences of those who believe they have been stopped because of racial profiling and, in turn, give rise to a set of common concerns about police stop-and-search practices. A 1999 report by David Harris, *Driving While Black: Racial Profiling on Our Nation's Highways*, cites numerous accounts of disparate treatment toward minorities by police from a variety of state and local jurisdictions.[6] A sample of these accounts illustrates the emotional impact of such incidents.

The concern that police stop drivers because they or their passengers do not appear to "match" the type of vehicle they occupy is common in racial profiling accounts. This "driving in the wrong car" concern is illustrated by the experiences of Dr. Elmo Randolph, a 42-year-old African-American dentist, who commutes from Bergen County to his office near Newark, New Jersey. Since 1991, he has been stopped by New Jersey troopers more than 50 times. Randolph does not drive at excessive speeds and claims he has never been issued a ticket.[7] Instead, troopers approach his gold BMW, request his license and registration, and ask him if he has any drugs or weapons in his car. The experience of Randolph and many other minority drivers on New Jersey's highways led to the recent consent decree and settlement between the state of New Jersey and DOJ. As a result of the settlement, New Jersey State Police (NJSP) are collecting data on the race and ethnicity of persons stopped by state troopers and improving their supervision and training.

Another common complaint is that police stop people of color traveling through predominately White areas because the police believe that people of color do not "belong" in certain neighborhoods and may be engaged in criminal activity. This type of profiling was reported by Alvin Penn, the African-American deputy president of the Connecticut State Senate. In 1996, a Trumbull, Connecticut, police officer stopped Penn as he drove his van through this predominately White suburban town. After reviewing Penn's license and registration, the officer asked Penn if he knew which town he was in (Bridgeport, the state's largest city, where Blacks and Latinos comprise 75 percent of the population, borders Trumbull, which is 98 percent White). Penn, recalling that he had been turning around on a dead-end street when the officer stopped him, responded by asking why he needed to know which town he was in. The officer told him that he was not required to give Penn a reason for the stop and that, if he made an issue of it, the officer would cite him for speeding.[8] Three years after this incident, Penn sponsored legislation that made Connecticut the second state to begin collecting data on the demographics of individuals stopped by state police.

By far the most common complaint by members of communities of color is that they are being stopped for petty traffic violations such as underinfl-ated tires, failure to signal properly before switching lanes, vehicle equipment failures, speeding less than 10 miles above the speed limit, or having an illegible license plate. One example of this is the account of Robert Wilkins, a Harvard Law School graduate and a public defender in Washington, D.C., who went to a family funeral in Ohio in May 1992. On the return trip, he and his aunt, uncle, and 29-year-old cousin rented a Cadillac for the trip home. His cousin was stopped for speeding in western Maryland while driving 60 miles per hour in a 55-mile-per-hour zone of the interstate. The group was forced to stand on the side of the interstate in the rain for an extended period while officers and drug-sniffing dogs searched their car. Nothing was found. Wilkins, represented by the ACLU, filed suit and received a settlement from the state of Maryland.[9]

Although this small sample of anecdotal evidence does not prove that police officers actively engage in racial profiling, it is representative of the thousands of personal stories cataloged in newspaper articles, interviews, ACLU commentary, and court battles.

Empirical Research on Racial Profiling

In addition to a growing body of individual accounts of racial profiling, scholars have begun examining the relationship between police stop-and-search practices and racial characteristics of individual drivers. The majority of empirical research collected to date has been used in expert testimony accompanying lawsuits. *Wilkins* v. *Maryland State Police* (1993) was one of the first cases to introduce empirical evidence of racial profiling into the court record.

In 1995 and 1996, as a result of Wilkins' settlement with the Maryland State Police (MSP), Dr. John Lamberth, a professor of psychology at Temple University, conducted an analysis of police searches along I–95 in Maryland.

Using data released by MSP pursuant to the settlement, Lamberth compared the population of people searched and arrested with those violating traffic laws on Maryland highways. He constructed a violator sample using both stationary and rolling surveys of drivers violating the legal speed limit on a selected portion of the interstate. His violator survey indicated that 74.7 percent of speeders were White, while 17.5 percent were Black.[10] In contrast, according to MSP data, Blacks constituted 79.2 percent of the drivers searched. Lamberth concluded that the data revealed "dramatic and highly statistically significant disparities between the percentage of Black I–95 motorists legitimately subject to stop by the Maryland State Police and the percentage of Black motorists detained and searched by troopers on this roadway."[11]

Empirical data on stop-and-search practices in New Jersey also originated through actions of the court. In the late 1980s and early 1990s, Black drivers were reporting that they were being stopped disproportionately by New Jersey troopers. In response to these complaints, in 1994, the Gloucester County public defender's office, while representing Pedro Soto and others, filed a motion to suppress evidence obtained in a series of searches, alleging that the searches were unlawful because they were part of a pattern and practice of racial profiling by New Jersey troopers.[12] As part of that litigation, the defendants received traffic-stop and arrest data compiled by NJSP in selected locations from 1988 through 1991.[13] Lamberth served as the statistical expert for the defendants and conducted a comparative violator survey to weigh the percentage of Blacks stopped and arrested by New Jersey troopers against a comparative percentage of Blacks who violated traffic laws on New Jersey highways. His analyses found that Blacks comprised 13.5 percent of the New Jersey Turnpike population and 15 percent of the drivers speeding. In contrast, Blacks represented 35 percent of those stopped and 73.2 percent of those arrested. In other words, in New Jersey, Black drivers were disproportionally more likely to be stopped and arrested than White drivers. The Superior Court of New Jersey relied on Lamberth's study in its decision to suppress the evidence seized by New Jersey troopers in 19 consolidated criminal prosecutions and concurred with his opinion that the troopers relied on race in stopping and searching turnpike motorists.

Recent data collection efforts in New Jersey and New York have confirmed the independent empirical findings used in court cases. In April 1999, the Attorney General of New Jersey issued a report indicating that New Jersey troopers had engaged in racial profiling along the New Jersey Turnpike.[14] This report tracked the racial breakdowns of traffic-stops between 1997 and 1998. The information indicated that people of color constituted 40.6 percent of the stops made on the turnpike. Although few stops resulted in a search, 77.2 percent of those individuals searched were people of color. An analysis of the productivity of these searches indicated that 10.5 percent of the searches that involved White motorists resulted in an arrest or seizure and that 13.5 percent of the searches involving Black motorists resulted in arrest or seizure. Finally, the New Jersey report demonstrated that minority motorists were more likely to be involved in consent searches than nonminority motorists. Eighty percent of consent searches involved minority motorists.[15]

In December 1999, New York Attorney General Eliot Spitzer released the results of an investigation by his office of the "stop and frisk" practices in New York City. It showed that Blacks and Latinos were much more likely to be stopped and searched even when the statistics were adjusted to reflect differing criminal participation rates in some neighborhoods.[16] After reviewing 175,000 incidents in which citizens were stopped by the police during the 15-month period that ended in March 1999, the attorney general found that Blacks were stopped six times more often than Whites, while Latinos were stopped four times more often. Blacks made up 25 percent of the city population but 50 percent of the people stopped and 67 percent of the people stopped by the New York City Street Crimes Unit.[17]

International data suggest that racial profiling is not an isolated American experience. A 1998 study by the British Government's Home Office examined the racial and ethnic demographics of the stop-and-search patterns of 43 police forces in England and Wales. The study indicated that Blacks were 7.5 times more likely to be stopped and searched and 4 times more likely to be arrested than Whites.[18] This is true even though, according to census population figures, Great Britain is 93 percent White and 7 percent ethnic minority.[19] Although the high proportion of searches of people of color has been a constant feature of police searches in London, England, and elsewhere, the proportion of searches that result in an arrest does not differ by race or ethnicity. That is, the arrest rate differs little regardless of whether the search was of a White or Black person. In London, the arrest rate was 11.1 percent for light-skinned Europeans, 11.4 percent for dark-skinned Europeans, and 11.7 percent for Black people. In the case of Asians, the arrest rate was lowest at 9.4 percent.[20]

Anecdotal and empirical evidence has helped state and local activists, community members, and government officials understand the problem of racial profiling and has raised new questions about police stop-and-search practices. However, more expansive and systematic data collection is needed to address the concerns surrounding police practices of racial profiling.

Origin of Racial Profiling and the Complexities of Police Discretion

Although empirical research, anecdotal evidence, and survey data confirm the existence of racial profiling as a social problem, many still question how such profiling could arise. Throughout all areas of their daily routine, police exercise a great deal of individual discretion. Within the area of traffic-stops, for example, police must use reasoned judgment in deciding which cars to stop from among the universe of cars being operated in violation of the law. Since many traffic enforcement and vehicle code laws apply to all cars on the road, and since more vehicles are being operated in violation of the local traffic laws than police have the resources to stop them, officers have a wide discretion in selecting which cars to stop.

Many traffic officers say that by following any vehicle for 1 or 2 minutes, they can observe a basis on which to stop it.[21] Many police departments have not developed formal, written, standards directing officers on how to use this discretion. Instead, officers often develop ad hoc methods of winnowing suspicious from innocent motorists. This intuition, often learned by young officers observing the actions of more experienced officers, can vary widely across individual officers even within a particular department. Police departments often use traffic-stops as a means of ferreting out illicit drugs and weapons. Consequently, some officers routinely use traffic stops as a means of tracking down drug or gun couriers. These discretionary decisions are seldom documented and rarely reviewed. As a result, individual officers are infrequently made accountable for these decisions.

Levels of Police Discretion

Several factors may influence an officer's decision to stop-and-search an individual, but the various types of potential scenarios can easily be broken down into high- and low-discretion realms. Traffic and pedestrian stops can be viewed on a continuum from low-discretion stops, in which an officer's decision not to make a stop is limited, to high-discretion stops, in which the decision to stop someone is often based on an officer's experiences in the field.

Low Discretion

Although the nature and scope of low-discretion stops vary by place and context, they are common in policing. Low-discretion stops can include those based on externally generated reports of a crime or suspicious activity, such as when a victim describes a particular suspect. In the traffic-stop context, for jurisdictions in which traffic enforcement is a priority, speeding more than 10 miles above the speed limit or running a red light may also be placed in the category of low-discretion stops. Some jurisdictions have actually calculated the percentage of stops that fall in this low-discretion category. The New York attorney general's *Stop and Frisk* study, for example, shows that only 30 percent of the stops were based on victims' descriptions.[22] Similarly, in London, England, only 25 percent of searches in selected study sites were considered low discretion.[23]

High Discretion

The complexities of police discretion emerge more often in the high-discretion stop category. In the traffic-stop context, these stops include checks for underinflated tires, safety belt warnings, failures to signal lane changes, and other minor vehicle code and nonmoving violations. In the pedestrian-stop context, high-discretion stops involve those who may look suspicious but are not engaged in any specific criminal violation or activities. These high-discretion stops invite both intentional and unintentional abuses. Police are just as subject to the racial and ethnic stereotypes they learn from our culture as any other citizen. Unless documented, such stops create an environment that allows the use of stereotypes to go undetected.

The Perception that Minorities are More Likely to Carry Contraband

The perception that African Americans, Hispanics, Asians, and other minorities are more likely to carry drugs than their White counterparts intensifies the complexities of police discretion in stops and searches.[24] The escalating pressure from the war on drugs has led some police officers to target people of color whom police believe to be disproportionally involved in drug use and trafficking. Although some members of the police community suggest that race-based searches are justified because more minority drivers are found with contraband, the empirical evidence amassed to date tends to discredit such arguments.[25] In Lamberth's study on I–95 in Maryland, he found that 28.4 percent of Black drivers and passengers who were searched were found with contraband and 28.8 percent of White drivers and passengers who were searched were found with contraband.[26] Thus, the probability of finding contraband was the same for Blacks and Whites. Race did not matter. According to the New Jersey attorney general's *Interim Report* (April 1999), the "hit rates" at which contraband was found among those searched did not differ significantly by race. Only 10.5 percent of the searches of Whites resulted in an arrest or seizure compared to a rate of 13.5 percent for Black motorists.[27] Similarly, in the New York study of "stop and frisk" practices, between 1998 and 1999, the attorney general found that 12.6 percent of Whites stopped were arrested, compared to only 10.5 percent of Blacks and 11.3 percent of Latinos.[28] In a recent U.S. Customs Service study, nationwide data revealed that, while 43 percent of those searched were either Black or Latino, the hit rates for Blacks and Latinos were actually lower than the hit rates for Whites. The study found that 6.7 percent of Whites, 6.3 percent of Blacks, and 2.8 percent of Hispanics had contraband. This finding is particularly surprising because the study does not involve car stops, but involves stops and searches in airports. Presumably, if the perception that drug couriers are more likely to be Black or Latino were true, a widespread survey of airport searches should reveal differing hit rates.[29] Similarly, in London, England, the probability of finding contraband as a result of a search did not significantly differ among races.[30] Although sound empirical research on the relationship between race and hit rates for contraband is limited, to date the evidence indicates that Blacks and Latinos are no more likely than Whites to be in possession of narcotics or other contraband.[31]

In many cases, disproportionate minority arrests for drug possession and distribution have fueled perceptions by police and others that race is an appropriate factor in the decision to stop or search an individual.[32] However, existing data on the productivity of searches across racial groups suggest that stop-and-search practices have become a game of "search and you will find." Police officers who aggressively and disproportionately search people of color will arrest more people of color than Whites, not because of differences in behavior, but because they are stopping and searching many more people of color than Whites. Regardless of whether the perception that Blacks and Latinos are more likely to be found in possession of contraband could be empirically verified, United States laws do not, and should not, permit race to be used as a basis for stopping and searching individuals.[33]

GENERAL DESCRIPTION OF DATA COLLECTION GOALS AND LIMITATIONS

In response to allegations of racial profiling, some communities have begun to track the race, ethnicity, and gender of those who are stopped and/or searched by police officers. This chapter examines the feasibility of having law enforcement collect data to determine whether racial profiling exists in a particular setting.

Data Collection Systems

Why would a law enforcement entity begin to collect data about the demographics of its stops? Reasons vary. The most obvious one is that in the long run the systematic collection of statistics and information regarding law enforcement activities support community policing by building trust and respect for the police in the community. The only way to move the discussion about racial profiling from rhetoric and accusation to a more rational dialogue about appropriate enforcement strategies is to collect the information that will either allay community concerns about the activities of the police or help communities ascertain the scope and magnitude of the problem. When police begin to collect information about the racial and ethnic demographics of their stops, they demonstrate that they have nothing to hide and retain their credibility. Once data are collected, they become catalysts for an informed community-police discussion about the appropriate allocation of police resources. Such a process promises to promote neighborhood policing.

Implementing a data collection system also sends a clear message to the entire police community, as well as to the larger community, that racial profiling is inconsistent with effective policing and equal protection. When implemented properly, this system helps to shape and develop a training program to educate officers about the conscious and subconscious use of racial and ethnic stereotypes and to promote courteous and respectful police-citizen encounters.

When implemented as part of a comprehensive early warning system, data collection processes can identify potential police misconduct and deter it. By detecting and addressing instances of disparate treatment of persons of color by the police, law enforcement organizations may be able to prevent the development of a systemic pattern and practice of discrimination.

Finally, a data collection system can also improve police productivity by enabling police to assess and study the most effective stop-and-search practices. It can provide police with information about the types of stops being made by officers, the proportion of police time spent on high-discretion stops, and the results of such steps. It may identify certain strategies to improve the likelihood that a stop will result in an arrest or seizure of contraband. It will also enable police and the community to assess the quantity and quality of police-citizen encounters.

Although no written policy can anticipate all situations and mechanistic adherence to formal procedures could chill the use of sound judgment and experience, data collection could help officers understand practices that they may be undertaking subconsciously. Additionally, data collection can assist departments in developing strategic ways to use the power at their disposal.

Potential Challenges in Implementing a Data Collection System

There are myriad benefits from implementing a data collection system, but there are also some potential challenges. The most common have been articulated as follows:

- How can officers determine the race or ethnicity of the citizens they stop in the least confrontational manner and without increasing the intrusiveness of the stop?
- What budgetary, time, and paperwork burdens will data collection impose on police departments?
- Will data collection procedures result in police "disengagement" by leading police officers to scale down the number of legitimate stops and searches they conduct?
- How can departments ensure the accuracy of data collection procedures and be certain that reporting requirements are not circumvented by officers who fail to file required reports or who report erroneous information?
- How can departments collect enough information to provide a refined, contextualized analysis without unduly burdening line officers?
- How can departments ensure full compliance by line officers and deal effectively with any officer resistance?
- Will the data that are collected be used for research and training purposes only or will they be used to discipline officers and facilitate lawsuits?
- Will the data be analyzed and compared with an appropriate measure of the statistically correct representative population? How do you ascertain and define the parameters of that population?

Since several jurisdictions have already begun to collect data on the race, ethnicity, and gender of the persons police stop, the next section of this guide provides information about existing data collection systems and how jurisdictions have addressed and overcome these potential challenges.

STUDY SITE EXPERIENCES AND ANALYSES

The San Jose Experience

San Jose is the 3rd largest city in California and the 11th largest city in the nation. Nestled in California's Silicon Valley, it is a large, culturally diverse urban community with a population estimated at 900,000. San Jose's population is approximately 43 percent White, 31 percent Hispanic, 21 percent Asian, and 4.5 percent African American.[34] In 1999, the officers of San Jose's police force made approximately 100,000 traffic-stops.[35]

Precipitating Events

Like other cities, San Jose was faced with rising community complaints about racial profiling. The city's independent police auditor, Teresa Guerreo-Daley, was receiving about 500 complaints each year concerning alleged profile stops.[36] However, these complaints were rarely sustained because there was no evidence about the reason for the stops other than police statements. Although some complaints were probably unwarranted and others might have been retaliation against the police, no one could determine whether there was a problem.

Meanwhile, in 1999, State Senator Kevin Murray reintroduced a bill into the California Legislature requiring that all state law enforcement agencies collect data on the racial and ethnic demographics of their traffic-stops.[37] The bill required police to collect information and data surrounding vehicle stops, including information on searches, the results of searches, and information about passengers. Although the bill was ultimately vetoed, it was part of what galvanized San Jose Police Chief William Landsdowne to create a simpler data collection system. He felt that the proposed legislatively created system was too onerous and thought that the implementation of a simpler system might convince legislators to modify the proposed system.

Another impetus for San Jose to begin gathering data about the demographics of their stops was a highly publicized incident that occurred on March 9, 1999. On that date, Michael McBride, a Black youth minister, asserted that he was the victim of a racial profiling stop and a subsequent search and assault by San Jose police officers. An internal affairs investigation concluded that the department could neither prove nor disprove McBride's allegations.

In response to community complaints and the prospect of a legislatively imposed data collection system, on March 24, Chief Lansdowne announced that San Jose would become the second California city to embark voluntarily on tracking the race, gender, age, and reason for stopping motorists. Chief Lansdowne wanted to respond to the community's perception that people of color were being stopped because of their race and to demonstrate to the community that the San Jose police did not "do business that way."[38]

Data Collection Process

On June 1, 1999, San Jose began to implement a data collection system that focused on four key pieces of information: race/ethnicity of the driver, gender, age (adult or minor), and the reason for the stop. It is a simple system designed to minimize the burden on line officers.

Since 1996, every patrol car in the San Jose Police Department (SJPD) has been equipped with a mobile data terminal (MDT). San Jose's data collection system, however, can be used with or without the MDT units. Using a system based on letter codes, the traffic-stop data collection system is designed to collect and relay information verbally (via police radio) or by typing the information into the MDT in the patrol car. This system eliminates the need for officers to complete or collect written forms or reports.

Traffic-stop Protocol before June 1999

Even before the data collection system was implemented, whenever officers made a traffic-stop, they advised the communications dispatcher via radio or MDT that a traffic-stop was being made. At that time, the officer would tell the dispatcher the driver's gender. After the stop was completed, the officer would use an alpha code to indicate to the dispatcher the result of the stop (e.g., whether a citation was issued, whether an arrest was made). For instance, the officer would clear a call by stating on the radio "10–98 D–David." The "10–98" meant that the call was being cleared, and the "D–David" meant that a traffic citation had been issued.

The New Data Collection System

Under the new data collection system, three additional alpha codes are being used by officers clearing a stop. These new alpha codes indicate the reason for the stop, the race of the driver, and whether the driver is an adult or a juvenile.[39] For example, under the new system an officer clears a call by stating "10–98 D–David, V–Victor, W–William, A–Adam." "D–David" means that a moving violation citation was issued; "V–Victor" means the reason for the stop was a vehicle code violation; "W–William" means the race of the individual driver was White; and "A–Adam" means the driver was an adult. This information can be relayed to the dispatcher via radio or the MDT unit.

SJPD uses the following codes to indicate race and ethnicity:

A   = Asian American.
B   = African American.
H   = Hispanic.
I   = Native American.
O   = Other.
P   = Pacific Islander.
S   = Middle Eastern/East Indian.
W   = White.

Additionally, SJPD uses letter codes to indicate the reasons for the stop based on four scenarios:

V–Victor. A violation of the California vehicle code.
P– Paul. A California penal code violation, e.g., an officer might have observed a person committing a criminal violation (picking up a known prostitute).
M–Mary. A municipal code violation.[40]
B– Boy. A notice or an all-points bulletin was broadcast on police radio channels, or a description of the suspect or car was issued in a report or bulletin by a police organization in the area.

Under both the pre-June vehicle-stop procedures and the new data collec-tion system, the officer clears a call by indicating the disposition or out-come of the traffic-stop. The codes used for the stop disposition are asfollows:

A   = Arrest made.
B   = Warrant arrest made.
C   = Criminal citation issued.
D   = Traffic citation issued—hazardous.
E   = Traffic citation issued—nonhazardous.
F   = Field interview card.
H   = Courtesy service/assistance.

N   = No report completed.[41]

Once the officer provides the information by computer or over the radio, it is relayed to an automated computer-aided dispatch system and automati-cally entered into a new database. By collecting the information immedi-ately after each stop on an already existing system, SJPD is able to keep up-to-date accurate information on all vehicle stops.

Identifying and Overcoming Perceived Difficulties

Racial and Ethnic Designations
San Jose determined that because an officer's perceptions gives rise to the problem of racial profiling, the officer's perception is an appropriate means of ascertaining race or ethni-city. It seemed unimportant whether the officer had correctly guessed the race or ethnicity of the driver; what seemed important was to analyze whether, having perceived the driver as a person of color, the officer treated the person fairly.

Costs
SJPD opted for a simple system that kept the quantity of information low, so that data could be gathered quickly without tremendous financial costs. The additional time an officer needs to clear a call is less than 3 seconds. Moreover, the system costs less than $10,000, which includes the software for the existing 1990 system and training, training materials, and plastic pocket-size reference cards issued to each officer. It does not include the cost for data analysis.

Disengagement
Police disengagement from duty or any reduction in stops, searches, and arrests is a concern of many local jurisdictions. In San Jose, initial analysis indicates that the number of traffic-stops has increased rather than decreased.[42] Thus, San Jose does not appear to have experienced any disengagement.

Data Integrity
San Jose employs only routine supervision of the data collection procedures. No systemic mechanism for spot-checking or crosschecking the data is currently in place.

Quantity of Data
The San Jose system covers all traffic-stops. Ideally, an officer cannot clear a call and get back in service without providing the reason for the stop, the race of the driver, the outcome of the stop, and whether the driver was an adult or a minor. As designed, neither the dispatcher nor the computer will clear the call without this information.[43] However, the system does not record whether a search was conducted or the basis or results of the search. It also does not cover pedestrian stops. Finally, it only provides a list of four possible reasons for the stop: all-points bulletin, municipal code violation, penal code violation, or vehicle code violation.[44] The system fails to distinguish, for example, between a high-discretion stop for underinflated tires and a low-discretion stop for traveling 20 miles over the speed limit. Thus, while it provides a fast, simple, inexpensive means of obtaining data on stops, it may

not provide sufficient information for a complete analysis of the problem. Still, the system deserves praise for its simplicity and ability to be adopted in jurisdictions without computerized facilities. San Jose is considering adding a code to indicate whether a search was conducted.[45] San Jose's dedication to a community-oriented response to the problem of racial profiling serves as a model for other police departments.

Officer Resistance

Recognizing that officers might feel insulted about collecting data and resist the implementation of the system, Chief Lansdowne established an extensive training program focused on line officers. During training, officers were instructed to explain the reason for a traffic-stop to each driver and to be respectful and courteous during the entire encounter. Lansdowne stressed that developing traffic-stop protocols and implementing data collection systems were ways to enhance the professionalism of the department. He emphasized that San Jose's system did not require any additional written reports and it was a simpler and less onerous alternative to the proposed legislative model for data collection. The data collection system has received support and active input from members of the police officers' union.

Use of the Data

To garner the support of the San Jose Police Officers' Association, the local police union, the identity of the citizen and the police officer involved in a stop must remain anonymous. Thus, the data will not be used to discipline or analyze the stops of individual officers but solely to evaluate the department on a systemwide basis.[46]

Data Analysis

On December 17, 1999, Chief Lansdowne issued SJPD's first preliminary analysis of the data collected from July 1 to September 30.[47] Although the study is ongoing, the preliminary report provides some initial analysis of the demographics of San Jose's traffic-stops.

To analyze the data, the department decided to compare the racial and ethnic demographics of those stopped with the racial and ethnic makeup of the residential population. Obtaining the residential demographics proved difficult. The demographics from the 1990 national census were criticized by many because the census failed to accurately count the minority population in many geographic areas.[48] Additionally, in 1995, the California Department of Finance issued some small-area race and ethnicity statistics. Thus, although actual statistics on the demographics of San Jose's residential population were unreliable, SJPD was able to use estimates from both the 1990 census and the 1995 California Department of Finance study to create a comparative residential population.[49]

Having created a residential benchmark population, SJPD then compared those population demographics with the demographics of their traffic-stops. Table 1 illustrates the results.

African Americans and Hispanics were stopped at a rate exceeding their percentage of the residential population. However, SJPD believes there are two reasons for this outcome: the number of officers per capita is concentrated in the police districts with more Hispanic and African-American populations, and socioeconomic factors in minority neighborhoods lead to more calls for service and interactions with police. Each factor is addressed below.

Table 1. Traffic Stops by Race

Race/Ethnicity	San Jose's Population (%)	Total Vehicle Stops (%)	Variation
African American	5%	7%	+2.0
Asian	21%	16%	−5.0
Hispanic	31%	43%	+12.0
White	43%	29%	−14.0

The Number of Officers per capita in Smaller Minority Police Districts

San Jose is made up of 16 police districts, each of which was created by using a computer model that allowed for the calls for police services to be spread out evenly among all districts. As a result, in areas where residents' 911 calls for police service per capita are higher, the geographic size of a district is smaller. These small districts, however, have the same number of officers assigned to them as larger geographic districts. Since the number of calls for police services is higher in minority neighborhoods, the number of officers per capita is concentrated in these small districts. SJPD examined traffic-stops by district and found that the percentage of stops by the police closely mirrors the racial population of these districts. These are only impressions since SJPD does not have the racial population percentages for individual police districts.

Socioeconomic Factors that Lead to More Interactions with Police

Other factors that may lead to more interactions with the police include social problems such as unemployment and poverty rates. SJPD suggests that these factors may lead to more stops being made on vehicles that have not been properly maintained.[50]

SJPD's preliminary report indicates that, although Hispanics and African Americans are stopped at rates higher than their percentage of the residential population, this overrepresentation may be explained when compared to other law enforcement-related data and statistics. However, using residential population statistics does not capture the racial demographics of the roadways in that both residents and nonresidents drive on the roadways. Additionally, the residential population data used in San Jose were not limited to the segment of the population that is within the legal driving age. Finally, the San Jose population statistics cannot account for differences in the driving behavior of individuals of different racial groups, if such differences exist. These concerns illustrate the need for additional research to refine the data analysis process.

Lessons Learned and Future Suggestions

Chief Lansdowne believes that a data collection system should be simple and not require officers to prepare additional written reports. Obtaining the police union's support enabled the system to be implemented smoothly. Informing officers about the need for data collection encouraged officers to accept the new system. Once training was completed, educating the media about the process became a critical activity for SJPD. SJPD would like to equip all of its cars with video cameras, which would contextualize the data collection process.[51] In addition, cameras might change the nature of police-citizen encounters because when parties know that their behavior is being recorded, both police and civilians are more likely to be on their best behavior. However, due to the high costs associated with installing video cameras, SJPD has not used video monitoring on a systemwide basis.

The San Diego Experience

San Diego, the nation's seventh largest city, has its share of crime problems. The San Diego Police Department (SDPD) routinely deals with violence along the border with Mexico and the drugs that travel across it. Its population is diverse, with a Hispanic community that comprises 23.2 percent of the population and sizable Black (8.8 percent) and Asian (5 percent) populations. It is one of the most lightly policed major cities in the United States. Only 2,683 police officers serve its population of roughly 1.25 million.[52]

The city of San Diego has enjoyed remarkable success in reducing crime, which has declined for 9 consecutive years. Since 1991, its homicide rate has declined 75 percent.[53] The city's style of policing emphasizes strong community bonds and relationships, assisted by 1,100 civilian volunteers who donate about 200,000 hours of service annually.[54] In 1998, SDPD made about 200,000 vehicle stops, issuing citations in 125,000 of these stops.[55]

In February 1999, SDPD became the first big-city police department in the nation to voluntarily record the racial and ethnic demographics of its traffic-stops to determine whether minority motorists were being pulled over at a higher rate than White drivers.[56]

Precipitating Events

As in other cities, for years local community groups complained that police were disproportionately stopping people of color for minor traffic offenses. 57 The perception that SDPD was using race as a basis for conducting traffic-stops was fueled by an incident in 1997. While driving his Jeep Cherokee, San Diego Chargers football player Shawn Lee was pulled over by the police because he was thought to be driving a vehicle that fit the description of a car stolen earlier that evening. Lee and his girlfriend were handcuffed and detained for half an hour. Later, however, the San Diego Union Tribune reported that the stolen vehicle had been, in fact, a Honda sedan.[58]

Former San Diego Police Chief Jerry Sanders recognized that the perception that police were engaged in racial profiling needed to be addressed if community policing was going to continue to be successful. Like other California police chiefs, he was aware that legislation was pending in the California legislature that would require state law enforcement agencies to begin tracking the race and ethnicity of motorists stopped for routine traffic violations.

During a meeting with Chief Sanders in July 1998, local African American leaders raised their concerns about racial profiling. In February 1999, Sanders met with leaders of the local ACLU, Urban League, National Association for the Advancement of Colored People, and Human Relations Commission who asked him to begin collecting data on all traffic-stops. He agreed to do so if it was not too costly. By March 1999, it was clear that data collection would be technically feasible and that the costs would not be excessive. Sanders announced his decision to collect the requested data.

When questioned about the initiative, Sanders said that he was not afraid of what the data might reveal and reiterated that he believed the police were doing their job professionally. However, he felt data collection was necessary to allay community perceptions about profiling and to retain SDPD's credibility and trust with the community. He told the press,

"This perception [of racial profiling], whether true or not, is eroding public trust and needs to be addressed."[59]

Data Collection Process

SDPD began collecting traffic-stop data in January 2000. Each of its 1,300 patrol, traffic, and canine officers has been issued a laptop computer that they can use inside or outside their patrol cars to enter data.[60] In addition, SDPD has 45 motorcycle officers who write about 50 percent of all traffic citations. These officers use wireless handheld computers to collect data.

San Diego's data collection program focuses on all traffic-stops, regardless of whether a citation or warning is issued. To tally the racial demographics of the traffic-stops in San Diego, SDPD decided to focus on 14 basic data elements:

- District.
- Date and time.
- Cause for stop—moving violation, equipment violation, radio call/ citizen complaint, personal observation/knowledge, suspect info (e.g., bulletin, log), or municipal/county code violation.
- Race.
- Gender.
- Age.
- Disposition of the stop—citation issued, oral warning, written warning, field interview, or other.
- Arrest (yes/no).
- Search (yes/no).
- Search type—vehicle, driver, or passengers.
- Basis for search—contraband visible, odor of contraband, canine alert, inventory search prior to impound, consent search, 4th waiver search, search incident to arrest, inventory search, observed evidence related to criminal activity, or other.
- Obtained consent search form (yes/no).
- Contraband found (yes/no).
- Property seized (yes/no).

These elements provide the information that would have been required in the 1999 California Traffic-stop Data Collection legislation, except San Diego elected not to collect information on the nature and amount of contraband discovered during a search.

In San Diego, an officer who makes a traffic-stop advises the radio communications dispatcher of the stop and its location. Next, the officer runs the car's license plate. The officer talks to the driver, asks for a license and registration, and goes back to the patrol car to make a decision on disposition. The officer informs the driver of the disposition and then completes the data entry form on the laptop or handheld computer. As a fail-safe procedure, officers must complete the forms before the dispatcher clears the call and allows the officer back in service.

Identifying and Overcoming Perceived Difficulties

Racial and Ethnic Designations and Categories

San Diego decided to use the officer's perception of the driver's race or ethnicity for its data collection program. If unsure, the officer may ask the driver. Because community groups had complained that officers treated drivers differently because of the way they perceived their race or ethnicity, the use of "officer perception" seemed appropriate. Current Police Chief David Bejarano thought that asking drivers about their race might exacerbate the community's perception that racial profiling was occurring and that many officers may not feel comfortable asking motorists their race.

The department uses the following racial categories on its incident reports:

A = Other Asian.	K = Korean.
B = Black.	L = Laotian.
C = Chinese.	O = Other.
D = Cambodian.	P = Pacific Islander.
F = Filipino.	S = Samoan.
G = Guamanian.	U = Hawaiian.
H = Hispanic.	V = Vietnamese.
I = Indian.	W = White.
J = Japanese.	Z = Asian Indian.

Cost

For SDPD, the system was relatively easy to implement because it was able to use a previously installed in-house data system. Since all patrol cars had a mobile dispatch terminal and each officer already had a laptop, the hardware costs were minimal. Because the department's computer software was already designed in a Windows environment, it was able to use Microsoft Access to develop a series of pulldown menus for each of the 14 data collection elements. The department developed its own in-house software, so there were no costs for programming. The data services department estimates that it will need two additional computer servers, bringing the data collection costs to approximately $30,000.[61]

It is estimated that it will take officers an additional 20 to 30 seconds to enter the data by making choices on the computer pulldown menus. Since most traffic-stops do not result in a search, officers will be completing only the first seven elements. The other elements will default to "no."

Disengagement

According to former Chief Sanders, disengagement was not a primary concern when adopting the data collection system. He did not believe that traffic-stops constitute an essential police enforcement activity. Sanders stated, "The officers should be out on the street working to prevent gang activity, getting to know the community, and helping to decrease truancy by making sure kids are in school. I never emphasized traffic enforcement as a primary activity. In fact, during my tenure, traffic-stops decreased more than 50 percent because I diverted my officers to other more important activities, and during that time, crime continued to go down despite a less aggressive 'traffic-stop' policy. Of course, my officers always enforced hazardous driving infractions such as excessive speeding or running a red light, but the vehicle equipment violations and failure to signal incidents were not high on my enforcement agenda."[62]

Consequently, in San Diego, disengagement was not viewed as a major concern, given the relative importance of traffic-stop enforcement versus other enforcement priorities. Former Chief Sanders explained that community policing meetings can be a better use of resources than random traffic-stop procedures.

Data Integrity

Officials in San Diego felt that, if they instituted a mechanism to establish multiple sources of information so that the data could be cross-checked through random or automated procedures, the police union would oppose the data collection effort. Therefore, there is no independent mechanism for checking the data's accuracy. Instead, traffic and patrol supervisors are responsible for ensuring that officers properly record and enter traffic-stop data. In addition, to enter the data in the computer, officers must also enter the information in their daily journals. Officers have been informed that entering information that the officer knows to be false is a violation of departmental policies that could result in disciplinary action.

Quantity of Data

SDPD elected to cover only traffic-stops. Since pedestrian stops constitute a significant percentage of all police-civilian stops, the analysis will focus on only one aspect of the potential problem. San Diego's data collection system will provide information on stops and searches, but it will not qualify or quantify the nature of contraband seized during a search.

Officer Resistance

When former Chief Sanders announced his decision to collect data, some traffic officers said that they were insulted by the idea that they made traffic-stops based on a person's race.[63] Although the idea of the data collection system was generally well received, according to current Police Chief Bejarano, about 10 percent of the officers expressed concerns about the system. Some of those concerns included the following:

– Would there be disciplinary activities associated with this data collection process?
– Would it apply to specialized units?
– Would there be fewer traffic-stops because officers feared being monitored for stopping too many minorities?
– Would officers be labeled "racists" if their traffic-stop patterns indicated they were stopping a disproportionate number of minorities?

To allay these fears, SDPD undertook an extensive training program to explain to officers the purposes of the program, the nature and extent of community perceptions, how the data would be analyzed, and how the program would affect each officer. The department chose not to include officer identification in the stop-and-search data collection system.

In addition to the data collection system training, officers were instructed to be courteous and tell drivers the reason for the stop. Sergeant Tony McElroy was put in charge of this training. He involved firstline supervisors in the process, was available during training sessions, and gave out his phone number so that officers could talk to him privately about their concerns.

Use of the Data

SDPD has ensured that, during the data collection process, neither the officer nor the motorist will be identified by name. The data will only be collected, used, and analyzed in the aggregate. The identification of officers was omitted from the data collection process to assure officers that data collection was to assess whether the department as a whole was acting professionally, rather than to isolate or punish individual conduct.

Data Analysis

San Diego plans to analyze the data by divisions, of which there are eight. Analysts fear a citywide analysis would not produce an accurate picture of police enforcement patterns, which vary by neighborhood. The department is struggling with how to create a comparative statistical measure and is not certain about how to calculate a potential violator population for each of the eight districts. However, the department is working with academic partners from the University of California at San Diego, University of San Diego, and San Diego State to develop appropriate benchmarks.

The North Carolina Experience

North Carolina is a state with both rural areas and medium-size metropolitan cities. Based on the 1990 census, North Carolina's population of 6.5u million is approximately 75.6 percent White, 22.2 percent Black, and 2.2u percent other racial groups.[64] The North Carolina Highway Patrol (NCHP) is the state's primary law enforcement organization and consists ofu 1,417 troopers and a 12-member interdiction team. Troopers patrol interstate highways and local roads. Last year, NCHP issued 684,721 traffic citations.[65]

Precipitating Events

For years, Black drivers in North Carolina complained that they were routinely stopped on flimsy pretexts and were subsequently questioned and searched for drugs far more often than White drivers.[66] On July 28, 1996, the *Raleigh News and Observer* reported that NCHP's drug interdiction team stopped and charged Black male drivers at nearly twice the rate of other troopers patrolling those same roads.[67] Subsequently, the newspaper reported that, based on 1998 statistics, Blacks and other minorities were twice as likely as White drivers to have their cars searched by the drug unit.[68]

In 1999, State Senator Frank Balance and State Representative Ronnie Sutton, working with the local ACLU office, introduced a bill requiring state law enforcement entities to collect data on all routine traffic-stops. On April 22, 1999, North Carolina became the first state to enact such a law.[69]

Data Collection Process

The data collection system is designed to be statewide and apply to all traffic-stops by any state police organization. Although NCHP is the largest state law enforcement entity, the data collection law applies to other state law enforcement organizations such as the Department of Fish and Wildlife and the State University Police. NCHP began collecting traffic-stop data on January 1, 2000. The data are collected in real time using a computerized system. Each trooper's car has an MDT, allowing the trooper to enter data on the stop. The trooper uses Access, a Windows-based software system, to record the required data. Using pulldown menus, each trooper completes the form electronically.

Under the law, state troopers are required to specify the race, age, and gender of every driver and passenger they stop, regardless of whether the occupants were arrested, cited, warned, or sent on their way. The law applies to all traffic-stops but not to pedestrian stops. It is one of the most comprehensive data collection laws, requiring troopers to collect the following data:

- The initial reason for the stop.
- The identifying characteristics of the drivers stopped, including race/ethnicity, gender, and approximate age.
- The type of enforcement action, if any, that was taken as a result of the stop.
- Whether any physical resistance was encountered.
- Whether a search was conducted.

Troopers rarely conduct searches, but if one occurs, the following additional information must be recorded:

- Type of search.
- Basis for the search.
- Whether vehicle, driver, or passengers were searched.
- Race/ethnicity and gender of those searched.
- A description of the contraband found and whether any property was seized.

Identifying and Overcoming Perceived Difficulties

Racial and Ethnic Designation and Categories

Race and ethnicity data are collected as separate variables. Troopers designate White, Black, Indian, Asian, or other as the racial categories and Hispanic or non-Hispanic as the ethnic categories. Currently, the plan is that troopers will use their best judgement regarding the race and ethnicity utilizing either:

- Perception of the person after the traffic-stop encounter.
- Information provided by the driver of the vehicle.
- Backup racial and ethnic information collected by the Bureau of Motor Vehicles.[70]

Time Burdens and Financial Costs

The time required to complete the form electronically is expected to be less than 5 minutes. NCHP Colonel Richard Holden believes this is not a significant burden. He stated, "How much is 5 minutes when it means stopping the perception that exists about police misbehavior? It is not much time to ask out of an officer's day."[71]

It cost NCHP $50,000 to implement this system, including the costs of a new computer server, hardware, and software. This cost excludes equipping each cruiser with an MDT unit. The software was developed with the help of the International Association of Chiefs of Police. Equipping all the cruisers with MDT units costs $8,000 per car. The units are being used for various purposes in addition to data collection. NCHP, for independent reasons, would have begun to equip each cruiser with an MDT unit, even without the data collection legislation.[72]

Disengagement

Prior to passage of the data collection law, NCHP collected racial data only on the number of written citations and warnings. The department did not collect any reliable information about traffic-stops resulting in verbal warnings.[73] Consequently, it may be difficult to gauge whether troopers stop fewer cars as a result of the new data collection system.

Data Integrity

Currently, there is no plan to audit or verify the data independently or to engage in systematic cross-checking procedures.

Officer Resistance

At first, some troopers were insulted by the suggestion that they were engaging in racist behavior. Colonel Holden met with troopers across the state to explain the goals of the data collection process and the department's commitment to fully participate in this effort. Once the data protocol was finalized, training workshops were provided to all troopers. As part of the training, Colonel Holden emphasized that the data would not be used for discipline of individual officers and expressed his hope that collecting the data would improve the training and performance of all the troopers. He said that the process can be used to understand and improve practices for NCHP.

Data Analysis

NCHP will not collect individual officer identification numbers. Consequently, the department plans to use the data to assess the prevalence of any systemwide problems in traffic-stops. Preliminary reports of traffic-stop data for January 2000 indicate that Black motorists were stopped in proportion to their representation in the state population.[74] However, Black motorists were disproportionally searched and arrested when compared with their percentage of the state population.

In addition to releasing monthly aggregate statistics for traffic-stops, NCHP is working with Professor Matthew Zingraff, associate dean at the Center for Crime and Justice Research, North Carolina State University. With the help of a National Institute of Justice grant, Zingraff is trying to identify a statistical benchmark that will enable him to compare the relevant violator population with the data from highway patrol stops. He is trying to identify the population at risk of being stopped in selected geographic areas. Since he cannot quantify the risk of being stopped for weaving, reckless driving, or following too closely, he will focus on the risk of being stopped for speeding. Having mapped certain segments of the interstates, he plans to identify the racial/ethnic demographics of an "at-risk" population by having troopers certified in the use of radar guns and two observers parked in stationary locations. The troopers will identify cars travelling in excess of 8 miles above the speed limit. Observers in the car will identify the race/ethnicity, age, and gender of the drivers (these will be estimates).

Another possibility is a "rolling carousel" model in which the researchers move with traffic. Again, troopers will have mounted radar guns concealed by tinted windshields and will identify the demographics of drivers traveling in excess of 8 miles above the speed limit.

Zingraff's study will help create a baseline against which to measure NCHP enforcement patterns. He also plans to conduct a survey asking citizens to describe their "perceived safe driving speed," that is, the speed at which they believe they can safely travel without being stopped.

Quantity of Data

North Carolina's data collection system is comprehensive. When a trooper indicates the initial reason for a stop, the data collection form creates separate categories for moving violations, speeding violations, vehicle equipment violations, and so on. This design enables NCHP to analyze high-discretion vehicle equipment stops separately from low-discretion stops for excessive speed and hazardous moving violations. It focuses only on traffic-stops, and it captures information about searches.

Collecting information about the duration and location of the stop might further enrich the ultimate analysis. Some members of NCHP believe cameras in patrol cars would be a useful adjunct to the data collection system. One of the problems with data collection is that it fails to provide a context for the stop. Adding cameras to a data collection system would provide a comprehensive integrated system.

The New Jersey Experience

New Jersey is a diverse eastern state with both medium-size cities and rural populations. Department of Labor and Management population demographic estimates for 1998 indicate that 79.4 percent of the state population is White, 15 percent is Black, and 4.2 percent is other racial groups.[75] The New Jersey State Police (NJSP) is the state's primary state law enforcement organization, with approximately 2,800 troopers. NJSP is 14 percent minority and 3 percent women. Troopers patrol both interstate highways and local roads and serve as the police force for approximately 50 rural jurisdictions.[76]

Precipitating Events

Allegations of racial profiling on the New Jersey state highways resulted in federal intervention. As a result of this intervention, the state of New Jersey and the U.S. Department of Justice reached a consent decree that included provisions for traffic-stop data collection and monitoring. The events leading up to the decree showed patterns of early warning signals of potential problems within NJSP.

The issue of racial profiling came to the public forefront more than a decade ago. In 1989, WWOR–TV Channel 9 carried a special segment titled "Without Just Cause" that highlighted the problem of racial profiling on highways in New Jersey. The investigative team surveyed tickets from the New Jersey Turnpike, interviewed drivers, and concluded that a disproportionate number of people ticketed on the turnpike were drivers of color. During this report, the investigative team presented interviews with state troopers who admitted that race was a factor in selecting which drivers to stop.[77] In 1996, a New Jersey Superior Court judge dismissed a case against 19 defendants following a motion to suppress evidence obtained in a series of searches, alleging that the searches were unlawful because they were part of a pattern and practice of racial profiling by the troopers.[78] As part of this litigation, Dr. John Lamberth testified that Blacks comprised 13.5 percent of the drivers on the southern portion of the turnpike and 15 percent of the drivers speeding. In contrast, Blacks represented 35 percent of those stopped. The court found that the defendants were unlawfully stopped and evidence presented against them was the result of an unlawful seizure.[79]

While this case was on appeal, on April 23, 1998, two troopers fired 11 shots into a van carrying 4 young Black males after a traffic-stop. Three of the young men were injured during the shooting.[80] Former State Police Superintendent Carl Williams reported that the van was pulled over because radar showed that the driver was speeding. However, later reports confirmed that the police patrol car was not equipped with a radar unit. Following the shooting, the two officers were brought before a state grand jury on charges of attempted murder and indicted for falsifying records to conceal the race of people they stopped and searched. In the months following the shooting, Governor Christine Whitman announced plans to secure funding for video cameras in police cars.

Attention to the issue of racial profiling peaked in February 1999 when the *Newark Star-Ledger* released statistics obtained from the state police documenting that three out of four motorists arrested on the turnpike in 2 selected months during 1997 were minorities.[81] Later that year, the newspaper published additional data for 1997 showing that four in five drivers arrested were minorities.[82] One dramatic illustration of the problem of racial profiling came during a *Star-Ledger* interview with then-NJSP Superintendent Williams, in which he explained, "The drug problem is cocaine or marijuana. It is most likely a minority group that is involved with that."[83] Governor Whitman fired Superintendent Williams shortly after this public statement.

On April 20, 1999, then-Acting New Jersey Attorney General Peter Verniero issued a 112-page report acknowledging the potential problems of racial profiling within the NJSP.[84] The attorney general's report recommended several internal reforms including an early warning system to detect patterns of discrimination by individual troopers or particular interdiction units. Facing a potential federal civil rights suit for racial bias in police stops and searches, New Jersey entered into a consent decree with DOJ mandating traffic-stop-and-search data collection.[85]

Data Collection Process

Pursuant to the federal consent decree, NJSP began gathering traffic-stop data on May 1, 2000. The data collection system is designed for use by state troopers engaged in patrol activities.[86] The initial data collection protocol relies on using the existing computer aided dispatch (CAD) system. Under this system, officers report the following information to the CAD operator:

- Name and identification number of all troopers who actively participated in the stop.
- Location, date, and time at which the stop commenced and ended.
- License plate number and state in which the car is registered.
- Description of the vehicle.
- Gender, race/ethnicity of the driver and date of birth of the driver (if known).
- Gender and race/ethnicity of any passengers.
- Whether the driver was issued a summons or warning and the category of violation (i.e., moving violation or nonmoving violation).
- Reason for the stop (i.e., moving violation, nonmoving violation, or probable cause).

The consent decree specifies that officers should make initial calls to the communication center before approaching the car, unless circumstances make this practice unsafe or impractical. CAD operators will manually enter data transmitted by troopers at the time of each stop. Eventually, NJSP plans to place laptops in all patrol cars, allowing officers to enter the traffic-stop data directly. At the end of the call, the communication center assigns an incident number to each motor vehicle stop. This number can be used to track information about poststop enforcement actions and can be useful in future auditing mechanisms.

The consent decree also specifies that troopers should notify the communications center prior to conducting searches. Any poststop enforcement action is recorded on a Motor Vehicle Stop Report (MVSR) for those traffic-stops in which the officer orders an occupant out of his or her vehicle, requests a consent search, conducts a search, requests a drug-detection canine, frisks an occupant, makes an arrest, recovers contraband or other property, or uses force. This additional stop report includes the race, gender, and date of birth of the occupants and an explanation concerning the process when one of these eight procedures is invoked.

Identifying and Overcoming Perceived Difficulties

Racial and Ethnic Designations and Categories
The traffic-stop data collection uses the following racial/ethnic categories:

- White.
- Black.
- Hispanic/Latino.
- Asian Indian (Asian subcontinent, e.g., India, Pakistan).
- Other Asian.
- American Indian/Native American.

In New Jersey, troopers do not ask drivers to identify their race or ethnicity. Instead, officers rely on their perceptions to provide the racial/ethnic data.

Time Burdens and Financial Costs

Although the state has not conducted a formal study concerning the additional radio transmission time, it is anticipated that little additional time will be required by troopers to relay the data collection information over the CAD system. The attorney general's office estimates that it will take several minutes for an officer to fill out the additional information on MVSR forms. However, poststop enforcement activities make up only a small percentage of an officer's daily duties.

The costs of such a wide-reaching, comprehensive data collection system are high. The state estimates that the modifications for the CAD system will cost $130,000. Also, the attorney general's office has estimated that $1.43 million will be spent on officer training. The training is designed to educate troopers about the data collection protocol and provides substantial additional training on criminal procedure and search and seizure law. Also, $12.581 million is budgeted for the purchase and installation of mobile video recorders and mobile data computers.

Disengagement

NJSP expressed concerns about officer disengagement. The attorney general's office reports that patrol-related arrests have decreased dramatically since the state began implementing its revised patrol practices and data collection system.[87] The reason for disengagement is currently under review. Because the consent decree was not implemented until May 2000, and the disengagement began much earlier, other factors such as the ongoing investigation of trooper misconduct may be responsible for the disengagement.

Data Integrity

Under the terms of the federal consent decree, the attorney general is responsible for auditing the traffic-stop data for accuracy. The attorney general's office is required to contact a sampling of persons who were the stopped by troopers to evaluate whether the stops were appropriately conducted and documented.[88] Additionally, the decree specifies that supervisors will regularly review trooper reports on poststop enforcement actions and videotapes of traffic-stops to ensure accuracy of the information and the appropriateness of their actions.

Officer Resistance

The publication of data was a primary concern of troopers. In the light of the tense political atmosphere around racial profiling and negative reports of officer behavior in the press, troopers expressed strong concerns that individual behavior would be reported to the press and that they would be labeled as racists.

Additionally, troopers raised concerns about the reliability of the CAD system and CAD officers. They feared that, if the CAD operators were short staffed, not trained, or inaccurate, the potential existed for misreporting traffic-stop data. The attorney general responded by hiring more CAD operators and adding training for troopers on the CAD system.

Data Analysis

The data from the New Jersey traffic studies will be collected and analyzed by individual officer identification numbers. This process allows the state attorney general to monitor both the prevalence of any systemwide problems in traffic-stops and flag individual officers who may be engaging in discriminatory traffic-stop practices. The data will be made available to both the state and an outside federal monitor.

Under the terms of the decree, NJSP will issue semiannual reports containing aggregate statistics on law enforcement activities.[89] These reports will include traffic-stop statistics. Attorney General Farmer explained that aggregate numbers alone would not dictate disciplinary action: "What we tried to move away from with the Justice Department was the idea that numbers alone dictate results. If it were the case that an officer had some proportion of a certain kind of stops, that would not trigger a conclusion of any kind; rather, it would trigger further investigation. So the numbers don't dictate results, they raise a red flag that we then pursue to see if there is a problem."[90]

The New Jersey Department of Law and Public Safety, in conjunction with DOJ, is conducting a survey of persons and vehicles traveling on the New Jersey Turnpike. The survey is designed to develop an objective sample of certain characteristics of persons and vehicles that travel on the turnpike. This traffic survey will serve as a tool to help the attorney general and other monitors determine whether an officer's stop patterns are disproportionate. At this time, the state has no plans to conduct an additional survey of the demographics of traffic violators on state highways.

Quantity of Data

New Jersey's data collection system captures a large amount of information, including detailed information on consent searches and the use of canines. However, the state police data collection system focuses only on traffic-stops, not pedestrian stops. Additionally, NJSP hopes to equip all trooper cars with video cameras by February 2001.

Lessons Learned

Collecting traffic-stop data is compatible with officer safety. Attorney General Farmer explained: "From our perspective, the fundamental point that we would want to communicate to others, and that I have said to several other of my colleagues, is that addressing this issue is not incompatible with promoting officer safety, or robbing law enforcement of its efficacy. When you make people accountable, who basically haven't been in the past because of antiquated record keeping and because of an institutional culture that didn't promote openness, of course there is a reaction and a recoiling."

Additionally, the New Jersey experience shows that allegations of racial profiling may be part of larger structural or organizational problems within a police organization. For example, in New Jersey, the state police were trained and rewarded for high numbers of arrests, as opposed to making quality arrests.[91] In addition to contributing to allegations of racial profiling, this emphasis may have undermined the effectiveness of police practices. In an interim report, the attorney general acknowledges two primary concerns: documented stop-and-search practices producing a "find" rate of only 10 percent were ineffective, and the find rates did not vary across races. Attorney General Farmer illustrated the costs of such ineffective policing. He explained that, during a recent highway drug interdiction program on the turnpike, an investigative team interdicted a tractor-trailer carrying approximately $1 million in contraband. This interdiction was supported with intelligence, wiretaps, and specific targets. Conversely, the attorney general explained, the nearly 500 seizures from traffic-stops in 1999 netted only $60,000 in contraband, illustrating the ineffectiveness of traffic "profiling" for high-level drug interdiction.

According to Attorney General Farmer, addressing the problem of profiling is just one piece of a much larger program of restructuring within NJSP. The traffic-stop data collection system is one critical part of its new effective management strategy.

The Experience in Great Britain

Currently, data collection on the racial and ethnic demographics of police searches is occurring throughout England and Wales, a region that includes a mixture of urban and rural areas. The largest urban center is London, with a population of 7 million. Great Britain is 81 percent White, 7.5 percent Black, 7.3 percent Asian, and 4.2 percent other.[92]

In London, the Metropolitan Police Service (MPS) numbers 26,000, plus a civilian staff of 15,000. The current MPS program to monitor the race and ethnicity of persons searched and (in seven pilot sites) stopped by police officers was developed after a period of racial unrest in the 1970s and early 1980s. Authorities within the British Government, concerned about increasing claims that police were disproportionally stopping and searching ethnic minorities, determined that a systematic data collection system was necessary to address questions about police legitimacy and ethnic bias. In 1991, the Criminal Justice Act was passed requiring the home secretary to publish "such information necessary to assess the existence of racial discrimination in police practices." The original program of ethnic monitoring required data collection on searches, arrests, cautions, and homicides.[93]

Precipitating Events: The Stephen Lawrence Murder and the MacPherson Report

Several high-profile events led MPS to expand the scope of race and ethnicity data collection required under the Criminal Justice Act of 1991. On April 22, 1993, in the southeastern London suburb of Elthram, two young Black men, Stephen Lawrence and Duwayne Brooks, were rushing to catch a bus when they were confronted by a gang of White youths. The gang, who did not know Lawrence, attacked him with knives. After being badly beaten, he managed to scramble free but was bleeding profusely. After 200 yards, he collapsed and died.[94]

The subsequent police investigation, or lack of investigation, of this hate crime sparked a long protest and inquiry. Although an inquest verdict indicated that Lawrence was killed in a completely unprovoked racist attack by five White youths, none of them was ever convicted.[95] MPS's investigation of the Lawrence murder was severely criticized as flawed by corruption, incompetence, and racism.[96] A subsequent private prosecution ended in an acquittal. In July 1997, the home secretary announced in Parliament that an investigation of Lawrence's murder would be undertaken,[97] and Sir William MacPherson was asked to chair the public inquiry into the murder. Released in 1999, the *MacPherson Report* criticized MSP for "institutionally racist" practices.

The report's recommendations dealt not only with the investigation and prosecution of hate crimes but also with the general problems and differing perceptions that exist between the minority ethnic communities and the police.[98] During the public inquiry, there were universal complaints from the minority community that police discriminate in the practice of stopping and searching civilians.[99] In his report, MacPherson recommended that police officers record, monitor, and analyze the racial and ethnic demographics of all police stops and searches.[100]

The Stephen Lawrence case and the MacPherson public inquiry and report were widely covered in the press, and these events were critical catalysts to Great Britain's current data collection efforts. In 1998, MPS began pilot data collection programs in seven jurisdictions.[101]

Data Collection Process

For the last 3 years, all police departments in Great Britain have been collecting data on all Police and Criminal Evidence (PACE) Act searches.[102] PACE provides British police with the power to stop-and-search any person or vehicle when the officer has reasonable grounds for suspecting that stolen or prohibited articles will be found.[103] While these vehicle and pedestrian stops may seem equivalent to the American stop-and-frisk practice, PACE powers are actually quite different: they allow officers to conduct a full search, as opposed to a mere pat down of outer clothing, for weapons. Consequently, police officers can conduct a full search of the person, as well as anything they may be carrying or any vehicle they are in.

While the current British data collection system records information on all PACE pedestrian and vehicle searches, it does not include PACE stops that do not result in a search or on-PACE stops and searches such as traffic-stops or voluntary stops. However, selected pilot locations have tested data collection programs collecting information on all police stops.[104]

Data Collection Mechanism

Police are using paper forms to collect the data. Each officer carries an Information for Persons Searched form, which the officer completes after a search has been conducted. The form consists of a yellow face sheet and a white carbon copy. Individuals searched are entitled to a full copy of the record of the search (the white copy) at the time of the search or, upon demand, within 12 months. Since the process of completing the form may take 5 to 10 minutes, most people do not wait for the officer to complete the form.

Elements Collected

After each search, police record the reason for the search; information about the person searched; a description of the person or vehicle searched; the location, date, and time of the stop; and the object and grounds for the search.

On the search form, police specify the grounds for the search as follows:

- Reasonable grounds exist to search for stolen property or offensive weapons.
- Reasonable grounds exist to search for drugs.
- Reasonable grounds exist to search for firearms.
- Reasonable grounds exist to search for certain dangerous weapons.
- A senior officer authorized searches in particular circumstances without reasonable grounds.[105]
- Terrorism searches are conducted.

Next, officers complete information about the person searched including name, address, date of birth, and telephone number. They describe the person searched including their clothing, height, and gender. The form asks whether clothing was searched or intimate parts exposed. The fourth section gathers information about the vehicle searched and whether property was found. A description of property found is required. Finally, the time, date, and location of the search are recorded. A separate line indicates whether the person was arrested.

Identifying and Overcoming Potential Difficulties

Racial and Ethnic Designations

Police have been using the following racial and ethnic categories:

- White-skinned European appearance, e.g., English, Scottish, Welsh, French, German, Swedish, Norwegian, Polish, and Russian.
- Dark-skinned European appearance, e.g., Mediterranean, Greek, Turkish, Sicilian, Sardinian, Spanish, and Italian.
- Black.
- Asian.

Police categorize persons searched based on the officer's perception. Initially, it was deemed impractical to ask individuals about their racial and/ or ethnic background. However, the McPherson report specifically recommended that, when an officer records information about stops and searches, the records include the reason for the stop, the outcome, and the self-identified ethnic identity of the person, in addition to a description of the person. Consequently, police will begin asking the person to self-identify using one of 17 self-identification categories:

1. White–Northern Europe.
2. White–Southern Europe.
3. White–other.
4. Black–British.
5. Black–Caribbean.
6. Black–African.
7. Black–other.
8. Asian–Indian.
9. Pakistani.
10. Bangladeshi.
11. Chinese.
12. Asian–other.
13. Arabic.
14. Other.
15. Mixed Origin–Black/White.
16. Mixed Origin–Asian/White.
17. Mixed Origin–Other.[106]

Costs

Searching is a relatively rare activity for British police officers. During an interview, one officer in Hounslow estimated that on any given day, less than 5 percent of his time involves searches. The search form itself takes 5 to 10 minutes to complete. In Hounslow, where they are completing forms on all stops and searches on an experimental basis, an officer can complete the stop portion of the form in approximately 2 minutes. Since the English system records data on paper, each police district pays for data entry, at an approximate cost of $8,000 per year.

Disengagement

Beginning in 1998, the official philosophy underlying searches changed. The new philosophy emphasized the quality rather than the quantity of searches.[107] This change meant focusing on the percentage of searches that resulted in arrests for serious offenses. As a result, the search productivity and arrest rates have improved.[108] Thus, by late 1999, in selected pilot sites, the proportion of recorded searches for which an arrest had also been recorded had gradually risen.[109] More recent figures demonstrate that the trend has been sustained. From 1998 to 1999, the arrest rate across the MPS force was 17 percent.[110]

An analysis of search records indicates that most of the searches conducted by police are high-discretion or proactive searches rather than low-discretion searches driven by information given to police from other sources.[111] The overall fall in searches has been far more marked with respect to high-discretion searches.[112]

However, the volume of arrests has decreased. Indeed, the overall number of arrests and searches has dropped by nearly 33 percent among the selected pilot sites.[113] Marian FitzGerald, a researcher who has studied this phenomenon, attributes the decrease in searches to the ongoing McPherson inquiry, as well as a reduced police presence on the streets.[114] Officers interviewed expressed a deep loss of morale that has influenced the effectiveness of MPS during and after the McPherson inquiry. FitzGerald reports, "Many officers felt a deep sense of personal injustice, perceiving their integrity systematically and relentlessly being called into question and believing they each stood indicted individually of institutional racism."[115] A number of events that required high-profile policing took 60 percent more officers in London away from normal street duties, so fewer officers were available to undertake routine searches. Also, during 1998 and 1999 fewer officers were on the street.[116] These factors indicate that, although there has been disengagement, a number of exogenous factors may account for the decrease in PACE searches.

Quantity of Data

Currently, other than in the seven pilot sites, police only collect data on PACE searches. Their data collection system will become broader when they begin to record all stops, regardless of whether the stop results in a search or an arrest. As noted earlier, once data collection is expanded to include all stops, a richer analysis of England's stop-and-search policy can occur.

Officer Resistance

As noted earlier, many officers feel frustrated by mounting paperwork and the barriers that constrain their professional judgment. Only part of this frustration is due to PACE data collection. In England, few officers have access to a computer, so most of their information processes require completion of paper forms.

Use of the Data and Analysis

The Information from Persons Searched forms are used to monitor, supervise, and discipline individual officers. The name and signature of the officer conducting the search is on the form. By collecting this information, police are able to identify officers engaging in "best practices" as well as officers whose search patterns seem questionable.

All analysis conducted on the British data has been based on residential population figures. Analysts have not yet developed a system for calculating a comparative benchmark that would incorporate differing criminal participation rates. This comparative population might differ from residential statistics because many individuals who are searched do not live in the neighborhood where the search occurred.

Lessons Learned

Three important lessons have been learned from the British data collection experience. First, research has begun to show that the manner in which searches are conducted may greatly influence any resulting racial animosity surrounding police action. Research indicates that, although a search may be procedurally correct, when it is conducted confrontationally or in an uncivil or authoritarian manner, the result can be profoundly alienating.[117] Thus, the manner in which a search is conducted may be a major cause of particular complaints or dissatisfaction.

Second, some searches are conducted in response to specific incidents, information, and/or calls from the public. These are low-discretion searches. Other high-discretion searches are the result of proactive policing. Recognizing these differences may allow for a richer and more complete analysis of the data once they are collected.

Third, the initial research on data collection in Great Britain illustrates the complexities of measuring police disengagement. FitzGerald argues that a clear statistical relationship exists between the reduction in searches and the rise in crime in spring 1999. For example, searches produced 12 percent of all arrests in 1998, and by mid-1999, the number had fallen to under 9 percent of all arrests.[118] FitzGerald cautions that additional analyses are necessary to determine whether the reduction of searches had any direct influence on the rise in crime.[119] The possibility of police disengagement in Great Britain underscores the need for more systematic research on the relationship between data collection, search rates, and increases in crime to fully evaluate the successes or problems of initial stop-and-search data collection efforts.

RECOMMENDATIONS FOR TRAFFIC-STOP DATA COLLECTION SYSTEMS

In implementing any data collection system, a primary consideration must be the feasibility of collecting the data. Police must collect sufficient data for meaningful analysis while creating a data collection system that is manageable and causes minimal inconvenience to citizens, officers, and other police administrators. For these reasons, each locality or jurisdiction may decide to balance considerations of time, officer safety, and convenience differently. This chapter offers recommendations for collecting data on traffic-stops and searches.[120] The recommendations are limited to traffic-stops for two reasons: all of the selected sites included in this analysis, with the exception of London, limited their data collection to traffic-stops; and jurisdictions that develop a successful traffic-stop protocol can then adjust their data collection mechanisms to meet the different needs of pedestrian-stop data collection.

For the purposes of this guide, a "stop" is defined as any time an officer initiates contact with a vehicle resulting in the detention of an individual and/or vehicle. Although jurisdictions may decide to widen or limit the scope of their data collection process, at a minimum data should be collected on all stops regardless of whether a warning or citation is issued. Much of the anecdotal evidence about racial profiling involves motorists who allege they were stopped for "driving the wrong car," "driving in the wrong place," or minor equipment violations. In many cases, these individuals were never issued a written warning or citation. Such incidents will only be captured in a data collection system that monitors all traffic-stops, regardless of outcome. Only by documenting all stops can a law enforcement organization gain information about the nature and scope of the alleged problem.

Local Task Force

Local jurisdictions will differ on the type of data that they will want to collect and the methodologies they will employ to collect information. However, a critical first step to any data collection design process is to convene a task force composed of representatives from law enforcement, members of the community, and citizen group representatives. Although this guide provides recommendations and models for data collection, a local task force is best able to recognize the specific needs of community members and police within a particular jurisdiction.

Additionally, we recommend that local jurisdictions develop a relationship with an academic or research partner. During the data collection design phase, local jurisdictions should consider who is going to analyze the stop-and-search data. When possible, the local jurisdiction should include members of the analysis team as part of the data collection design process. Knowing how the analysis will be conducted and what is needed for analysis is a critical step in the data collection design process.

Data Collection Pilot Program

In addition to gaining valuable guidance from a local task force, individual jurisdictions should allow 3 to 6 months as a test period for any data collection program. A pilot phase for data collection allows local jurisdictions to modify data collection elements, methodologies, and auditing procedures as needs arise.

If the first round of analysis determines that new elements need to be collected or changes need to be made to the data collection procedure, the data collection system should be flexible enough to allow for changes with minimal inconvenience and expense.

Data Collection Design

Any opportunity to streamline data collection efforts should be seized, and at least two opportunities exist. First, for those jurisdictions that have laptop computers or MDTs capable of running software, the easiest way to collect the data will be to use pulldown menus for each data collection category. For those jurisdictions that do not have such capabilities, San

Jose's simple alpha code system enables the relevant data to be captured easily and quickly via the dispatcher or an MDT unit that cannot run windows. In San Jose, officers carry a pocket-sized laminated, color-coded card that assists them in recording the appropriate alpha codes for each designated category.

Additionally, we recommend that jurisdictions use existing data collection systems (dispatch information, citations, officer logs) to minimize the burden of additional data collection efforts. By linking current data collection processes with new study-specific information, local jurisdictions can minimize both cost and officer inconvenience.

Data Collection Elements

To discuss which data should be collected by local jurisdictions, we have categorized elements into two parts. The first set of elements in any traffic-stop study should be data that are routinely collected during normal traffic-stop operations. The second set of elements is to be collected specifically to assess questions of racial profiling in stop-and-search practices.

We recommend that jurisdictions assign a stop identification code to each dispatch or MDT communication for traffic-stops. The stop identification code should correspond to a unique identification number on new stop-and-search data collection forms or computer entries. This process allows jurisdictions to link information that they routinely collect on traffic-stops with additional information (either forms or computerized entries) specifically recommended for stop-and-search data collection. For example, if an officer normally calls in the license number and description of the vehicle stopped, the location of the stop, and his or her badge number, the officer would simply add a number identifying the data collection sheet or computerized entry to this dispatch. To further reduce officer workload, the unique identification numbers could also be attached to citations, search/ inventory forms, or other routinely collected sources of information to be automatically linked with study-specific data elements.

The unique identification number can be used at a later date to match dispatch and study-specific information. During the analysis phase of their study, jurisdictions may determine which information from the dispatch records will be matched with stop-and-search study-specific records. The elements recommended for collecting routine dispatch or traffic-stop operations are described in the following section.

Routine Data Collection Elements

Date, Time, and Location of the Stop

Collecting these items is essential for analyzing traffic-stop data. The data assist law enforcement by providing a context for stops made by enabling staff to determine where and when stops are occurring. This information could include the police precinct, the street address or intersection, and mile marker or exit. Some of the officers who have reacted negatively to the collection of stop-and-search data have raised an important issue. To fully understand why an officer chooses to stop a particular vehicle one must know the context of the situation. Was the stop part of a particular operation? Was the officer in a neighborhood of predominantly one race or ethnicity? By collecting basic information on the date and location of the stop, a department can begin to measure it in context. Additionally, the date, time, and location of the stop are critical components of future audits of traffic-stop data.

License Number, State, and Description of Vehicle Stopped

To ensure the accuracy of data collection procedures, a systematic mechanism for crosschecking data should be implemented. By recording the car's license number and state in which it is registered, staff can cross-check the data entered with department of motor vehicle (DMV) information.

In addition, many officers report that the decision to stop a vehicle may sometimes be due to the type of vehicle (e.g., rental) or a combination of the type of vehicle and the characteristics of its driver. Collecting this information allows departments to understand how often this type of stop occurs.

Length of Stop

Anecdotal evidence includes incidents involving stops for extended periods. To discern whether this is a problem in a particular jurisdiction, officers should, with the assistance of the dispatcher, record the time at which a stop commenced and at which it ended.

Name and Identification Number of the Officers who Initiated or Participated in the Stop

One of the most controversial aspects of stop-and-search data collection is whether to collect the identity of the officer making the stop. There are several analytical advantages to recording these data. Adopting such an approach enables organizations to identify potential problem officers who may be disproportionately stopping minorities. In this sense, the data collection process functions as an early warning system, alerting management to problems and allowing them to investigate possible extenuating circumstances and, if necessary, to intervene early with counseling, training, or some other intervention.

Within this selected site analysis, San Jose, San Diego, and North Carolina do not collect the identity of the officers involved in a stop. By contrast, in New Jersey and Great Britain, the name and identity of the officer is included in the data collection process. Research from the few sites suggests that collection of officer identification can engender considerable officer and/or union opposition and disengagement.

An alternative to officer identification may be the use of unit or district information. This option provides a way to analyze the data within a meaningful unit of analysis (section/specific force) but allows agencies to collect data without requiring the identity of the officer. The purpose of recording the identity of the officer should be to diagnose and remedy problems as part of an early warning system. As New Jersey Attorney General Farmer stated: "It [data collection] is definitely supposed to be part of an early warning system that enables us to identify a potential problem, go in and fix it rather than waiting for it to fester. For it to be an early warning system, we didn't see any way to do it unless we had officer identification."

Departments should consider a procedure that requires the officer's identity to be recorded but uses the data primarily for training and support. Officers identified as engaging in any unusual pattern of vehicle stops would review the information with their immediate supervisors. If this pattern (or a similarly unusual pattern) persists, the behavior would be brought to the attention of the human resources unit of the department, and assistance/training would be offered to the officer. If these two steps are followed and the officer still behaves in a disturbing manner in traffic-stops, the matter should be dealt with using the department's normal disciplinary procedures.

Study-Specific Data Collection Elements

It is recommended that this second set of data be collected on all traffic-stops, regardless of whether a citation, search, or arrest is made. These elements could also be linked to existing forms or data entry.

Date of Birth

Some jurisdictions collect age in two general categories, juvenile or adult, but it is recommended that officers record the exact age of the individual being stopped. This can be accomplished by having the officer record the date of birth that appears on the driver's license.

The reason for collecting exact age is two general categories such as juvenile or adult may conceal age distinctions. For example, the preliminary analysis of San Jose's data indicates that 97 percent of persons stopped were labeled adults, compared to 3 percent who were classified as minors. This finding indicates a need for more precise measurement. Additionally, national survey data indicate that young Black Americans disproportionally report the perception of being stopped by the police because of both their race and their age.[121] To address these concerns, data on the age of the person stopped should be available for analysis.

Gender

Many departments already collect information on the gender of persons stopped. This practice was established in some departments after the filing of several lawsuits alleging sexual harassment by male officers toward female motorists they stopped. Information about the gender of individuals stopped is important in stop-and-search data collection systems. Analysis of national survey data indicates that Black males perceive that they are being stopped more often than Black females or Whites of either sex.[122] Thus, the ability to disaggregate gender can be an important analytical tool.

Race or Ethnicity

Unlike age and gender, which appear on an individual's driver's license, discerning race or ethnicity requires either a verbal inquiry of the individual or an officer's subjective determination. Since a verbal inquiry risks exacerbating tensions during a potentially tense encounter, to minimize inconvenience and maximize officer safety, we recommend using the officer's perception of race or ethnicity. Since an officer's perception of race or ethnicity gives rise to the problem of racial profiling, the officer's perception is an appropriate means of ascertaining race or ethnicity. Whether the officer correctly ascertains the race or ethnicity of the driver is less important than being able to analyze whether, having perceived the driver is a person of color, the officer treats the person fairly.

For data collection purposes, we recommend the following racial and ethnic categories:

- White.
- Black.
- Asian, Pacific Islander.
- Native American.
- Middle Eastern, East Indian.
- Hispanic.

Local jurisdictions may choose to alter these racial categories to more appropriately reflect the racial and ethnic demographics of their population. To assist the officer in assessing the ethnicity of an individual, it is suggested that the officer assess and record any racial identification information after using both of the following subjective tools: visual and verbal contact with the individual and the surname of the individual. Additionally, jurisdictions may want to consider whether an officer should be able to check two racial categories when the individual appears to be of mixed racial origin. While intending to more accurately reflect the ethnic diversity of a community, we believe that detailed ethnic breakdowns inevitably miss some groups and do an injustice to the rich ethnic heritage of most Americans.

Reason for the Stop

The reason an officer gives for stopping a vehicle is one of the most important pieces of information that will be collected. Although there are many reasons why an individual might be stopped, a key design issue is not only to simplify this category sufficiently to allow manageable collection but also to provide for measurement precise enough to accurately monitor discretion. Discretion is at the core of a law enforcement officer's job, and it permits innovative, flexible problem solving. However, it also provides opportunities for conscious and subconscious racial discrimination to affect decisionmaking. The level of discretion involved in traffic-stops varies considerably. At times, officers respond to externally generated information. For example, when a person places a 911 call providing a description of a crime, officers have little discretion but to respond. This type of low-discretion situation might be analyzed differently from other law enforcement actions because it is based on an external source rather than an individual officer's discretionary determination. Similarly, if an officer observes a driver failing to stop at a red light or driving 30 miles above the speed limit, the officer may feel obliged to pull over the driver. This type of officer-initiated low-discretion situation differs dramatically from an officer-initiated high-discretion stop such as when an officer stops a vehicle with underinflated tires, a soiled license plate, or traveling 4 miles above the speed limit. In both the low-discretion and the high-discretion stops, the driver has violated the law, but officers vary more often in their responses to high-discretion situations.

Disparate treatment is more likely to occur in high-discretion than low-discretion circumstances. Consequently, the data collection systems should be designed so that analysts can disaggregate the level of discretion available to the officer at the time of the stop and whether the stop was based on external information such as an all-points bulletin or a 911 call.

Although jurisdictions and/or localities may collect different elements that correspond appropriately with local enforcement patterns, we recommend the categories listed in table 2.

Departments should review stop and citation practices within their own jurisdiction to determine appropriate reasons for stopping motorists.

Unfortunately, the reason for the stop category is often oversimplified. San Jose's preliminary analysis demonstrates the problems of narrowly defining this category. San Jose designated only four reasons that a vehicle was stopped: vehicle code violation, penal code violation, municipal code violation, and a stop based on an all-points or be-on-the-lookout notice. Its first analysis revealed that 99 percent of the time the reason for the stop was a vehicle code violation, a broad category that fails to distinguish among moving violations, nonmoving violations, equipment violations, and hazardous moving violations. This type of broad categorization obfuscates distinctions among the various types of violations and indicates the need for a more precise measurement.

Disposition or Outcome of the Stop

The disposition of each traffic-stop should be collected. While there are many police disposition codes relevant to traffic-stops, departments should use a system that limits the complexity and volume of codes to be collected. Officers should be allowed to designate more than one disposition code, if necessary. The following disposition codes are recommended:

Table 2 Reasons for Stopping Motorists

Reason for Stop	Examples
Hazardous moving violation	Stoplight or stop sign violation, driving 10 miles or more above the speed limit
Nonhazardous moving violation	Failure to signal when changing lanes, driving less than 10 miles above the speed limit
Externally generated information stop	911 call or all-points bulletin
Vehicle equipment violations/defects	Broken headlight or brake light, underinflated tires, etc.
Investigatory stop	Belief of criminal activity based on observation
Seat belt violation	
Driving while impaired	
Courtesy stop/citizen assistance	
Other motor vehicle violation	

- Oral warning.
- Written warning (where used).
- Arrest made.
- Arrest by warrant.
- Criminal citation.
- Traffic citation—hazardous.
- Traffic citation—nonhazardous.
- Courtesy service/citizen assist.
- No action taken.

Whether a Search was Conducted

This is a complex but valuable item to collect. While there are sundry legal and operational factors involved in collecting information about searches, such information should be col-lected. For most officers, searching is a relatively rare activity; so, ordi-narily, most officers will not be completing the series of inquiries that follow. Still, the following information should be collected:

- Was a search conducted (yes/no)?
- What type of search was conducted?
  - Vehicle
  - Driver
  - Passenger or passengers
- What was the basis for the search?
  - Visible contraband
  - Odor of contraband
  - Canine alert
  - Inventory search prior to impoundment
  - Consent search
- Was contraband found (yes/no)?
- Was property seized (yes/no)?
- Describe the nature and quantity of the contraband seized or found.[123]
- Comment Box that allows officers to put in any contextual information that appears relevant to the search, such as a strategic initiative.

For some of the above categories, an officer can check more than one cat-egory. When using a computerized data collection system, the categories can be defaulted to "no" to speed data collection in cases where a search was not conducted.

Although it may seem easier to omit search information from the process, it serves two valuable functions. First, search information provides local jurisdictions with a sense of the quantity and quality of searches being conducted, the characteristics of those searches, and their productivity. Productivity refers to the number of searches that result in arrests or seizures, the nature of those arrests, and the quality of the seizures. Such information allows local jurisdictions to appropriately allocate resources to productive search techniques. Second, information about searches allows departments to assess whether certain groups are disproportionally targeted for searches.

Mechanisms for Ensuring Data Integrity

To ensure the accuracy of data collection processes, departments should implement a mechanism for spot-checking or cross-checking the data. Several possibilities exist. Nearly all traffic-stops conducted by officers in the United States involve an officer transmitting to the dispatcher that a stop isu being made. This is normal police procedure in most communities. It increases officer safety by notifying the dispatcher that the officer is leaving the police vehicle to talk to a citizen. It also informs the dispatcher that the officer is involved with an action and may not be available to take another call. These stops are part of the CAD file in most agencies and could be reviewed to ensure that all stops result in a traffic-stop data form being completed.

Using the license plate number and the state the vehicle is registered in, staff can spot-check reports by cross-checking data collected with the relevant state DMV information. Some DMVs have on file the race of the licensee or a photograph of the license holder. This information could be used on a limited basis to verify the race and ethnicity information on the completed data collection forms.

An additional auditing mechanism involves ongoing customer satisfaction surveys that many departments use. Most of these surveys randomly poll those who have called the police for assistance. The respondents are asked a few questions about the quality of the service they received and their satisfaction with it. This approach could be useful in traffic-stops. During this survey, information could be acquired about the race of the person stopped and the reason for the stop. This information could be used to verify the information collected by the officer.

Such a survey helps to ensure the accuracy of data and provides management with useful information about the quality of stops and searches from the perspective of the individual stopped. As in earlier instances, the information should be used principally for training purposes and not for officer discipline.

Data Analysis and Future Research

The limited studies available concerning disparate stop-and-search patterns during traffic-stops raise complex analytical issues. Local jurisdictions must coordinate data collection design efforts with a designated data collection team. Where possible, local jurisdictions should partner with statisticians at local universities, colleges, or junior colleges or work with members of internal research units.

The three most vexing problems involve assessing why an individual officer decides to stop a particular vehicle, measuring the populations that put themselves at risk of being stopped by their actions or the actions of others (a base violation rate), and comparing pedestrian stops to appropriate street populations (or street violator populations).

Assessing Police Discretion

Many officers have spoken of the difficulty in quantifying the decision to stop. They have noted that the decision to stop a vehicle is the result of several factors including the behavior of the operator of the vehicle, the officer's experience, the departmental policies and procedures, the crime problems faced by a particular neighborhood, and specific police tactics. Although no quantitative survey can accurately measure all the factors involved in an officer's decision, the collection of data can provide some aggregate estimates about the behavior of officers as well as the criminal behavior of certain population groups.

By collecting information about a phenomenon that is almost invisible to review at the moment, a law enforcement agency can identify a typical pattern of behavior of its officers and discern if outliers exist. This analysis could be done for individual officers or for individual neighborhoods. Data collection could determine, for example, that a typical officer stops 10 cars per shift and issues 4 citations. Once this information is known, the behavior of all officers can be evaluated by this measure. If an officer is stopping 50 cars in a shift, that officer may be working very hard in an area or may be causing increased community resentment in a particular neighborhood. Similarly, if the officer who stops 50 motorists only issues 4 citations, this may identify a training issue regarding why the hit rate of this officer is so much lower than others. There may be legitimate reasons for this kind of variation, but currently, most police departments do not even know whether this kind of variability exists.

The collection of this kind of information enables an agency to track changes over time. If departments were regularly collecting information on the characteristics of traffic-stops, they would be able to detect trends in the use of this law enforcement tactic. If the number of stops decreased drastically in one section of a community, the data would alert officials to this change. Similarly, if one area is marked by an increase in stops of Asian motorists, a department could investigate to determine the cause of this increase. In addition, having the data would allow departments to respond more quickly to complaints from community groups of racial profiling.

Constructing a Comparative Benchmark

Once a law enforcement agency begins to gather traffic-stop data, what steps should be undertaken to understand and interpret the data? One important step is to bring the agency, community members, and other interested persons together to construct a comparative benchmark to determine whether minority individuals are being stopped disproportionately. This benchmark is also important for determining whether poststop law enforcement actions are being directed at minorities in a disproportionate manner. If a substantial disparity is found, is there a nondiscriminatory explanation or justification for the disparity?

By themselves, the characteristics of traffic-stops are difficult to interpret. For example, if, after collecting data, a particular city discovers that 65 percent of its traffic-stops on a particular highway are of Hispanic drivers, that percentage by itself does not reveal much. The city must compare that percentage to an appropriate benchmark, which ideally could be the proportion of Hispanic traffic violators on the highways where the stops occurred. Thus, the 65 percent stopping rate would be proportionate if 65 percent of the violators on this highway were Hispanic but would be disproportionate if only 20 percent of the violators were Hispanic. The city could determine whether the disparity correlates with a disproportionate allocation of police resources to minority residential areas and, if it does so, whether this correlation explains the disparity.

Generally, there are two different types of comparative benchmarks: those that are external to the traffic-stop data and those that may be generated from within the data set. These benchmarks can be used in conjunction or separately.

External benchmarks involve developing an estimate of the percentages ofu persons who are at risk for being stopped on roads that are patrolled by the law enforcement agency by racial or ethnic group. These benchmarks may be used to measure persons who are violating traffic laws on particular roadways or, alternatively, may simply travel on these roads. In analyzing police activity on a particular highway or road, the stationary and rolling surveys planned by Zingraff and conducted by Lamberth provide ways to calculate a violator rate broken down by race. However, it may be appropriate to construct benchmarks that simply measure the racial percentages of vehicle drivers on particular roadways.

Some jurisdictions have sought to use residential population data, broken down by race, to estimate the racial percentages of persons using the jurisdiction's roads. This breakdown may be useful, if done properly. First, it is important to ensure that the population data are sufficiently current. The 2000 census would be a more appropriate description of population demographics than older census estimates. Second, because the age demographics for different racial groups may vary, it is vital that the residential benchmark be applied only to individuals who are of legal driving age. Other available data concerning a person's access to vehicles reported by race may help jurisdictions refine the residential population benchmark. Third, residential population benchmarks are least appropriate for examining the racial demographics of individuals stopped by the police who reside outside that particular jurisdiction.

Various internal benchmarks may be developed. For example, a jurisdiction could compare traffic-stop data of the same unit (or the same officer) over time or could compare that data for several units (or several individual officers) that patrol the same or similar areas. Additionally, data on speeding tickets and searches may be analyzed to determine if minority drivers are disproportionately ticketed or searched. Finally, data on searches may be analyzed to compare the percentages of persons searched, by race, with the corresponding hit rates (searches producing contraband) for different racial groups.

More research is needed to determine the most useful way to analyze data on stops and searches. By experimenting with various benchmark comparisons, practical methods can be designed.

CONCLUSION AND RECOMMENDATIONS

The challenge that confronts American police organizations is how to sustain the historic decline in rates of criminal activity while enhancing police legitimacy in the eyes of the communities they serve. Appropriately addressing allegations of racial profiling is central to this new mission. Historically, police have defined their purpose as regulatory—ensuring the greatest possible order. Their task was reactive and involved responding to obvious signs of disorder, such as emergency calls. Realizing the profound limitations of this model, the community policing strategy began to use information, technology, research, and data to engage officers in more effective and better managed policing by anticipating and disrupting the causes of disorder. Nationwide, police departments have begun using information and technology to measure and identify crime clusters and develop strategies to intervene and disrupt violent crime before it occurs.

Local and state jurisdictions that have begun to collect data point to a number of benefits of a well-planned traffic-stop data collection system. Some of these advantages include the following:

- Police forces committed to improving legitimacy find that measurement of police activity is a critical first step toward effective management.
- Data collection sends a clear message that racial profiling is inconsistent with effective policing and equal protection.
- Having available data moves the conversation within the community away from rhetoric and accusations to a discussion about the effective deployment of police resources.

- In contrast to a rigid set of guidelines, the data collection approach allows a fluid and local determination of how to deploy law enforcement resources.
- The process of collecting data begins to change behavior of line officers and supervisors.

As state and local law enforcement agencies develop data collection designs to address community concerns about racial profiling in police stops and searches, DOJ can play an increasingly important role. By providing information and technical assistance to state and local law enforcement agencies, DOJ can encourage localities to adopt suitable racial profiling data collection systems. To facilitate this goal, the authors recommend that DOJ should:

- Sponsor a Web site for disseminating up-to-date information about racial profiling data collection system designs, providing sample data collection forms, and allowing a forum for discussion of common obstacles.
- Encourage and fund demonstration projects for determining best practices for data collection and analysis. At the time this guide was drafted, only a few jurisdictions had developed and implemented comprehensive data collection systems. Since then, and as this guide goes to press, numerous law enforcement jurisdictions have started collecting data. In the light of this increased data collection activity, and as a followup to this guide, DOJ should fund a Best Practices Guide to examine and evaluate emerging traffic-stop policies, data collection strategies, training, and analysis techniques.
- Assist jurisdictions in designing statistical benchmarks and determining comparative populations. Such projects might include an academic workshop on the ways to construct a statistical benchmark and meaningfully analyze traffic-stop data.
- Recognize and reward pioneering efforts in racial profiling data collection, and provide encouragement for other jurisdictions to follow their lead.
- Create requirements in federal funding to ensure design and implementation of state and local traffic-stop data collection protocols.
- Develop federal funding programs for software, technical assistance, and data analysis grants for state and local agencies.
- Foster partnerships between DOJ and the U.S. Attorney's Ofices that would encourage U.S. Attorneys to meet with their local community policing partners to discuss the prospect of voluntary data collection efforts. To further this goal, DOJ could host an information session on current data collection efforts and strategies.
- Develop a traffic-stop training curriculum that specifically address the issues of racial profiling for use by state and local departments.

ACKNOWLEDGMENTS

Deborah Ramirez, Jack McDevitt, and Amy Farrell would like to acknowledge the assistance of many individuals and agencies. In particular, we thank Attorney General Janet Reno and the U.S. Department of Justice for supporting research on racial profiling data collection efforts. We appreciate the support of Richard Jerome, Deputy Associate Attorney

General, and Karen Stevens, Counsel to the Assistant Attorney General, who facilitated development of this project; the Bureau of Justice Assistance for providing the resources for this research; and Northeastern University for enabling our involvement with this project. Most of all we are grateful to the members of those law enforcement and state agencies who generously shared their time and knowledge with us.

ENDNOTES

[1.] Attorney General's Conference on Strengthening Police-Community Relationships, Report on the Proceedings, Washington, DC: U.S. Department of Justice, June 9–10, 1999, at 22–23.

[2.] The U.S. Supreme Court has addressed the issue of ethnicity and immigration stops in United States v. Brignoni-Ponce 422 U.S. 873 (1975) and United States v. Martinez-Fuerte 428 U.S. 543 (1976). More recently, the Ninth Circuit addressed the use of race in border stops in United States v. Montero-Camargo, 208 F. 3d 1122 (9th Cir. 2000).

[3.] Gallup Poll Organization Poll Release, Racial Profiling Is Seen as Widespread, Particularly Among Young Black Men, Princeton, NJ: Gallup Poll Organization, December 9, 1999, at 1.

[4.] Gallup Poll Organization Poll Release, see note 3, at 1.

[5.] Bureau of Justice Statistics, Criminal Victimization and Perceptions of Community Safety in 12 Cities, 1998, Washington, DC: U.S. Department of Justice, May 1999 (NCJ 173940).

[6.] David Harris, Driving While Black: Racial Profiling on Our Nation's Highways, Washington, DC: American Civil Liberties Union, 1999.

[7.] Mark Hosenball, "It Is Not the Act of a Few Bad Apples: Lawsuit Shines the Spotlight on Allegations of Racial Profiling by New Jersey State Troopers," Newsweek, May 17, 1999, at 34–35.

[8.] Richard Weizel, "Lawmaker Pushes for Racial Profiling Bill," Boston Globe, May 2, 1999, at D21.

[9.] Wilkins v. Maryland State Police, Civil Action No. CCB–93–483, Maryland Federal District Court (1993). For a discussion of the settlement, see John Lamberth, "Driving While Black: A Statistician Proves That Prejudice Still Rules the Road," Washington Post, August 16, 1999, at C1.

[10.] Lamberth, see note 9. For a discussion of the Lamberth study, see David Harris, "The Stories, the Statistics, and the Law: Why Driving While Black Matters," Minnesota Law Review 84(2), 1999, at 280–281.

[11.] Lamberth, see note 9, at 4.

[12.] State of New Jersey v. Pedro Soto et al., Superior Court of New Jersey, 734 A.2d 350, 1996.

[13.] The stop and arrest information was compiled using patrol charts, radio logs, and traffic tickets for selected dates from April 1988 to May 1991.

[14.] Peter Verniero and Paul Zoubek, New Jersey Attorney General's Interim Report of the State Police Review Team Regarding Allegations of Racial Profiling (N.J. Interim Rep.), April 20, 1999.

15. Verniero and Zoubek, see note 14, at 27–28.

16. Kevin Flynn, "State Cites Racial Inequality in New York Police Searches," New York Times, December 1, 1999, at 22.

17. New York Attorney General, New York City Police "Stop and Frisk" Practices: A Report to the People of New York From the Office of the Attorney General, New York, NY: December 1, 1999, at 95.

18. Statistics on Race and the Criminal Justice System: A Home Office Publication Under Section 95 of the Criminal Justice Act of 1991, London, England: Home Office, 1998, chapters 3 and 4.

19. The UK in Figures, London, England: Office of National Statistics, Government Statistical Service, 1999.

20. Marian FitzGerald, Searches in London, Interim Evaluation of Year One of the Programme of Action, London, England: Home Office, August 1999, at 21.

21. For a discussion of this practice, see Gary Webb, "Driving While Black," Esquire Magazine, April 1999, at 119–127.

22. New York Attorney General, see note 17, at 141–145.

23. Marion FitzGerald, Final Report Into Stop-and-Search, London, England: Metropolitan Police, 1999.

24. This idea has been perpetuated by some police training materials. For example, in the mid-1980s, the Florida Department of Highway Safety and Motor Vehicles issued guidelines for the police on common characteristics of drug couriers that warned officers to be suspicious of drivers who do not "fit the vehicle" and "ethnic groups associated with the drug trade." For a discussion of this practice, see O.W. Wisotsky, Beyond the War on Drugs: Overcoming a Failed Public Policy, Buffalo, NY: Prometheus Books, 1990.

25. Note that only a limited number of empirical studies have examined the relationship between an individual's race and the probability that they are carrying contraband. More research is needed to address such questions.

26. Lamberth, see note 9.

27. Verniero and Zaubek, see note 14. Note that the New Jersey report is based on a sample size of only 78 searches. Although the hit rate of 38 percent for Latinos was higher than for Whites or Blacks, the smaller number of searches involving Latinos makes any conclusion about the proportionality of those searches more difficult to determine statistically.

28. New York Attorney General, see note 17, at 111.

29. U.S. Customs Service, Personal Searches of Air Passengers Results: Positive and Negative, Washington, DC, 1998, at 1. For a discussion of the Customs study, see Harris, note 10, at 277–288.

30. FitzGerald, see note 23.

31. National research conducted by the Substance Abuse and Mental Health Services Administration (SAMHSA) National Household Survey of Drug Abuse indicates that the rate at which Blacks use illegal drugs is 8.2 percent, only slightly higher than the White or Hispanic rates, both at 6.1 percent. This research indicates that the vast majority of people across all racial groups do not use drugs and should not be seen as targets of suspicion. Similarly, the National Institute of Drug Abuse found that 12 percent to 14 percent of those who abuse drugs are Black. This percentage mirrors the proportion of Blacks in the general population. For more information, see National Clearinghouse for

Alcohol and Drug Information, Research and Statistics, National Household Survey on Drug Abuse, Washington, DC: U.S. Department of Health and Human Services, 1998, at 16.

[32.] The racial demographics of arrest statistics for narcotics show more Blacks, Hispanics, and minorities tend to be arrested on drug charges than Whites. However, most drug possession and distribution go undetected. Those activities are private and conducted outside the ambit of police view. Only a small percentage of these crimes are given the attention of law enforcement. Thus, the number of drug arrests may only reflect law enforcement patterns.

[33.] Just as we do not allow insurance companies to charge differential life insurance rates to women because they live longer than men, we ought not allow empirical racial profiling to impose costs on the entire community of color. It would be unfair to stigmatize an entire community based on the conduct of a few. By allowing police to use race as a factor in determining whom to stop-and-search, many innocent Black and Hispanic individuals are subjected to searches. For more discussion on this issue, see Randall Kennedy, Race, Crime and the Law, New York, NY: Pantheon Books, 1997, at 147.

[34.] San Jose Police Department, Vehicle Stop Demographic Study: First Report, San Jose, CA, December 1999.

[35.] Julie Lynem, "San Jose Police Study: Race in Arrest Patterns," San Francisco Chronicle, March 25, 1999, at A17.

[36.] Joe Rodriques, "No Refuge From Racism Behind the Wheel," San Jose Mercury News, March 29, 1999, at 1B.

[37.] Julie Ha, "Groups Seek Data on Race-Based Police Stops," Los Angeles Times, April 16, 1999, at B3.

[38.] Ha, see note 37, at B3.

[39.] SJPD's prior protocol already required officers to indicate whether the stop was being made on a male or female. Under that protocol, an officer used a code to indicate whether the driver was a female (11–95X) or male (11–95).

[40.] In San Jose, a municipal code violation refers to laws that forbid activities such as cruising or continuing to drive in circles on a main road.

[41.] This code is used when no enforcement action is taken, such as when an officer stops a driver for a moving or equipment violation and issues a verbal warning instead of a citation.

[42.] Lynem, see note 35.

[43.] However, San Jose's initial analysis of its data collection indicates that many calls were cleared with incomplete information, sometimes due to special enforcement activities such as radar patrols.

[44.] After preliminary analysis of the first 3 months of data, San Jose determined that they would need to refine the traffic-stop categories because nearly all calls fell into the vehicle code violation category, making any analysis of the reason for the stop less meaningful.

[45.] Including the type of contraband seized and a description of it should not be difficult. Once contraband is seized, police must record such information in their routine police reports.

[46.] Of course, even though the data are not tabulated by officer identification number, since the name of the officer, the time, date of the stop, and the computer on which the data were recorded are potentially available, the identification of the officer is not truly anonymous. It could be obtained, but it is not routinely collected and analyzed.

47. Although the study began on June 1, 1999, the Crime Analysis Unit decided to conduct its first report for stops generated from July 1 to September 30. This time period allowed SJPD to look at corresponding quarterly reports so that the data collection could be correlated with existing crime statistics.

48. Local news reports and editorials suggest that 1990 census estimates incorrectly represent the minority populations in California. See "Are Our Cops Colorblind," San Jose Mercury News, December 23, 1999; "Blacks and Latinos Stopped More: San Jose Police Release Traffic-Stop Report," San Jose Mercury News, December 18, 1999.

49. This was done by using 1990 census data and 1995 California Department of Finance data estimates on population increases in the state. SJPD then applied the same data population projections for the 1990–95 period to the 1995–99 period.

50. Note that the vast majority of citations during the study period were for speeding, not for equipment failure or vehicle code violations.

51. Some law enforcement organizations have put video cameras in patrol cars. They are usually located inside the car near the rearview mirror. Tapes are then stored for a certain period. Supervisors review some tapes and use them for training purposes.

52. San Diego Police Department, Budget and Personnel, 1999.

53. San Diego Police Department, Historical Crime Rates, 1950–1999.

54. George Will, "Takes More Than Good Policing To Cut Crime," Houston Chronicle, August 23, 1999, at A18.

55. David Bejarano, Racial Profiling: The San Diego Police Department's Response, Internal Memo, Chief of Police, San Diego Police Department, November 9, 1999.

56. Michael Stetz and Kelly Thorton, "Cops To Collect Traffic Stop Racial Data," San Diego Union Tribune, February 5, 1999, at A1.

57. Stetz and Thorton, see note 56.

58. Doc Anthony Anderson, "They're Guilty of Driving—While Being Black or Brown," San Diego Union Tribune, December 24, 1998, at B9; Michael Stetz, "Stopped for Driving While Black: People of Color Commonly Are Pulled Over by Police for Little Apparent Reason," San Diego Union Tribune, December 13, 1999, at A1.

59. Stetz and Thorton, see note 56.

60. At the time of the drafting for this guide, San Diego officers were using paper forms to collect data because laptops had not yet been installed in patrol cars.

61. Stetz and Thorton, see note 56.

62. Interview with former San Diego Police Chief Jerry Sanders, March 1, 2000.

63. Stetz and Thorton, see note 56.

64. North Carolina Office of State Planning, State Demographics, 1997.

65. Demographic information provided by NCHP.

66. Lynn Bonner, "Bill Probes Traffic Stops for Driving While Black," Raleigh News and Observer, February 18, 1999.

67. The drug interdiction team is a small and distinct unit of troops whose mission is to uncover drug traffickers on the state and interstate highways. For a description of racial disparities in drug charges by the interdiction team, see Joseph Neff and Pat Stith, "Highway Drug Unit Focuses on Blacks," Raleigh News and Observer, July 28, 1996, at A1.

[68.] Joseph Neff, "Who's Being Stopped?" Raleigh News and Observer, February 19, 1999, at A2.

[69.] Press Release, Office of North Carolina Governor Jim Hunt, April 22, 1999.

[70.] There are no racial or ethnic data on North Carolina driver's licenses, but there is backup information available from the state bureau of motor vehicles. They collect it by asking an optional question about race and ethnicity. If unanswered, bureau staff record what they perceive.

[71.] Interview with NCHP Colonel Richard Holden, September 27, 1999.

[72.] These figures do not include the costs of additional training associated with using the data collection system.

[73.] The only indication of the number of verbal warning stops is based on estimates by individual troopers.

[74.] Blacks in North Carolina represent approximately 22 percent of the state population, and 22.6 percent of the motorists stopped by NCHP in January 2000 were Black. In the same study, of those searched, 31 percent were Black, and of those arrested 27 percent were Black. For a description of the preliminary data report, see "Spotlight on Stops," Raleigh News and Observer, March 9, 2000, at A16; Craig Jarvis, "Traffic Stops Aren't Linked to Race, First Report Shows," Raleigh News and Observer, March 3, 2000, at A3.

[75.] Annual Demographic Profile for New Jersey, New Jersey Department of Labor and Management, March 1999.

[76.] Interview with New Jersey Attorney General John Farmer, April 4, 2000.

[77.] Ralph Seigel, "Racial Profiling Anatomy of a Scandal," New Jersey Reporter, 28, May 1999, at 17–29.

[78.] New Jersey v. Soto, 734 A.2d 350, Superior Court of New Jersey (1996).

[79.] New Jersey v. Soto, 734 A.2d 350, Superior Court of New Jersey (1996).

[80.] Details of events leading up to the shooting are unclear. Troopers report that the van backed away from the officers and veered into the patrol car before sideswiping a car in oncoming traffic and that they fired shots because they perceived that the van was trying to get away. The occupants of the van claim that the van shifted out of gear, and they only backed into traffic as a response to police drawing their weapons. For a description of the event, see John Kifner and David Herszenhorn, "Racial Profiling at Crux of Inquiry Into Shooting by Troopers," New York Times, May, 8, 1998, at B1.

[81.] Michael Raphel and Kathy Barrett Calter, "State Police Reveal 75% of Arrests Along Turnpike Were of Minorities," Star-Ledger, February 10, 1999, at News 01.

[82.] Michael Raphel and Joe Donahue, "Turnpike Arrests 73% Minority," Star-Ledger, April 8, 1999, at News 01.

[83.] Joe Donahue, "Trooper Boss: Race Plays Role in Drug Crimes," Star-Ledger, February 28, 1999, at News 01.

[84.] In New Jersey, the attorney general oversees the activities of the state police.

[85.] Joint Application for Entry of Consent Decree, United States v. State of New Jersey, Civil Action 99–5970 (MLC), December 20, 1999 (consent decree).

[86.] Consent Decree, see note 85, at 29–33.

[87.] Letter from Martin Cronin, assistant attorney general, director of State Police Affairs in New Jersey, June 13, 2000 (on file with author).

[88.] Joint Application for Entry of Consent Decree, see note 85, at section 110.

[89.] Joint Application for Entry of Consent Decree, see note 85.

90. Interview with John Farmer, see note 76.

91. The attorney general cited the Officer of the Year Award within the state police as an example of past departmental emphasis on arrests. Traditionally, the award went to the officer making the highest number of arrests rather than any qualitative measure of good behavior, acts of valor, or assisting motorists.

92. The "other" category includes Pakistani, Somalian, and Indian.

93. Marian FitzGerald and Rae Sibbitt, Ethnic Monitoring in Police Forces: A Beginning, London, England: Home Office, Research and Statistics Directorate, 1997, at 12.

94. Sir William MacPherson, The Stephen Lawrence Inquiry, London, England: The Stationary Office, 1999, at 1.

95. MacPherson, see note 94, at 2, 3.

96. MacPherson, see note 94, at 4.

97. MacPherson, see note 94, at 6.

98. MacPherson, see note 94, at 4.

99. MacPherson, see note 94, at 312.

100. MacPherson, see note 94, at 334.

101. The seven pilot sites are Brixton, Charing Cross, Hounslow, Kingston, Limehouse, Plumstead, and Tottenham.

102. Great Britain has collected data on searches from 1996 to 2000.

103. Police and Criminal Evidence Act of 1983. For a discussion of PACE and its implementation, see FitzGerald, note 23.

104. For example, in Hounslow, voluntary stops and traffic stops will be included, but "stop and talks," where police and people on the street stop to converse, will not be included. Hence, most officer-initiated contacts will be recorded. Hounslow is just one of seven pilot sites participating in experimental data collection strategies.

105. English law allows this in limited circumstances. For example, when there is a gang fight, such searches might be authorized within 1 square mile for a short period. Such an action must be ratified in 24 hours by a superintendent.

106. In Hounslow, these 17 self-identification codes are already being used. Note that the self-identification categories are not the same as the ones police use to describe persons searched.

107. FitzGerald, see note 23, at 29.

108. Marian FitzGerald, Stop-and-Search Interim Report, London, England: The Stationary Office, 1999, at 63.

109. FitzGerald, see note 23, at 29.

110. FitzGerald, see note 23, at 29.

111. FitzGerald, see note 23, at 24. 112. FitzGerald, see note 23, at Figure 3:5. 113. FitzGerald, see note 23, at Figure 3:5. 114. FitzGerald, see note 23, at 21. 115. FitzGerald, see note 23, at 49. 116. FitzGerald, see note 23, at 52. 117. FitzGerald, see note 23, at 54.

118. Presentation to MPS Lay Advisor's Group—Written Remarks, February 15, 2000 (on file with author).

119. Marion FitzGerald, The Relationship Between Police Searches and Crime, January 24, 2000 (on file with author).

120. The recommendations offered in this guide arise from research on the selected sites highlighted in Chapter 4. Additionally, Houston, Philadelphia, Richmond, and many

other local jurisdictions have graciously volunteered information and samples of their data collection forms, which were useful in designing these recommendations.

[121.] Gallup Poll, December 9, 1999. Seventy-two percent of Black men between the ages of 18 and 34 report that they perceived they were stopped by the police because of their race.

[122.] Gallup Poll, see note 121. Only 40 percent of Black women between the ages of 18 and 34 reported a perception that they were stopped by the police because of their race compared to 72 percent of men of the same age category.

[123.] The question of nature and quantity of contraband could be categorized by local jurisdictions. Most officers will be unable to give exact quantities of drugs or other contraband, but it is important to distinguish small amounts of drugs, guns, or other contrabands from major quantities. As we saw in the example from the New Jersey attorney general, officers may be making many stops that result in small "finds" of drugs or guns, but such stops do not uncover higher quantities of contraband associated with trafficking. By having some qualitative information about the quantities seized in searches, departments can monitor the effectiveness of their traffic-stop efforts.

In: Racial Profiling: Issues, Data and Analyses
Editor: Steven J. Muffler, pp. 109-153

ISBN 1-59454-547-2
© 2006 Nova Science Publishers, Inc.

Chapter 7

RACIAL PROFILING: LIMITED DATA AVAILABLE ON MOTORIST STOPS[*]

U.S. General Accounting Office

ABBREVIATIONS

ACLU	American Civil Liberties Union;
BJS	Bureau of Justice Statistics;
DEA	Drug Enforcement Administration;
III	Interstate Indentification Index;
INS	Immigration and Naturalization Service;
LEMAS	Law Enforcement Management and Administrative Statistics;
MSP	Maryland State Police;
NJSP	New Jersey State Police.

RESULTS IN BRIEF

We found no comprehensive, nationwide source of information that could be used to determine whether race has been a key factor in motorist stops. The available research is currently limited to five quantitative analyses that contain methodological limitations; they have not provided conclusive empirical data from a social science standpoint to determine the extent to which racial profiling may occur. However, the cumulative results of the analyses indicate that in relation to the populations to which they were compared, African American motorists in particular, and minority motorists in general, were proportionately more likely than whites to be stopped on the roadways studied. Data on the relative proportion of minorities stopped on a roadway, however, is only part of the information needed from a social science perspective to assess the degree to which racial profiling may occur.

---

[*] Excerpted from http://www.gao.gov/new.items/gg00041.pdf

A key limitation of the available analyses is that they did not fully examine whether different groups may have been at different levels of risk for being stopped because they differed in their rates and/or severity of committing traffic violations.[1] Although we have no reason to expect that this occurred, such data would help determine whether minority motorists are stopped at the same level that they commit traffic law violations that are likely to prompt stops. The best studies that we identified sought to determine the racial composition of motorists at risk of being stopped and collected data on the population of travelers and traffic violators on specific roadways. However, even these well-designed studies made no distinction between the seriousness of different traffic violations, and it is not clear that all violations are equally likely to prompt a stop. There appears to be little comparative research on traffic violations committed by different racial groups, including possible differences in the type or seriousness of traffic violations. In addition, none of the studies provided information on which traffic violations, if any, were more likely to prompt a stop. More information is needed to determine the extent to which race, as opposed to other factors, may be the reason for the traffic stop.

Several analyses compared the racial composition of stopped motorists against that of a different population, but the validity of these comparison groups was questionable. In addition, missing data may have skewed the results of some analyses. Finally, because only a few locations have been studied, and these locations were not selected to be generally representative of motorist roadways, the results cannot be generalized to roadways and locations other than those reviewed. These limitations notwithstanding, we believe that in order to account for the disproportion in the reported levels at which minorities and whites are stopped on the roadways, (1) police officers would have to be substantially more likely to record the race of a driver during motorist stops if the driver was a minority than if the driver was white, and (2) the rate and/or severity of traffic violations committed by minorities would have to be substantially greater than those committed by whites. We have no reason to expect that either of these circumstances is the case.

Federal, state, and local agencies are in various stages of gathering data on motorist stops, and these efforts should augment the empirical data available from racial profiling studies. The federal government, which has a limited role in making motorist stops, is undertaking several efforts to collect data. For example, the Justice Department's Bureau of Justice Statistics (BJS) is conducting a national household survey that should provide aggregate data on the characteristics of stopped motorists and the nature of the traffic stops. BJS is also conducting other surveys that should identify the motorist stop information maintained by state and local law enforcement agencies. In accordance with a presidential directive, three federal departments are preparing to collect data on the race, ethnicity, and gender of individuals whom they stop or search. State and local agencies are in the best position to provide law enforcement data on motorist stops because most motorist stops are made by state and local law enforcement officers. A number of state legislatures are considering bills to require state and/or local police to collect race and other data on motorist stops, and Connecticut and North Carolina have passed such legislation. Several local jurisdictions are also making efforts to collect motorist stop data.

Given the paucity of available data for assessing whether and to what extent racial profiling may exist, current efforts to collect information on who is stopped and why are steps in the right direction. Getting more and better data involves a variety of methodological considerations and information needs. Whether the efforts that are currently under way will produce the type and quality of information needed to answer questions about racial profiling remains to be seen.

BACKGROUND

The Fifth and Fourteenth Amendments prohibit law enforcement officers from engaging in discriminatory behavior on the basis of individuals' race, ethnicity, or national origin. The Fifth Amendment protects against discrimination by federal law enforcement officers, and the Equal Protection Clause of the Fourteenth Amendment protects against discrimination by state and local law enforcement officers. Two federal statutes also prohibit discrimination by law enforcement agencies that receive federal financial assistance. Title VI of the Civil Rights Act of 1964[2] prohibits discrimination on the basis of race, color, or national origin by all recipients of federal financial assistance. The Omnibus Crime Control and Safe Streets Act of 1968[3] prohibits discrimination on the basis of race, color, national origin, sex, or religion by law enforcement agencies that receive federal funds pursuant to that statute. In addition, a 1994 statute grants the Attorney General the authority to seek injunctive relief when a state or local law enforcement agency engages in a pattern or practice of conduct that violates the Constitution or federal law, regardless of whether the agency is a recipient of financial assistance.[4]

The Fourth Amendment guarantees the rights of people to be secure from unreasonable searches and seizures. The temporary detention of individuals during the stop of an automobile by police constitutes a seizure of persons within the meaning of the Fourth Amendment. The Supreme Court recently held that regardless of an officer's actual motivation, a stop of an automobile is reasonable and permitted by the Fourth Amendment when the officer has probable cause to believe that a traffic violation occurred.[5] The Court noted, however, that the Constitution prohibits selective enforcement of the law based on considerations such as race, but the constitutional basis for objecting to intentionally discriminatory application of laws is the equal protection provisions of the Constitution, not the Fourth Amendment.

Some have expressed concern that the escalation of this country's war on drugs has placed minorities at increased risk of discriminatory treatment by law enforcement. The allegation is that law enforcement officers stop minority motorists for minor traffic violations when, in reality, the stop is a pretext to search for drugs or other contraband in the vehicle.

In 1986, the Drug Enforcement Administration (DEA) established Operation Pipeline, a highway drug interdiction program that trains federal, state, and local law enforcement personnel on indicators that officers should look for that would suggest possible drug trafficking activity among motorists. In a 1999 report,[6] the American Civil Liberties Union (ACLU) stated that Operation Pipeline fostered the use of a racially biased drug courier profile, in part by using training materials that implicitly encouraged the targeting of minority motorists. DEA's position is that it did not and does not teach or advocate using race as a factor in traffic stops. Further, according to DEA officials, a 1997 review of Operation Pipeline by the Justice Department's Civil Rights Division, which is responsible for the enforcement of statutory provisions against discrimination, concluded that Operation Pipeline did not instruct trainees to use race as a factor in traffic stops.

Representatives of organizations representing law enforcement officers have stated that racial profiling is unacceptable. The National Association of Police Organizations, representing more than 220,000 officers nationwide, has expressed opposition to pulling over an automobile, searching personal property, or detaining an individual solely on the basis of the individual's race, ethnicity, gender, or age. The International Association of Chiefs of Police, one of the largest organizations representing police executives, stated that stopping and searching an individual simply because of race, gender, or economic level is unlawful and unconstitutional and should not be tolerated in any police organization. Neither group supports federally mandated collection of data on motorist stops.

Lawsuits alleging racial profiling have been filed in a number of states, including Oklahoma, New Jersey, Maryland, Illinois, Florida, Pennsylvania, and Colorado. For example, in Colorado, a class action suit filed on behalf of 400 individuals asked the court to halt racially based stops by a Sheriff's Department highway drug interdiction unit. Traffic infractions were cited as the reason for stopping the motorists, but tickets were not issued. The court ruled that investigatory stops based solely on motorists' match with specified drug courier indicators violated the Fourth Amendment's prohibitions against unreasonable seizures.[7] A settlement was reached that awarded damages to the plaintiffs and disbanded the drug unit. In another case, a class action lawsuit filed by ACLU against the Maryland State Police resulted in a settlement that included a requirement that the state maintain computer records of motorist searches. These records are intended to enable the state to monitor for any patterns of discrimination.[8] In yet another case, a Superior Court in New Jersey ruled that the New Jersey State Police engaged in discriminatory enforcement of the traffic laws.[9]

The Justice Department's Civil Rights Division has recently completed investigations in New Jersey and Montgomery County, MD, which included reviewing complaints of discriminatory treatment of motorists. In the New Jersey case, Justice filed suit in U.S. District Court alleging that a pattern or practice of discriminatory law enforcement had occurred. The parties filed a joint application for entry of a consent decree, which the judge approved in December 1999. Under the consent decree, state troopers in New Jersey will be required to collect data on motorist stops and searches, including the race, ethnicity, and gender of motor vehicle drivers. In the Maryland case, the Justice Department and Montgomery County signed a Memorandum of Understanding in January 2000 that resolved the issues raised in Justice's investigation. The agreement included the requirement that the Montgomery County Police Department document all traffic stops, including information on the race, ethnicity, and gender of drivers.

Lack of empirical information on the existence and prevalence of racial profiling has led to calls for local law enforcement to collect data on which motorists are stopped, and why. To support local data collection efforts, the Bureau of Justice Assistance plans to release a Resource Guide in spring of 2000. The guide is expected to focus on how data can be collected to monitor for bias in traffic stops, with specific "lessons learned" and implementation guidance from communities that have begun the data collection process.

SCOPE AND METHODOLOGY

Our objectives were to provide information on (1) analyses that have been conducted on racial profiling of motorists by law enforcement; and (2) federal, state, and local data currently available, or expected to be available soon, on motorist stops.

To obtain information on analyses that have been conducted on racial profiling of motorists, we did a search of on-line databases and reviewed all of the quantitative analyses that we identified that attempted to address whether law enforcement officers stop motorists on the basis of race. We also contacted the authors of the analyses and obtained references to any other analysis or research sources they considered to be pertinent. Our criterion for selecting analyses to be included in this report was that they provide quantitative information on motorist stops, although these analyses might have also measured searches, arrests, and/or other activities. We used social science research principles to assess the methodological adequacy of the available analyses and to discuss factors that should be considered in collecting stronger empirical data. Our review is not intended to constitute a statement regarding the legal standard for proving discrimination in this context.

To obtain information on the federal government's efforts to collect data on racial profiling of motorists, we reviewed published and electronic literature and discussed data sources with officials at the Justice Department's Bureau of Justice Statistics (BJS), officials in the office of the Attorney General, academic experts, the American Civil Liberties Union (ACLU), and several police associations.

To obtain information on states' efforts to collect data on racial profiling of motorists, we conducted Internet searches and reviewed the literature. We also held discussions with academic experts, state officials, ACLU officials, and representatives of the National Conference of State Legislatures.

To obtain information on local efforts to collect data on racial profiling of motorists, we reviewed the literature and held discussions with academic experts, interest groups, local police officials, and knowledgeable federal officials. On the basis of these discussions, we judgmentally selected several communities that had voluntarily decided to require their police departments to collect motorist stop data. In September 1999, we visited four police departments in California—in San Diego, San Jose, Alameda, and Piedmont. We selected these police departments because they appeared to be furthest along in their plans for collecting data, could provide examples of different data collection methods, and varied greatly in size.

We performed this work from August through February 2000 in accordance with generally accepted government auditing standards.

FEW STUDIES OF RACIAL PROFILING

We found no comprehensive, nationwide source of information on motorist stops to support an analysis of whether race has been a key factor in law enforcement agencies' traffic stop practices. We identified five quantitative analyses on racial profiling that included data on motorist stops. The quantity and quality of information that these analyses provided varied, and the findings are inconclusive for determining whether racial profiling occurred.

Although inconclusive, the cumulative results of the analyses indicate that in relation to the populations to which they were compared, African Americans in particular, and minorities in general, may have been more likely to be stopped on the roadways studied.

A key limitation of the available analyses is that they did not fully examine whether the rates and/or severity of traffic violations committed by different groups may have put them at different levels of risk for being stopped. Such data would help determine whether minority motorists are stopped at the same level that they commit traffic law violations that are likely to prompt stops. Most analyses either compared the proportion of minorities among stopped motorists to their proportion in a different population (e.g., the U.S. population, the driving age population of a state) or did not use a benchmark comparison at all. There appears to be little comparative research on traffic violations committed by different racial groups, including possible differences in the type or seriousness of traffic violations. Therefore, there are no firm data indicating either that the types and seriousness of driving violations committed by whites and minorities are comparable, nor that they are not.[10] Although we have no reason to expect that such differences exist, collecting research data on this issue— though difficult to do—could help eliminate this as a possible explanation for racial disparities in the stopping of motorists.

The studies with the best research design collected data on the population of travelers on sections of interstate highways and on the portion of those travelers who violated at least one traffic law. The studies compared the racial composition of these groups against that of motorists who were stopped. However, the studies made no distinction between the seriousness of different traffic violations. Although violating any traffic law makes a driver eligible to be stopped, it is not clear that all violations are equally likely to prompt a stop.

None of the available research provided information on which traffic violations, if any, were more likely to prompt a stop. We recognize that it is difficult to determine which traffic violations specifically prompt a law enforcement officer to stop one motorist rather than another. Different jurisdictions and officers may use different criteria, and candid information on the criteria may be difficult to obtain. Pursuing such information would be worthwhile, however, as would analyses that considered the seriousness of the traffic violation. Below, we summarize the reported results and our judgment of the key limitations of each analysis. More detail on each analysis is provided in appendix I.

- An analysis by Lamberth of motorists traveling along a segment of the New Jersey Turnpike[11] found the following: (1) 14 percent of the cars traveling the roadway had an African American driver or other occupant; (2) 15 percent of cars exceeding the speed limit by at least 6 miles per hour had an African American driver or other occupant; (3) of stops where race was noted by police, 44 percent of the individuals in one section of the roadway and 35 percent of the individuals in this section and a larger section combined were African American.[12] Lamberth also reported that 98 percent of all drivers violated the speed limit by at least 6 miles per hour. This study is notable in that it attempted to determine the percentage and characteristics of drivers who put themselves at risk for being stopped. However, we are uncertain whether traveling over the speed limit by at least 6 miles per hour on a major highway is the violation for which most police stops occurred.
- In a similar analysis of motorists traveling along a segment of Interstate 95 in northeastern Maryland,[13] Lamberth found the following: (1) 17 percent of the cars

had an African American driver; (2) 18 percent of cars exceeding the speed limit by at least 1 mile per hour or violating another traffic law[14] had an African American driver; (3) 29 percent of the motorists stopped by the Maryland State Police were African American. This study also found that 92 percent of all motorists were violating the speeding law, 2 percent were violating another traffic law, and 7 percent were not violating any traffic law.[15] However, we are uncertain whether Lamberth's criteria for traffic violations were the basis for which most police stops were made.

- Another analysis examined motorist stops in Florida. Using data that were first presented in 1992 in two Florida newspaper articles, Harris[16] reported that more than 70 percent of almost 1,100 motorists stopped over a 3-year period in the late 1980s along a segment of Interstate 95 in Volusia County, FL, were African American or Hispanic. In comparison, African Americans made up 12 percent of Florida's driving age population and 15 percent of Florida drivers convicted of traffic offenses in 1991. Harris also reported that African Americans and Hispanics made up 12 percent and 9 percent, respectively, of the U.S. population.

- The findings reported by Harris were based on videotapes of almost 1,100 motorist stops made by Volusia County Sheriff deputies. However, videotapes of stops were not made for much of the 3-year period, and sometimes deputies taped over previous stops. Because no information was provided on other motorist stops made by the deputies over the 3-year period, we do not know whether the videotaped stops were representative of all stops made during that period. In addition, no information was provided on drivers who put themselves at risk for being stopped.

- The Philadelphia ACLU reported that motorists stopped by Philadelphia police in selected districts during 2 weeks in 1997 were more likely to be minority group members than would be expected from their representation in census data.[17] Limitations of this analysis included the use of census data as a basis for comparison and an absence of information on drivers who put themselves at risk for being stopped. In addition, there were substantial amounts of missing data. The race of the driver was not recorded for about half of the approximately 1,500 police stops made during the 2 weeks.

- The New Jersey Attorney General's Office reported that African Americans and Hispanics, respectively, represented 27 percent and 7 percent of the motorists stopped by New Jersey State Police on the New Jersey Turnpike.[18] Interpreting these results is difficult because no benchmark was provided for comparison purposes.

Because of the limited number of analyses and their methodological limitations, we believe the available data do not enable firm conclusions to be made from a social science perspective about racial profiling. For example, we question the validity of comparing the racial composition of a group of stopped motorists on a given roadway in a given location with the racial composition of a population that may be vastly different. It would be more valid to compare the racial characteristics of stopped motorists with those of the traveling population who violated similar traffic laws but were not stopped. This is what Lamberth did, although we are not certain that the traffic violations committed by the motorists observed in his studies were the same as those that prompted police stops. Nonetheless, Lamberth's analyses went furthest by attempting to determine the racial composition of motorists at risk of being stopped by police as a function of traveling on the same roadways and violating traffic laws. We believe that the state of knowledge about racial profiling would be greater if Lamberth's well-designed research were augmented with additional studies looking at the racial characteristics of persons who commit the types of violations that may result in stops.

Other significant limitations of the available analyses were that the results of some analyses may have been skewed by missing data and may not have been representative of roadways and locations other than those reviewed. These limitations notwithstanding, we believe that in order to account for the disproportion in the reported levels at which minorities and whites are stopped on the roadways, (1) police officers would have to be substantially more likely to record the race of a driver during motorist stops if the driver was a minority than if the driver was white, and (2) the rate and/or severity of traffic violations committed by minorities would have to be substantially greater than those committed by whites. We have no reason to expect that either of these circumstances is the case.

Appendix II contains a discussion of some of the methodological considerations and information needs involved in getting stronger original data from empirical research on the racial profiling of motorists. These include the need for high-quality data from multiple sources, such as from law enforcement records, surveys of motorists and police, and empirical research studies. By high quality, we mean data that are complete, accurate, and consistent and that provide specific information on the characteristics of the stop and the individuals involved in the stop in comparison to those who are not stopped. The accumulation of these data would form a better foundation for assessing whether, and to what extent, racial profiling exists on the roadways.

FEDERAL EFFORTS TO COLLECT DATA ON MOTORIST STOPS

Although the federal government has a limited role in making motorist stops, several federal activities currently planned or under way represent the first efforts to collect national level information. The Police Public Contact Survey conducted by BJS will include information on the characteristics of individuals reporting they were subject to traffic stops and other information about the stop. BJS is also conducting surveys of state and local law enforcement agencies to determine what motorist stop data they maintain. In addition, to help determine whether federal law enforcement agencies engage in racial profiling, three federal departments are under a presidential directive to collect information on the race, ethnicity, and gender of individuals whom they stop or search.[19]

Population Survey of Motorist Contacts With Law Enforcement

A national household survey now under way asks respondents to discuss their contacts with police during motorist stops. As part of BJS' 1999 Police Public Contact Survey, BJS is conducting interviews with 90,000 people aged 16 or older to ask them up to 36 questions pertaining to the most recent occasion (if any) during the prior 12 months that their motor vehicles were stopped by police officers. For example, the interview questions ask for information on the race of the motorist and police officer, the reason for the stop, whether a search was conducted, and whether the officer asked what the person was doing in that area. (See app. III for the survey questions to be asked.) BJS completed the survey in December 1999, and expects the results to be available in September 2000.

Surveys of Motorist Stop Data Collected by Law Enforcement Agencies

BJS is conducting two surveys in an effort to determine whether law enforcement agencies collect stop data that can be used to address the question of racial profiling. One survey targets state police agencies; the other survey targets both state and local law enforcement agencies.

In April 1999, BJS administered a survey of all state police agencies in the nation. The Survey of State Police Agencies asked, in general, whether the agency required its officers to report demographic information on the driver or other occupants of every vehicle stopped for a routine traffic violation. If the agency reported that it did collect such information, then more detailed questions were to be answered, such as whether individual records were kept detailing the driver's race and immigration status and whether a search was conducted. BJS issued the results of the state police survey in February 2000. BJS found that 3 of the nation's 49 state law enforcement agencies whose primary duties included highway patrol reported that they required officers to collect racial/ethnic data for all traffic stops. Of the three states, Nebraska and New Mexico reported storing the racial/ethnic data electronically, and New Jersey reported that it did not store the data electronically.

BJS administers the Law Enforcement Management and Administrative Statistics (LEMAS) survey to a sample of state and local law enforcement agencies every 3 to 4 years. The survey collects information on the budget, salaries, and administrative practices of the agencies. The 1999 survey included a single question asking if the agencies collected data on traffic stops. The survey was sent to a sample of about 3,000 police/sheriff departments and was to include all agencies with 100 or more employees. The 1999 survey results are expected to be available during the summer of 2000. According to a BJS official, the 2000 LEMAS survey will contain more questions about what records are kept on motorist stops and whether they contain information on race.

Data Collection on Motorist Contacts With Federal Law Enforcement

Pursuant to a presidential directive, three federal departments are to collect data on contacts between their law enforcement officers and the public. The directive did not instruct the departments to focus solely on motorist stops, but data on motorist stops are to be included.

In June 1999, the President issued a memorandum on fairness in law enforcement that addressed the issue of racial profiling. The memorandum directed the Departments of Justice, the Interior, and the Treasury to design and implement a system for collecting and reporting statistics on the race, ethnicity, and gender of individuals who are stopped or searched by law enforcement. The three departments were tasked with developing data collection plans within 120 days and implementing field tests within 60 days of finalizing the plans. After 1 year of field testing, the departments are to report on complaints received that allege bias in law enforcement activities, the process for investigating and resolving complaints, and their outcome. The memorandum also required a report to the President within 120 days of the directive concerning each department's training programs, policies, and practices regarding the use of race, ethnicity, and gender in law enforcement activities, as well as recommendations for improvement.

The departments submitted data collection plans and proposed locations for the field tests to the White House in October 1999. (See app. IV for the list of data elements to be collected and all federal data collection test sites.) Federal law enforcement offices and proposed locations likely to be involved in motorist stops included the following:

- INS inspectors at the land border crossing at Del Rio, TX;
- INS border patrol agents from San Diego, CA; Yuma, AZ; and El Paso, TX;
- National Park Service officers at eight national parks; and
- National Park Service officers on three federally maintained memorial highways.

According to Department of Justice plans, officials will also pursue a variety of techniques at some sites to try to determine if the characteristics of those stopped differed from populations encountered at the field site in general.

SEVERAL STATES PROPOSED TRAFFIC STOP DATA COLLECTION LEGISLATION, BUT FEW BILLS PASSED

Most traffic stops are made by state and local law enforcement officers. Consequently, state and local agencies are in the best position to collect law enforcement data on the characteristics of stopped motorists. Several states have introduced legislation that would require their state and/or local police departments to collect data on motorists' traffic stops. However, few bills have passed.

As of October 15, 1999, at least 15 states had taken some action to address concerns about racial profiling of motorists. Two of the 15 states—North Carolina and Connecticut—enacted legislation requiring the collection and compilation of data on motorist traffic stops. Similar legislation requiring the collection of specific stop data was introduced in 11 states. The legislation was pending in 7 of those 11 states and was either not carried over to the next legislative session or vetoed in 4. The two remaining states, New Jersey and Virginia, issued resolutions. New Jersey's resolution calls for the investigation of racial profiling, and Virginia's resolutions call for data on traffic stops to be compiled and analyzed. See table 1 for a list of the states that had proposed or enacted traffic stop bills or resolutions and their status as of October 15, 1999.

All 13 states with data collection legislation proposed to collect data on driver's race or ethnicity, the alleged traffic violation that resulted in a motorist stop, and whether an arrest was made. Most of these states also proposed to collect data on age, on whether a search was conducted, and on whether an oral warning or citation was issued. The number of data elements that each state proposed to collect ranged from 6 to 16. For a list of data elements that each of the 13 states proposed to collect, see appendix V.

North Carolina passed legislation in April 1999 that called for the collection of statistics on a variety of law enforcement actions. Part of the legislation detailed what information on routine traffic stops by state law enforcement officers should be collected, maintained, and analyzed. All of the state's approximately 40 state law enforcement agencies are to collect the data, although about 90 to 95 percent of all traffic stops are made by the North Carolina State Highway Patrol.

Table 1. Status of Traffic Stop Bills Introduced in State Legislatures

State	Bill number	Date introduced	Bill status
Arkansas	HB 1261	January 1999	Referred to committee; session adjourned, no carryover
California	SB 78	December 1998	Vetoed by Governor 9/99
Connecticut	Sub. SB 1282	March 1999	Bill became law 6/99 – Public Act No. 99-198
Florida	HB 177	September 1999	Pending – referred to committee 10/99
Illinois	HB 1503	February 1999	Pending – referred to committee 3/99
Maryland	SB 430	February 1999	Passed House; session adjourned; no carryover,
Massachusetts	SB 1854	June 1999	Pending – referred to committee 6/99
New Jersey	Concurrent Resolution No. 162	March 1999	Pending – referred to Committee 3/99
North Carolina	SB 76	February 1999	Bill became law 4/99 – Session Law 1999-26
Ohio	HB 363	May 99	Pending – referred to Committee 5/99
Oklahoma	SB 590	February 1999	Referred to Committee; no carryover
Pennsylvania	HB 873	March 1999	Pending – referred to Committee 3/99
Rhode Island	SB 131	January 1999	Pending – referred out of Committee, 5/99
South Carolina	SB 778	April 1999	Pending – Referred to Committee; session adjourned; bill carried over
Virginia	Joint Resolutions 736 and 687	Both January 1999	Both referred to committee; session adjourned; no carryover

Source: Professor David Harris, University of Toledo College of Law; National Conference of State Legislators; Internet search of state legislatures; WESTLAW database.

Connecticut's legislation passed in June 1999 and requires collection of certain traffic stop data on stops made by state as well as local police departments. In addition, Connecticut's legislation bans the practice of racial profiling and calls for the collection of data on complaints that were generated as a result of law enforcement officer actions at traffic stops. North Carolina and Connecticut were both in the process of developing specifications for data collection. They planned to begin data collection January 1, 2000.

Local Initiatives to Collect Motorist Stop Data

We visited four California police departments—San Diego, San Jose, Alameda, and Piedmont—to learn about local efforts to collect traffic stop data. These departments had either begun or planned to begin to voluntarily collect traffic stop data. Some officials told us that their departments were interested in collecting traffic stop data because they wanted to address community concerns about racial profiling. San Jose began collecting data in June 1999, Alameda and Piedmont began collecting data in October 1999, and San Diego began collecting data January 2000.

The departments generally planned to collect similar data; however, their data collection methods and plans for analyzing the data differed. All four police departments planned to collect data on five data elements: race or ethnicity, age, and gender of the driver; the reason for the traffic stop; and whether the stop resulted in a warning or citation or an arrest. In addition, Alameda, Piedmont, and San Diego planned to collect data on searches conducted during traffic stops. San Diego planned to collect six additional pieces of information. Table 2 summarizes the data that the four police departments will collect.

Table 2: Traffic Stop Data Elements Collected by Four California Police Departments

Data element	San Diego	San Jose	Alameda	Piedmont
Driver's race or ethnicity	X	X	X	X
Age	X	X	X	X
Gender	X	X	X	X
Reason for stop	X	X	X	X
Location of stop			X	
Search conducted	X		X	X
Legal basis of search	X			
Obtain consent search form	X			
Result of stop/stop disposition (e.g. oral warning or citation Issued, arrest made)	X	X	X	X
Property seized	X			
Contraband found	X			
Officer on special assignment	X			
Total number of data elements to be collected	11	5	7	6

Source: GAO summary of police department information.

In San Jose, officers use their police radios to report traffic stop information to the dispatcher, who then enters the data into a computer system. Officers can also use mobile computers located in their patrol cars to report traffic stop information, and this can be transmitted directly to the computer system. In San Diego, officers initially are collecting vehicle stop data using manually completed forms, and plan later to use a wireless system to transmit information to the department's database. The Alameda police department also planned to use its computer-assisted dispatch system to collect data, but only on stops where citations are not issued, such as stops resulting in warnings or arrests. For stops in which the motorist receives a citation, traffic stop data are to be abstracted from patrol officers' ticket books and from motor officers' hand-held computer printouts and input into a citations database. Police officials in Piedmont, a police department consisting of 21 officers, decided that manually recording traffic stop information on paper forms would work best for its small department.

Three of the four departments indicated that they expect to analyze their traffic stop data. A preliminary report, issued in December 1999 and providing analysis results on data collected between July and September 1999 in San Jose, indicated some racial disparity in traffic stops.[20] According to the San Jose Police Department, the differences were due to socioeconomic factors rather than ethnicity. The report noted that more police were assigned to areas of San Jose that generated more police calls, and those neighborhoods tended to have more minorities. Because more police were available in these areas to make traffic stops, more stops were made there than in districts with a lower police presence. Within each police district, the stops reportedly reflected the demographics of the district. In the report, the San Jose Police Chief emphasized that more data were needed, along with the cooperation of the community to analyze what the data mean. Alameda officials told us they had no current plans to analyze their data, but the data will be available should there be a public request. None of the four departments planned to independently validate the accuracy of the data provided by the police officers. They said they rely on the integrity of the officers and supervisory oversight to ensure that the data are correct.

Officials from two of the departments reported that the amount of data to be collected was limited so as not to be burdensome for officers. However, a lack of information may limit the types of analyses possible. For example, the data collection efforts do not require data on the specific violation for which a motorist was stopped, so questions about whether minorities were stopped more often for less serious violations cannot be answered. None of four localities planned to collect this information. Officials noted, however, that trade-offs needed to be considered: police officers would be more likely to record motorist data if the data collection requirements imposed on them were not overly detailed or burdensome.

For a more detailed discussion on each of the four police departments' traffic stop data collection plans, see appendix VI.

CONCLUSIONS

The five quantitative examinations of racial profiling that we identified did not produce conclusive findings concerning whether and to what extent racial profiling exists. Although methodologically limited, their cumulative results indicate that in relation to the populations to which they were compared, African Americans in particular, and minorities in general, may have been more likely than whites to be stopped on the roadways studied. Because of methodological weaknesses in the existing analyses, we cannot determine whether the rate at which African Americans or other minorities are stopped is disproportionate to the rate at which they commit violations that put them at risk of being stopped. Although definitive studies may not be possible, we believe that more and better research data on the racial characteristics of persons who commit the types of violations that may result in stops could be collected.

To date, little empirical information exists at the federal, state, or local levels to provide a clear picture of the existence and/or prevalence of racial profiling. Data collection efforts that are currently planned or under way should provide more data in the next few years to help shed light on the issue. These efforts are steps in the right direction. However, it remains to be seen whether these efforts will produce the type and quality of information needed for answering questions about racial profiling.

AGENCY COMMENTS AND OUR EVALUATION

We requested comments on a draft of this report from the Justice Department. Based on a January 18 meeting with a Deputy Associate Attorney General and other Justice officials, and technical comments provided by Justice, we made changes to the text as appropriate. In addition, Justice's Acting Assistant Attorney General for Civil Rights provided us with written comments, which are printed in full in appendix VII. Justice agreed with us that there is a paucity of available data for assessing whether and to what extent racial profiling of motorists may exist. Justice also agreed that current data collection efforts by law enforcement agencies, as well as additional research studies, could generate information that may help answer questions about racial profiling. Justice felt, however, that our report set too high a standard for proving that law enforcement officers discriminate against minority motorists.

We believe that Justice's letter mischaracterized the conclusion of our report. Justice states that it disagrees with the "draft report's conclusion that the only 'conclusive empirical data indicating' the presence of racial profiling would be data that proved the use of race to a scientific certainty." Our conclusion, however, was that the "available research is currently limited to five quantitative analyses that contain methodological limitations; they have not provided conclusive empirical data from a social science standpoint to determine the extent to which racial profiling may occur" (page 1). We also noted that to account for the disproportion in the reported levels at which minorities and whites are stopped on roadways, (1) police officers would have to be substantially more likely to record the race of a driver during motorist stops if the driver was a minority than if the driver was white, and (2) the rate and/or severity of traffic violations committed by minorities would have to be substantially greater than those committed by whites. We do not believe that our approach to reviewing the research studies was so rigorous that we required "scientific certainty" in the data to draw conclusions about the occurrence of racial profiling. And we make clear in the report that our review was not intended to comment on the legal standard for proving discrimination in this context (see our Scope and Methodology section).

With respect to Justice's suggestion that we required research studies to provide scientific certainty of racial profiling, we would note that the concept of scientific certainty is generally not applicable to social science research. This is because social science research data are generally imperfect because they are collected in the "real world" rather than under controlled laboratory conditions. A fundamental, universally accepted, social science research principle that we did incorporate into our assessment of study results was whether the studies ruled out plausible alternative explanations for findings. We found that the available research on the racial profiling of motorists did not sufficiently rule out factors other than race—that is, other factors that may place motorists at risk of being stopped— that may have accounted for differences in stops. We observed that the two studies by Professor Lamberth were well-designed and went further than others in attempting to determine whether race was related to traffic violations that increased the risk of being stopped. But Lamberth established a criterion in each study that cast the net so wide that virtually the entire population of motorists was eligible to be stopped (i.e., traveling at least 1 and 6 miles above the speed limit, respectively, on two major interstate highways), and his studies provided little information about why motorists actually were stopped. Although law enforcement officers can use their discretion in deciding whom to stop, more information is needed on the actual reasons why they stop motorists before a firm conclusion can be made that the reason was race. As we indicate in the report, current data collection efforts by local, state, and federal law enforcement agencies may provide information on the reasons for stops that may help answer this question.

With respect to what kind of data would be needed to "prove" the use of race in motorist stops, this issue was outside the scope of our work. We recognize that the evidentiary standards that a court may apply in ruling on an allegation of race-based selective enforcement of the law may be different from the social science principles that we used to review these studies. It was not our intention to express or imply anything about legal standards to prove discrimination.

Justice also criticized our work for failing "to recognize or comment on the extensive scholarly debate on the subjects of the degree of statistical certainty, and the extent to which potential variables must be examined in order to demonstrate discrimination from a social science perspective." We did not comment on the matter of statistical certainty because it was not the basis for our determination that the available research on racial profiling is inconclusive. The problems that we identified with the research studies dealt primarily with the design of the studies; that is, using inappropriate or questionable benchmarks to isolate race from other factors. More and better data are needed on what traffic violations trigger stops and whether race is related to them.

Justice agrees that it is important to use an appropriate benchmark against which to compare the racial composition of stopped motorists. Justice disagrees, however, about the importance of examining whether certain driving behaviors or characteristics of vehicles may affect the likelihood of being stopped. In this context, Justice suggests that we make the unwarranted assumption in our report that severe traffic violations account for such a large proportion of traffic stops that they have a significant effect on the data. We did not intend, nor do we believe, that the report makes any assumptions about the reasons for which motorists are stopped. We simply believe that if the objective is to determine whether minority motorists are disproportionately more likely to be stopped than whites, then it is important to know what portion of the driving population on that roadway or in that jurisdiction commits the traffic offenses for which motorists are actually stopped—as opposed to being eligible to be stopped. This is the type of benchmark information that would isolate, to the extent possible, race from other variables that could influence traffic stops.

As arranged with your office, unless you publicly announce the contents of this letter earlier, we plan no further distribution until 15 days after the date of this report. At that time, we will send a copy to other appropriate congressional parties, the Honorable Janet Reno, the Attorney General, and to others upon request. If you or your staff have any questions concerning this report, please contact me or Evi L. Rezmovic, Assistant Director, on 202-512-8777. Other key contributors to this report are listed in appendix VIII.

APPENDIX I: STUDIES OF RACIAL CHARACTERISTICS OF DRIVERS STOPPED BY POLICE

A Summary of Analysis Design, Results, and Limitations

As part of our work, we reviewed all available quantitative analyses that we could identify pertaining to the use of race as a factor in motorist stops. This appendix provides a summary of the design, results, and limitations for each of the five analyses.

Source
Lamberth, J.L (1994, unpublished). *Revised Statistical Analysis of the Incidence of Police Stops and Arrests of Black Drivers/ Travelers on the New Jersey Turnpike Between Exits or Interchanges 1 and 3 From 1988 Through 1991.*

Study Design/Results
This analysis, done as part of a research study for a court case, provided a comparison of the races of vehicle occupants who were involved in traffic stops and arrests, drivers who violated traffic laws, and motorists in general who traveled along a segment of the southern end of the New Jersey Turnpike. The study involved three types of data collection: (1) direct observation of motorists from fixed observation points along the side of the road; (2) a moving survey in which an observer drove on the roadway and noted the races of drivers and whether they were speeding; and (3) obtaining law enforcement records from the New Jersey State Police (NJSP).

In the first data collection effort, observers were stationed beside the road. Using binoculars, they noted the number of cars that passed the observation point, the race of the driver and/or any other occupant, and the vehicle's state of registration. One observer was assigned to each lane of traffic, and a data recorder was present to record their observations. Observations were made in 18 randomly selected 3-hour blocks of time at 4 locations between 8 a.m. and 8 p.m. over a 2-week period in June 1993. The author noted that "most if not all" of the 26 pending cases in Gloucester County Superior court arose between these hours. Observers were reported to have been between 14 and 45 feet from the roadway.

According to the observations, 42,706 cars were counted as traveling on the turnpike, and the race(s) of the occupants were recorded for nearly 100 percent. An African American driver and/or other occupant were in 14 percent of the cars. Seventy-six percent of the cars were registered out of state.

In the second data collection effort, a moving survey was conducted to identify the racial distribution of all drivers on the road who violated the speed limit. In this phase, one observer drove at a constant 60 miles per hour (5 miles per hour above the speed limit at the time), and he recorded onto a tape recorder the race of each driver who passed him and whom he passed.

The observer noted all cars that passed him as violators and all cars that he passed as nonviolators.

In the moving survey, 1,768 cars were counted. More than 98 percent were speeding and classified as "violators." Fifteen percent of the cars observed speeding had an African American driver or other occupant.

A third data collection effort involved gathering data from NJSP. The data included the race of drivers who were stopped or arrested on randomly selected days between April 1988 and May 1991 along the section of the Turnpike covered by the traffic surveys and an additional section of the roadway. These data included 1,128 arrest reports from turnpike stops; 2,974 stops from patrol activity logs from 35 randomly selected days; and police radio logs from 25 of the selected days. (The 1988 radio logs had been destroyed.) Of the 2,974 stops, 870 were from the section covered by the traffic surveys. Data were not provided on the number of arrests from this section.

Of 1,128 NJSP reports, the race of the driver/occupants was noted in 1,059 of them. According to these 1,059 reports, 73 percent of those arrested were African American. The patrol logs and radio logs noted 2,974 events as "stops." Of the 2,974 stops, all but 78 noted the state of the registration of the car. Twenty-three percent of the stops were of New Jersey cars.

Lamberth noted that race was "rarely if ever" noted on the patrol activity logs and that in the radio logs, race appears about one-third of the time for the records that had not been destroyed. (Out of 2,974 stops, race was not noted in 2,041, or 69 percent of the stops. Of the 870 stops that were in the sections covered by the traffic surveys, race was not recorded in 649, or 75 percent of them.) According to the available race data on all stops, 35 percent of drivers stopped were African American; 29 percent of all race-identified stops involved out-of-state African Americans; and 6 percent of the same stops involved in-state African Americans. Of the 221 race-identified stops from the section covered by the traffic surveys, 44 percent of the drivers were African American.

In a separate analysis, Lamberth examined the race of individuals who were ticketed by three different units of the Moorestown, New Jersey State Police barracks.[1] He compared the proportion of tickets issued to African Americans by the (1) Radar Unit, which used a remote van and left no discretion in the hands of patrol officers; (2) Tactical Patrol Unit, which concentrated on traffic problems at specific locations on the roadway and exercised more discretion on whom to stop than the Radar Unit; and (3) Patrol Unit, which was responsible for general law enforcement and exercised the most discretion among the three units. Lamberth found that African Americans received 18 percent of the tickets issued by the Radar Unit, about 24 percent of the tickets issued by the Tactical Patrol Unit, and about 34 percent of the tickets issued by the Patrol Unit. These results suggested that increasing levels of trooper discretion translated into increasing percentages of African American stops.

Limitations

Although the data suggest that African Americans may have been disproportionately represented among motorists stopped and arrested, because of several limitations in the study's methodology, this study does not provide clear evidence of racial profiling of African American drivers.

First, the percentage of drivers violating traffic laws was measured by determining the percentage of drivers who were driving at least 6 miles per hour over the posted speed limit.

The study did not attempt to distinguish motorists who were driving 6 miles per hour over the speed limit from those who were speeding more excessively. On the basis of the criterion used to indicate speeding violation, the report concluded that 98 percent of the cars were violating at least one traffic law. We are uncertain whether this is an adequate indication of the type or seriousness of traffic violations that put motorists at risk for being stopped by police. We also do not know the reasons for which motorists were stopped.

Second, the traffic surveys and the data on police stops and arrests were not from comparable time periods. The police data were from about 2 to 5 years prior to when the traffic surveys were conducted—the traffic surveys were done in June 1993, and the police data were from randomly selected days from April 1988 to May 1991.

Third, the observed differences in the percentage of African Americans ticketed by Radar, Tactical Patrol, and general Patrol units may or may not have been due to discriminatory practices on the part of law enforcement officers. For the Tactical and general Patrol units, we do not know the reasons why tickets were issued, nor do we know if different groups may have been at different levels of risk for being stopped because they differed in their rates and/or severity of committing traffic violations.

Fourth, among stopped vehicles, the occupants' race was not recorded for three-fourths of cases along the portion of the highway where the traffic surveys were conducted; race was not recorded for two-thirds of cases along a larger portion of the highway. Therefore, the race of most motorists stopped is unknown. Statisticians performed calculations to determine the implications of the missing data for drawing conclusions about racial disparities in stops.[2] The calculations revealed that if the probability of having race recorded if one was African American and stopped was up to three times greater than if one was white and stopped, then African Americans were stopped at higher rates than whites. Because we do not know what factors affected officers' decisions to record race, the true extent to which officers tended to record race for African Americans versus whites is unknown.

Source

Report of John Lamberth, Ph.D. From ACLU Freedom Network, *http:-//www.aclu.org/court/Lamberth.html*

Study Design/Results

This analysis, done as part of a research study for a court case, provided a comparison between the racial distribution of motorists stopped by the Maryland State Police (MSP) on I-95 in northeastern Maryland, motorists whose cars were searched by MSP, all motorists on the roadway, and motorists on the roadway who violated traffic laws. The study involved two types of data collection: (1) a moving survey in which a team of researchers drove on the roadway and noted the race of drivers and whether they were speeding, and (2) obtaining law enforcement records from the Maryland State Police.

In the first data collection effort, a moving survey was conducted to determine the races of highway motorists and the races of highway motorists who violated traffic laws. A team of observers drove separately at the posted speed limit (either 55 or 65 miles per hour) and recorded the race of each driver who passed him or her and whom he or she passed. The observer noted all cars who passed him or her as violators and all cars that he or she passed as nonviolators (unless they were observed violating some other traffic law.) Twenty-one observation sessions were conducted on randomly selected days between 8 a.m. and 8 p.m. during the period June to July 1996.

In the moving survey, over 5,700 cars were counted. The author reported that driver's race was identified for 97 percent of cars. Seventeen percent of cars had African American drivers, and 76 percent had white drivers. Ninety-three percent of cars were observed violating traffic laws. Eighteen percent of the violators were African American, and 75 percent were white.

In the second data collection effort, data on motorists traveling a segment of I-95 were obtained from MSP. These data included information on (1) motorist stops made between May and September 1997 in Baltimore, Cecil, and Harford counties; (2) searches conducted between January 1995 and September 1997; (3) searches by MSP on roadways outside this corridor; and (4) drug arrests resulting from these searches.

The MSP data indicated that along the I-95 segment studied, 11,823 stops were made by MSP between May and September 1997. Of the 11,823 vehicles stopped, it was reported that 29 percent had an African American driver, 2 percent had a Hispanic driver, 64 percent had a white driver, and 5 percent had a driver of another race/ethnicity. With respect to searches, 956 motorists were searched between January 1995 and September 1997. It was reported that 71 percent were African American, 6 percent were Hispanic, 21 percent were white, and 2 percent had a driver of another race/ethnicity. The proportion of searched cars in which contraband was found was the same for whites and African Americans and the same for I-95 as compared to the rest of Maryland.

In comparison, there were 1,549 motorist searches outside the I-95 segment. Of these searches, 32 percent were African American, 4 percent were another minority, and 64 percent were white.

Limitations

Although the data suggest that African Americans may have been disproportionately represented among motorists stopped and/or searched, because of several limitations in the study's methodology, this study does not provide clear evidence of racial profiling of African American drivers.

First, we are uncertain whether the study adequately measured the type or seriousness of traffic violations that put motorists at risk for being stopped by police. For example, motorists who greatly exceed the speed limit, commit certain types of violations, or commit several violations simultaneously may be more likely to be stopped than others. The measure used to determine whether a car was speeding was whether it was traveling at any speed over the posted limit. As with the New Jersey study by the same researcher, this study did not attempt to distinguish between motorists who drove 1 mile over the speed limit and those who sped more excessively. Furthermore, this study recorded whether traffic violations other than speeding were committed but treated them as equal in seriousness and equally likely to prompt a stop. This may or may not have been a valid assumption. In addition, we do not know the reasons for which motorists were stopped.

Second, the data on police stops and police searches were not from comparable time periods. The data for stops were from May through September of 1997, and the data on searches were from January 1995 through September 1997. Lamberth noted in a correspondence to us that the stop data were not provided in time for his initial report. These problems do not necessarily indicate a systematic bias, however.

Source

Harris, David A.; Driving While Black and All Other Traffic Offenses: The Supreme Court and Pretextual Traffic Stops. Published in *The Journal of Criminal Law and Criminology* 87 (2): 1997.

Study Design/Results

The analysis provides quantitative data from Florida and Maryland. The Florida data first appeared in two Florida newspaper articles in 1992. The Maryland data were obtained by the author from lawyers involved in a Maryland lawsuit.

The journal article compares the racial characteristics of drivers involved in videotaped stops on a segment of I-95 in Volusia County, FL, over 3 years in the late 1980s (obtained from the County Sheriff's Department by the Orlando Sentinel) with population and observational data. It was reported that videotapes of stops were not made for much of the 3-year period and sometimes deputies taped over previous stops. More than 70 percent of the persons stopped among nearly 1,100 videotaped stops on I-95 were African American or Hispanic. African Americans, however, made up 12 percent of the driving age population in Florida, 15 percent of the traffic offenders in Florida in 1991, and 12 percent of the U.S. population. (Hispanics were 9 percent of the U.S. population.) Moreover, according to the Orlando Sentinel's observations of 1,120 vehicles on I-95, about 5 percent of the drivers were dark-skinned.

The article also noted that of the nearly 1,100 stops, 243 were made for swerving, 128 for exceeding the speed limit by more than 10 mph, 71 for burned-out tag lights, 46 for improper license tags, 45 for failure to signal, and a smattering of other offenses. Roughly half of the cars stopped were searched, 80 percent of the cars searched belonged to African American or Hispanic drivers, and African American and Hispanic drivers were detained for twice as long as whites. Only 9 of the 1,100 drivers stopped received tickets.

In Maryland, the only data provided in the article are the percentages of African Americans and Hispanics among 732 motorists stopped and searched by 12 Maryland State Police officers with drug-sniffing dogs between January 1995 and June 1996. The article stated that 75 percent of the persons searched were African American; and 5 percent were Hispanic. Of the 12 officers involved, 2 stopped only African Americans. Over 95 percent of the drivers stopped by one officer were African American and 80 percent of the drivers stopped by six officers were African American.

Limitations

Because of several methodological limitations, this analysis does not provide clear evidence of racial profiling of African American or Hispanic drivers.

For the Florida data, the validity of the comparisons made is questionable. For example, the data from the videotaped stops combined African Americans and Hispanics, but the comparison data for the driving age population of Florida included African Americans only. More importantly, no information was provided on the percentage of African Americans and Hispanics among traffic offenders. It is also not clear how accurately information on "dark-skinned" drivers was captured. In addition, there was an unknown amount of missing data because videotapes of stops were not made for much of the period. Therefore, we do not know whether the videotaped stops were representative of all stops.

For the Maryland data, no comparative data are provided on the percentage of African Americans and Hispanics among motorists generally, among stopped motorists, or among motorists who violated traffic laws. The data for drivers in Maryland included only motorists who were stopped and consented to being searched.

Source

Plaintiffs' Fourth Monitoring Report: Pedestrian and Car Stop Audit, Philadelphia Office of the American Civil Liberties Union, July 1998.

Study Design/Results

This was an analysis of the racial characteristics of motorists and pedestrians stopped by the Philadelphia Police Department in selected districts and persons stopped by the department's Narcotics Strike Force.

All police incident reports recording interactions between police and civilians that involved stops and investigations of pedestrians or automobiles in the 8th, 9th, 18th, and 25th Police Districts for the week of October 6, 1997, were obtained. Hardcopy and computerized records were reviewed and coded according to whether tickets or arrests resulted from the stops and, if not, whether the record indicated any legal explanation for the stop. Previously unreported data were also provided on pedestrian and automobile stops in the 9th, 14th, and 18th Police Districts for the week of March 7, 1997. All reports filed by the Narcotics Strike Force for incidents in the 4th, 12th, 17th, 25th, and 35th Police Districts that involved a pedestrian or a vehicle stop during August 1997 were obtained. Records were coded in the same way as described above. Demographic data for all Philadelphia residents from a 1995 census were provided as a benchmark for the city as a whole, and demographic data by census tract from the 1990 U.S. census were provided as benchmarks for the district-specific analyses. (The report mentions that Philadelphia Police Districts approximately encompass specific census tracts.)

For the week of March 7, there were police records of 516 motorist stops in the 3 districts. Overall, the race of the driver was recorded for only 51 percent of these stops, with race being recorded for between 40 and 58 percent of the stops in the three districts. For the week of October 6, there were police records of 1,083 motorist stops in the 4 districts. Overall, race of the driver was recorded for only 48 percent of these stops, with race being recorded for between 44 and 46 percent of the stops in three of the districts. (No separate data were provided for the 25th District, and no explanation was given for this omission.) In both weeks in each district, for stops with race of driver recorded, the driver was more likely to be a member of a minority group than would be expected on the basis of racial characteristics of the district as indicated by 1990 census tract data. Additionally, for stops with race recorded, the report indicated that minorities were more likely than whites to be involved in stops that were judged as not having a legally sufficient explanation than in stops judged to have a legally sufficient explanation for the March data, but not for the October data.

There were records of 214 stops by the Narcotics Strike Force in August 1997. (Task Force data were not presented separately for motorists and pedestrian stops.) However, the race of the individual stopped was recorded for only 68 percent of the stops. For stops with race recorded, the report indicated that minorities were more likely to be involved in stops judged not to have a legally sufficient explanation—43 percent African American, 39 percent

Hispanic, and 18 percent white—than in stops judged to have a legally sufficient explanation—33 percent African American, 47 percent Hispanic, and 20 percent white.

Limitations

Because of several methodological limitations, this analysis does not provide clear evidence of discriminatory targeting of minority drivers.

First, data on the racial characteristics of most motorists covered in the study were not available. The absence of these data is a severe limitation because the race of most drivers stopped is unknown.

Second, 1990 census tract data were used as benchmarks for the racial characteristics of the residents of the selected police districts. However, as the study notes, these census tract data were several years old at the time the study was conducted, and it is unknown how well these 1990 census data portrayed the 1997 population of these parts of Philadelphia. More importantly, no information was provided on the race of drivers who put themselves at risk for being stopped.

Source

Interim Report of the State Police Review Team Regarding Allegations of Racial Profiling, New Jersey Attorney General's Office, April, 20, 1999.

Study Design/Results

The report provides the racial characteristics of drivers stopped, searched, and arrested by the New Jersey State Police (NJSP) along the New Jersey Turnpike. Data were obtained from NJSP on the numbers of stops and searches made by troopers assigned to the Moorestown and Cranbury police barracks—two of three barracks assigned to the turnpike. Motorist stop data were from April 1997 through November 1998 (except February 1998). Data on motorist searches resulting from stops were from the same two barracks. Only data on searches for which motorists gave their consent for the search were available. Motorist search data were from selected months in 1994, all months in 1996 except February, and every month from April 1997 to February 1999. Data were obtained on motorist arrests made by troopers assigned to the Cranbury, Moorestown, and Newark barracks. Data on these arrests were from January 1996 through December 1998.

Over 87,000 motorists were stopped by NJSP. Twenty-seven percent of motorists stopped were African American, 7 percent were Hispanic, 7 percent were another minority, and 59 percent were white. Little difference was reported between the two NJSP barracks in the racial characteristics of motorists stopped. Only 627, or less than 1 percent, of these stops involved a search, but the racial characteristics of the motorists searched were not reported separately.

Racial characteristics were available for 1,193 motorists who gave consent for searches. Fifty-three percent of motorists searched were African American, 24 percent were Hispanic, 1 percent were another minority, and 21 percent were white. Little difference was reported between the two NJSP barracks in the racial characteristics of motorists searched.

Approximately 2,900 motorists were identified in the state's Computerized Criminal History Database as being arrested[3] by troopers assigned to all three barracks. Sixty-two percent of motorists arrested were African American, 6 percent were of another minority, and

32 percent were white. Little difference between the three NJSP barracks in the racial characteristics of motorists arrested was reported.

Limitations

Because of several methodological limitations, this analysis does not provide clear evidence of racial profiling of minority drivers.

First, direct comparisons between the racial characteristics of drivers stopped, drivers searched, and drivers arrested are problematic because comparable data for stops, searches, and arrests were not reported. Although there is some overlap, data for stops, searches, and arrests were reported for different time periods.

Second, search data were provided for consent searches only. Data on instances when motorists denied troopers' search requests were not available. Without data on denied search requests, it is not possible to know the racial characteristics of all motorists from which nonwarrant and nonprobable cause searches were requested.

Overall, as the report acknowledges, it is difficult to interpret the significance of the study's results because of the absence of any benchmark data, such as data from a survey to determine the racial or ethnic characteristics of turnpike motorists or the racial characteristics of motorists who put themselves at risk for being stopped.

APPENDIX II: METHODOLOGICAL ISSUES IN STUDYING RACIAL PROFILING OF MOTORISTS

Determining whether and to what extent racial profiling may occur on the nation's roadways is a complicated task that would require collecting more and better data than are currently available. Additional studies using comparison groups that are similar to the stopped motorist group in terms of their risk of being stopped for a traffic violation would contribute to our understanding of this issue. Federal, state, and local data collection efforts currently under way should augment the available information provided that the data are complete, accurate, consistent, and specific. To the extent that such data are gathered by a number of jurisdictions, a more complete picture of which motorists are stopped and why may emerge. Surveys of motorists and police officers and reviews of police protocols and training guides can also contribute to the state of knowledge about racial profiling. In our judgment, such a multifaceted examination of the issues is the means for developing a full and meaningful answer to questions about racial profiling.

We have noted that some of the existing analyses may have made comparisons that were not valid. These analyses generally compared the racial characteristics of motorists who were stopped with the racial characteristics of a larger population. The larger population may have been a state's driving age population or the U.S. population as a whole, among others. The limitation of such analyses is that they do not address whether different groups may have been at different levels of risk for being stopped because they differed in their rates and/or severity of committing traffic violations. Although discretion may play a part in an officer's decision to pull over a driver, the justification for initiating a stop is a violation or infraction committed by drivers. The available research on racial profiling, however, has given very little attention to potential differences across groups in the relative risk of being stopped.

Lamberth's studies[1] have been important steps in the direction of estimating the relative risks of being stopped, but they did not provide conclusive results. In both studies, Lamberth found that more than 9 out of 10 motorists violated a traffic law and were thus legally eligible for being stopped by the police. However, it is not clear that the driving violations that made motorists legally eligible for being stopped were the same violations that would prompt actual stops by law enforcement officers. For example, one of Lamberth's studies considered only speeding, although this type of infraction is not the only reason that motorists are stopped. The extent to which motorists exceed the speed limit and/or the number of violations they commit simultaneously may also affect their likelihood of being stopped. Lamberth's other study considered speeding plus other traffic law violations. However, this study also did not differentiate between the type or seriousness of different violations. For example, motorists who greatly exceeded the speed limit, committed certain types of violations, or committed several violations simultaneously may have been more likely to be stopped than others. None of the analyses that we identified examined whether there may be racial disparities in motorist stops that are related to the type or seriousness of the traffic violation committed. We recognize that it is difficult to determine which traffic violations specifically prompt a law enforcement officer to stop one motorist rather than another. Different jurisdictions and officers may use different criteria, and candid information on the criteria may be difficult to obtain. Nonetheless, to understand the extent to which motorist stops may have a discriminatory basis, data are needed on traffic violations—including the type and seriousness of those violations—that produce stops and the relative rates at which different groups of drivers in a particular jurisdiction commit those violations. Although we have no reason to expect that there are racial differences in committing traffic violations, such data would enable the most appropriate comparisons to be made in order to answer a key question; that is, how do the racial characteristics of motorists who are stopped for a particular traffic violation compare with the racial characteristics of all drivers who commit the same violation but are not stopped? Both observational studies and driver surveys may be useful in developing such comparative information.

Federal, state, and local efforts to collect data on motorist stops should increase the amount of information on law enforcement practices on the roadways. However, the usefulness of such data for addressing research questions about racial profiling will depend on the extent to which the data are complete, accurate, consistent, and sufficiently specific to provide meaningful information. Although we recognize that no empirical data are likely to be perfect, it would be difficult to draw conclusions about racial profiling if (1) stop data were selectively recorded, (2) race or other stop information is inaccurately recorded, (3) different jurisdictions capture different information, and/or (4) the information recorded is too broad to understand what happened. For example, recording "vehicle code violation" as the reason for the stop—when such a code can represent anything from failing to signal a lane change within a designated distance to a serious speeding offense—could make it difficult to discern whether and how the traffic violations for which motorists are stopped differ between racial groups.

In addition, confidence in the quality of data would be enhanced if provisions were made to validate the accuracy and completeness of data that are collected. Also, it would be constructive to have a mechanism in place for agencies to communicate and coordinate with one another to ensure that they are collecting comparable information, and at a sufficient level of specificity, to be useful for answering questions about racial profiling in a meaningful way.

It could also be instructive to examine whether there was a correlation between the race of the law enforcement officer and that of the stopped motorist. In addition, information is needed on the extent to which officers exercise discretion in the process of stopping, citing, and searching drivers. Toward this end, a review of established police protocols and training guides could be useful. In addition, a survey of officers could provide information on what observations and judgments they factor into their decisions to make stops. Although survey data of this sort would be subject to response biases, including the possibility that respondents would offer socially acceptable responses, well-designed surveys of police officers could be a useful supplement to official data. Further, in addition to querying drivers about the frequency with which they were stopped, cited, and searched, driver surveys could also ask about how many miles the drivers typically drove and how often they committed infractions that were likely to prompt stops. Data from police records and surveys could then be compared with them.

APPENDIX III:
BUREAU OF JUSTICE STATISTICS POLICE PUBLIC CONTACT SURVEY

OMB No. 1121-0111: Approval Expires 06/30/2000

ASKOFALLPE RSONS16+

We estimate that it will take from 5 to 10 minutes to complete this interview with 10 minutes being the average time. If you have any comments regarding these estimates or any other aspect of this survey, send them to the Associate Director for Management Services, Room 2027, Bureau of the Census, Washington, DC 20233 or to the Office of Information and Regulatory Affairs, Office of Management and Budget, Washington, DC 20503.

NOTICE ± Your report to the Census Bureau is confidential by law (U.S. code 42, Sections 3789g and 3735). All identifiable information will be used only by persons engaged in and for the purposes of the survey, and may not be disclosed or released to others for any purpose.

FORM **PPCS -1**
(5-14-99)

U.S. DEPARTMENT OF COMMERCE
BUREAU OF THE CENSUS
ACTING AS COLLECTING AGENT FOR THE
U.S. DEPARTMENT OF JUSTICE

POLICEPU BLICCONTACTSU RVEY

SUPPLEMENTTOTHE

NATIONALC RIME
VICTIMIZATIONSU RVEY

1999

Sample	Control number			
J ____	PSU	Segment	CK	Serial

A. Field Representative's Code

B. Respondent's characteristics

Last name
_____

First name
_____

| 001 | | 002 | Line no. | 003 | Sex
 1 ☐M
 2 ☐F | 004 | Age | 005 | Race
 1 ☐White
 2 ☐Black
 3 ☐American Indian, Aleut, Eskimo
 4 ☐Asian, Pacific Islander
 5 ☐Other | 006 | Hispanic Origin
 1 ☐Yes
 2 ☐No |

FIELD REPRESENTATIVE ± *Complete a PPCS-1 for all persons 16+ in all interviewed households. Complete a PPCS-1 through Item D for each NCVS Type Z person or NCVS proxy interview. DO NOT complete any PPCS-1 forms if the household is a Type A.*

C. Type of PPCS interview

007   1 ☐Personal (Self)
 2 ☐Telephone (Self) } **SKIP** to Intro 1
 3 ☐Noninterview ± *FILL ITEM D*

Proxy unacceptable for PPCS

D. Reason for PPCS noninterview

008   1 ☐NCVS Type Z noninterview
 2 ☐Refused PPCS only
 3 ☐Not available for PPCS only
 4 ☐NCVS proxy interview

FIELD REPRESENTATIVE ± *Read introduction*

INTRO 1 ± Now I have some additional que stion s about any contact s you may have had with the police at any time during the last12 month s, that is, any time since _____ 1, 19 98. E xclude contact s with private security guard s, police officer s you see on a social ba sis, police officer s related to you, or any contact s that occurred out side the U nited S tate s.

Include contact s which occurred as a re sult of being in a vehicle that wa s stopped by the police . H owever , plea se exclude tho se contact s which occurred becau se your employment or volunteer work brought you into regular contact with the police .

CONTACTSC REENQUESTIONS

1a. Did you have any contact with a police officer during the la st12 month s, that is, any time since _____ 1, 1998 ?

009   1 ☐Yes
 2 ☐No ± *END INTERVIEW*

1b. Were any of the se contact s with a police officer in per son, that is face -to -face ?

010   1 ☐Yes
 2 ☐No ± *END INTERVIEW*

| CONTACTSC REENQUESTIONS   ± Continued | | | | |

1c. How would you best describe the reason or reasons for these in-person contacts with the police during the last12 months, that is, any time since _____1,1998 ?

As I read some reasons, tell me if any of the contacts occurred once, more than once, or not at all.

Mark (X) all that apply.

A motor vehicle stop:

Transcribe entries from box 1 or box 2 to the FLAP on page 11.

		ONCE	MORE THAN ONCE	NOT AT ALL
(1) You were in a motor vehicle stopped by the police	011	₁☐	₂☐	₃☐

You contacted a police officer :

		ONCE	MORE THAN ONCE	NOT AT ALL
(2) To report a crime	012	₁☐	₂☐	₃☐
(3) To report a crime you had witnessed	013	₁☐	₂☐	₃☐
(4) To ask for assistance or information	014	₁☐	₂☐	₃☐
(5) To let the police know about a problem in the neighborhood	015	₁☐	₂☐	₃☐
(6) To tell the police about a traffic accident you had witnessed	016	₁☐	₂☐	₃☐
(7) For some other reason ± *Please specify* ↗	017	₁☐	₂☐	₃☐

A police officer contacted you because:

		ONCE	MORE THAN ONCE	NOT AT ALL
(8) You were involved in a traffic accident	018	₁☐	₂☐	₃☐
(9) You were a witness to a traffic accident	019	₁☐	₂☐	₃☐
(10) You were the victim of a crime which someone else reported to the police	020	₁☐	₂☐	₃☐
(11) The police thought you might have been a witness to a crime	021	₁☐	₂☐	₃☐
(12) The police asked you questions about a crime they thought you were involved in	022	₁☐	₂☐	₃☐
(13) The police had a warrant for your arrest	023	₁☐	₂☐	₃☐
(14) The police wanted to advise you about crime prevention information	024	₁☐	₂☐	₃☐
(15) Some other reason we haven't mentioned ± *Please specify* ↗	025	₁☐	₂☐	₃☐

CHECK ITEMA1	Was the motor vehicle stopped only once? (Is box 1 marked in Item 1c(1)?)	026	₁☐Yes ± *SKIP to Item 2* ₂☐No ± *Go to Check Item A2*
CHECK ITEMA2	Was the motor vehicle stopped more than once? (Is box 2 marked in Item 1c(1)?)	027	₁☐Yes ± *Ask Item 1d* ₂☐No ± *SKIP to Item 37*

1d. You said that you were in a motor vehicle that was stopped by the police on more than one occasion in the last12 months. How many different times were you stopped ?

(Record actual number.)

| 028 | _____ Number of times |

| MOTO RVE HICLESTOPS | |

FIELD REPRESENTATIVE ± *Read introduction*

INTRO 2 ± You reported that you were in a motor vehicle that was stopped by the police on more than one occasion. For the following questions, please tell me about the most recent occasion.

2. How many people age16 or over, INCLUDINGYOU RSELF, were in the vehicle ?

| 029 | _____ Number of persons |

3. Were you the driver ?

| 030 | ₁☐Yes
₂☐No ± *SKIP to Item 37* |

4. How many police officers were present during (this/the most recent) incident ?

(Record actual number.)

| 031 | ₁☐One ± *SKIP to Item 6*
More than one ↗

_____ Number of police officers |

FORM PPCS-1 (5-14-99)

MOTO RVE HICLESTOPS ± Continued	
5. Were the police officer sW hite , Black , or some other race ?	032 1☐All White 2☐All Black 3☐All of some other race 4☐Mostly White 5☐Mostly Black 6☐Mostly some other race 7☐Equally mixed 8☐Don't know race of any/some **SKIP** to Item 7
6. Was the police officer W hite , Black , or some other race ?	033 1☐White 2☐Black 3☐Some other race 4☐Don't know
7. Were you arre sted ?	034 1☐Yes ± **SKIP** to Item 9 2☐No 3☐Don't know
8. Did the police officer (s) threaten to arre st you?	035 1☐Yes 2☐No 3☐Don't know

VEHICLE/PE RSONALSEA RCH	
9. Did the police officer (s) search the vehicle ?	036 1☐Yes ± Ask Item 10 2☐No 3☐Don't know } **SKIP** to Item 14
10. At any time during (thi s/the mo st recent) incident did the police officer (s) ask permi ssion to search the vehicle ?	037 1☐Yes ± Ask Item 11 2☐No 3☐Don't know } **SKIP** to Item 12
11. Did you give the police officer (s) permi ssion to search the vehicle ?	038 1☐Yes 2☐No 3☐Don't know
12. Did the police officer (s) find any of the following item s in the vehicle ? *(Read answer categories.)* *Mark (X) all that apply.*	039 1☐Illegal weapon s 040 2☐Illegal drug s 041 3☐Open container s of alcohol , such as beer or liquor 042 4☐Other evidence of a crime ± *Please specify* ⟋ _____ 043 5☐None of the above
13. Do you think the police officer (s) had a legitimate rea son to search the vehicle ?	044 1☐Yes 2☐No 3☐Don't know
14. At any time during (thi s/the mo st recent) incident , did the police officer (s) search you, fri sk you, or pat you down ?	045 1☐Yes ± Ask Item 15 2☐No 3☐Don't know } **SKIP** to Item 19
15. At any time during (thi s/the mo st recent) incident , did the police officer (s) ask permi ssion to search you, fri sk you, or pat you down ?	046 1☐Yes ± Ask Item 16 2☐No 3☐Don't know } **SKIP** to Item 17
16. At any time during (thi s/the mo st recent) incident , did you give the police officer (s) permi ssion to search you, fri sk you, or pat you down ?	047 1☐Yes 2☐No 3☐Don't know
17. Did the police officer (s) find any of the following item s on or near you? *(Read answer categories.)* *Mark (X) all that apply.*	048 1☐Illegal weapon s 049 2☐Illegal drug s 050 3☐Open container s of alcohol , such as beer or liquor 051 4☐Other evidence of a crime ± *Please specify* ⟋ _____ 052 5☐None of the above
18. Do you think the police officer (s) had a legitimate rea son to search you , fri sk you, or pat you down ?	053 1☐Yes 2☐No 3☐Don't know

REASONFO RT RAFFICSTOP	
19. Did the police officer (s) give a reason for stopping the vehicle ?	054 ₁☐Yes ± *Ask Item 20* ₂☐No ₃☐Don't know } **SKIP** *to Item 22*
ASK OR VERIFY 20. What was the reason or reasons? Anything else? *Mark (X) all that apply.*	055 ₁☐Speeding 056 ₂☐Some other traffic offense 057 ₃☐A vehicle defect, such as a burned out tail light or an expired license plate 058 ₄☐Roadside check for drunk drivers ₅☐To check the respondent's license plate, driver's license, or vehicle registration 059 ₆☐The police officer suspected the respondent of something 060 ₇☐Some other reason ± *Please specify* ↗ _____
21. Would you say that the police officer (s) had a legitimate reason for stopping you?	061 ₁☐Yes ₂☐No ₃☐Don't know
OUTCOMEOFT RAFFICSTOP	
22. During (this/the most recent) incident were you: *(Read answer categories.)* *Mark (X) all that apply.*	062 ₁☐Given a warning ? 063 ₂☐Given a traffic ticket ? 064 ₃☐Tested for drunk driving ? 065 ₄☐Charged with driving while under the influence of drugs or alcohol ? 066 ₅☐Questioned about what you were doing in the area ? 067 ₆☐None of the above
23. Not including anything just mentioned , were you charged with any of the following ? *(Read answer categories.)* *Mark (X) all that apply.*	068 ₁☐Assaulting a police officer 069 ₂☐Resisting arrest 070 ₃☐Drug offense 071 ₄☐Possession of a firearm or concealed weapon 072 ₅☐Disorderly conduct 073 ₆☐Something else ± *Please specify*↗ _____ 074 ₇☐None of the above
24. At any time during (this/the most recent) incident were you handcuffed ?	075 ₁☐Yes ± **SKIP** *to Item 25b* ₂☐No ₃☐Don't know
USEOFFO RCEINT RAFFICSTOPS	
25 a. During (this/the most recent) incident , did the police officer (s) for any reason use or threaten to use physical force against you, such as grabbing you or threatening to hit you?	076 ₁☐Yes ± **SKIP** *to Item 26* ₂☐No ₃☐Don't know } **SKIP** *to Item 34*
25 b. Aside from being handcuffed , did the police officer (s) for any reason use or threaten to use physical force against you, such as grabbing you or threatening to hit you?	077 ₁☐Yes ± *Ask Item 26* ₂☐No ₃☐Don't know } **SKIP** *to Item 34*

FORM PPCS-1 (5-14-99)

	USE OF FORCE IN RECENT TRAFFIC STOPS ± Continued

26. What type of physical force did the police officer(s) use or threaten to use during (this/the most recent) incident? Did the police officer(s):

(Read answer categories)

Mark (X) all that apply.

078	1 ☐ Actually push or grab you in a way that did not cause pain?
079	2 ☐ Actually push or grab you in a way that did cause pain?
080	3 ☐ Actually kick you or hit you with the police officer's hand or something held in the police officer's hand?
081	4 ☐ Actually unleash a police dog that bit you?
082	5 ☐ Actually spray you with a chemical or pepper spray?
083	6 ☐ Actually point a gun at you but did not shoot?
084	7 ☐ Actually fire a gun at you?
085	8 ☐ Actually use some other form of physical force? ± *Please specify* ↗

086	9 ☐ Threaten to push or grab you?
087	10 ☐ Threaten to kick you or hit you with the police officer's hand or something held in the police officer's hand?
088	11 ☐ Threaten you with a police dog?
089	12 ☐ Threaten to spray you with a chemical or pepper spray?
090	13 ☐ Threaten to fire a gun at you?
091	14 ☐ Threaten to use some other form of physical force? ± *Please specify* ↗

27. Do you feel that any of the physical force used or threatened against you was excessive?

092	1 ☐ Yes ± *Ask Item 28*
	2 ☐ No — *SKIP to Item 29a*
	3 ☐ Don't know

28. FIELD REPRESENTATIVE ± *Mark without asking when ONLY ONE box is marked in Item 26.*

Specifically, what type of physical force do you feel was excessive? *(Read items marked in Item 26.)*

Mark (X) all that apply.

093	1 ☐ Actually pushing or grabbing the respondent in a way that did not cause pain?
094	2 ☐ Actually pushing or grabbing the respondent in a way that did cause pain?
095	3 ☐ Actually kicking the respondent or hitting the respondent with the police officer's hand or something held in the police officer's hand?
096	4 ☐ Actually unleashing a police dog that bit the respondent?
097	5 ☐ Actually spraying the respondent with a chemical or pepper spray?
098	6 ☐ Actually pointing a gun at the respondent but did not shoot?
099	7 ☐ Actually firing a gun at the respondent?
100	8 ☐ Actually using some other form of physical force? ± *Please specify* ↗

101	9 ☐ Threatening to push or grab the respondent?
102	10 ☐ Threatening to kick the respondent or hit the respondent with the police officer's hand or something held in the police officer's hand?
103	11 ☐ Threatening the respondent with a police dog?
104	12 ☐ Threatening to spray the respondent with a chemical or pepper spray?
105	13 ☐ Threatening to fire a gun at the respondent?
106	14 ☐ Threatening to use some other form of physical force? ± *Please specify* ↗

	USEOFFO RCEINT RAFFICSTOPS ± Continued

29 a. Were you injured as a result of (thi s/the mo st recent) incident ?

| 107 | 1 ☐ Yes |
| | 2 ☐ No ± *SKIP* *to Item 30* |

29 b. Did your injurie s include any of the following ?

(Read answer categories.)

Mark (X) all that apply.

108	1 ☐ Gun shot wound
109	2 ☐ Broken bone s or teeth knocked out
110	3 ☐ Internal injurie s
111	4 ☐ Brui ses, black eye s, cut s, scratche s, or swelling
112	5 ☐ Any other injury ± *Please specify* ⟋

_____

29 c. What type of care did you receive for your (injury /injurie s)?

113	1 ☐ No care received
	2 ☐ Respondent treated self
	3 ☐ Emergency services only
	4 ☐ Hospitalization
	5 ☐ Other ± *Please specify* ⟋

_____

30. Do you think any of your action s during (thi s/the mo st recent) incident may have provoked the police officer (s) to use or threaten to use phy sical force ?

114	1 ☐ Yes
	2 ☐ No
	3 ☐ Don't know

31. At any time during (thi s/the mo st recent) incident did you :

(Read answer categories.)

Mark (X) all that apply.

Verbal

115	1 ☐ Argue with or di sobey the police officer (s)?
116	2 ☐ Curse at, in sult, or call the police officer (s) a name ?
117	3 ☐ Say something threatening to the police officer (s)?

Cooperation

118	4 ☐ Resist being handcuffed or arre sted ?
119	5 ☐ Resist being searched or having the vehicle searched ?
120	6 ☐ Try to escape by hiding , running away , or being in a high -speed cha se?

Physical Resistance

121	7 ☐ Grab , hit , or fight with the police officer (s)?
122	8 ☐ Use a weapon to threaten the police officer (s)?
123	9 ☐ Use a weapon to assault the police officer (s)?
124	10 ☐ Do anything el se that might have cau sed the police officer (s) to use or threaten to use phy sical force again st you ? ± *Please specify* ⟋

_____

32. Were you drinking at the time of (thi s/the mo st recent) incident ?

125	1 ☐ Yes
	2 ☐ No
	3 ☐ Don't know

33. Were you using drug s at the time of (thi s/the mo st recent) incident ?

126	1 ☐ Yes
	2 ☐ No
	3 ☐ Don't know

34. Looking back at (thi s/the mo st recent) incident , do you feel the police behaved properly or improperly ?

127	1 ☐ Properly ± *SKIP* *to Check Item B1*
	2 ☐ Improperly
	3 ☐ Don't know ± *SKIP* *to Check Item B1*

35. Did you take any formal action , such as filing a complaint or law suit ?

128	1 ☐ Yes ± *Ask Item 36*
	2 ☐ No
	3 ☐ Don't know } *SKIP* *to Check Item B1*

36. With whom did you file a complaint or law suit ?

(Read answer categories.)

Mark (X) all that apply.

129	1 ☐ Civilian C omplaint Review Board
130	2 ☐ Law enforcement agency employing the police officer (s)
131	3 ☐ Local pro secutor 's office
132	4 ☐ The F BI or the U. S.A ttorney 's office
133	5 ☐ Law enforcement agency or the local government
134	6 ☐ Police officer involved in the contact
135	7 ☐ Took other formal action

FORM PPCS-1 (5-14-99)

USEOFFO RCEINT RAFFICSTOPS ± Continued	
CHECK ITEM B1 Was respondent the driver during the traffic stop? (Is box 1 marked in Item 3?) **AND** Was physical force used or threatened? (Is box 1 marked in Item 25a OR 25b?)	136 ₁☐Yes ± *END INTERVIEW* ₂☐No ± *Go to Check Item B2*
CHECK ITEM B2 Other than a motor vehicle stop, did the respondent have any other in-person contacts with the police? (Are there any entries marked in categories (2) through (15) on the FLAP on page 11?)	137 ₁☐Yes ± *Ask Item 37* ₂☐No ± *END INTERVIEW*

USEOFFO RCEINOTHE RFA CE-TO-FACECONTACTS	
37. Earlier you reported you had a face-to-face contact with the police for the following reason(s), *(Read items marked on the Flap on page 11.)* Did (this/any of these) contact(s) result in the police handcuffing you or using or threatening to use physical force against you, such as by grabbing you or threatening to hit you during the last 12 months, that is, any time since _____1,1998 ?	138 ₁☐Yes ± *Ask Item 38* ₂☐No ₃☐Don't know } *END INTERVIEW*
38. On how many different occasions did the police handcuff you or use or threaten to use physical force against you?	139 ₁☐Once ± *SKIP* to Item 39 More than once ⬎ _____ Number of times

FIELD REPRESENTATIVE ± *Read Introduction*

INTRO 3 ± You reported that, on more than one occasion, you had contact with the police in which the police handcuffed you or used or threatened to use physical force against you. For the following questions, please tell me about the most recent occasion.

| 39. FIELD REPRESENTATIVE ± *Mark without asking when ONLY ONE box is marked on the FLAP on page 11.*

Which of these contacts that you reported earlier resulted in a police officer using or threatening to use physical force? | **A motor vehicle stop:**
140   ₁☐Respondent was in a motor vehicle stopped by the police

Respondent contacted a police officer:
141   ₂☐To report a crime
142   ₃☐To report a crime respondent had witnessed
143   ₄☐To ask for assistance or information
144   ₅☐To let the police know about a problem in the neighborhood
145   ₆☐To tell the police about a traffic accident respondent had witnessed
146   ₇☐For some other reason ± *Please specify* ⬎

_____

A police officer contacted you because:
147   ₈☐Respondent was involved in a traffic accident
148   ₉☐Respondent was a witness to a traffic accident
149   ₁₀☐Respondent was the victim of a crime which someone else reported to the police
150   ₁₁☐The police thought the respondent might have been a witness to a crime
151   ₁₂☐The police asked the respondent questions about a crime they thought you were involved in
152   ₁₃☐The police had a warrant for the respondent's arrest
153   ₁₄☐The police wanted to advise the respondent about crime prevention information
154   ₁₅☐For some other reason ± *Please specify* ⬎

_____ |
| 40. How many police officers were present during (this/the most recent) incident?

Record actual number. | 155   ₁☐One ± *SKIP* to Item 42
More than one ⬎
_____ Number of police officers |

APPENDIX IV:
FEDERAL LAW ENFORCEMENT EFFORT TO COLLECT MOTORIST STOP DATA: FIELD TEST LOCATIONS AND DATA ELEMENTS

Presidential Directive

President Clinton directed the Attorney General, Secretary of the Treasury, and Secretary of the Interior in a June 9, 1999, memorandum to design and implement a system to collect and report statistics relating to race, ethnicity, and gender for law enforcement activities in their departments. Within 120 days of the directive, in consultation with the Attorney General, the departments were to develop proposals for collecting the data; and within 60 days of finalizing the proposals, the departments were to implement a 1-year field test. This appendix presents the field locations and data elements that the Attorney General's October 1999 proposal indicated would be collected during the field test.

Locations of Field Testing

Five agencies in three federal departments are to be involved in collecting data on individuals who are stopped or searched by law enforcement. The agencies include the Department of Justice's Drug Enforcement Administration and the Immigration and Naturalization Service; the Department of the Interior's National Park Service; and the Department of the Treasury's U.S. Customs Service and uniformed division of the Secret Service.

Department of Justice
Between six and nine of the following Drug Enforcement Administration *Operation Jetway*[1] sites are to be included in the field test:

- Detroit Metropolitan Airport;
- Newark International Airport;
- Chicago-O'Hare International Airport;
- George Bush Intercontinental Airport (Houston);
- Miami International Airport;
- Charleston, SC, bus station;
- Cleveland, OH, train station;
- Albuquerque, NM, train station; and
- Sacramento, CA, bus station.

The following Immigration and Naturalization sites are to be included in the field test:

- John F. Kennedy International Airport (New York City);
- George Bush Intercontinental Airport (Houston);
- Seattle/Tacoma Airport;

- El Cajon, CA, Station;
- Yuma, AZ, Station;
- El Paso, TX, Station; and
- Del Rio, TX, land-border crossing.

Department of the Interior

The National Park Service was the only agency identified by the Department of the Interior with regular public contact. The following Park Service sites are to be included in the field test.

- Lake Mead National Recreation Area (Nevada and Arizona);
- Yosemite National Park (California);
- Grand Canyon National Park (Arizona);
- Glen Canyon National Recreation Area (Arizona and Utah);
- National Expansion Memorial Park (Missouri);
- Indiana Dunes National Lake Shore (Indiana);
- Natchez Trace Parkway (Mississippi and Tennessee);
- Blue Ridge Parkway (Virginia and North Carolina);
- Valley Forge National Historical Park (Pennsylvania);
- Delaware Water Gap National Recreation Area (Pennsylvania and New Jersey); and
- Baltimore Washington Parkway (Washington, D.C., and Maryland).

Department of the Treasury

The Department of the Treasury identified the U.S. Customs Service and the uniformed division of the Secret Service as the agencies with regular public contact. The following sites are to be included in the field test:

U.S. Customs:
- Chicago O'Hare International Airport;
- JFK International Airport (New York City);
- Newark International Airport;
- Miami International Airport; and
- Los Angeles International Airport.

The Secret Service uniformed division will collect data in Washington D.C..

Data Elements

Agencies are to collect data describing demographic characteristics, such as gender, race, ethnicity, national origin, and date of birth based on agent's observation, or from official documents such as drivers' license when available. All participating agencies are to collect a core set of data elements, but they may collect additional data as they deem appropriate. Following is a core set of data elements contained in the data collection proposal:

- date of encounter,
- start time of contact,
- motorist's gender,
- motorist's race and ethnicity,
- motorist's national origin,
- location of contact,
- motorist's suspected criminal activity,
- reason for contact,
- external sources of information on person contacted,
- law enforcement action taken, and
- end time of contact.

APPENDIX V :
STATE LEGISLATION AND PROPOSED STATE LEGISLATION TO COLLECT TRAFFIC STOP DATA: ELEMENTS TO BE COLLECTED

	Arkansas	California	Connecticut[a]
Proposed data elements	**HB 1261**	**SB 78**	**P.L. 99-198**
Race or ethnicity	-	-	-
Age	-		-
Gender			-
Reason for stop/violation	-	-	-
Search conducted	-	-	-
Who, what searched	-		
Legal basis of search	-		
Oral warning or citation Issued	-	-	-
Arrest made	-	-	-
Contraband; type, amount	-		
Property seized			
Resistance to arrest			
Officer use of force			
Resulting injuries			
Location, time of stop			
Investigation led to stop			
Officer demographics			
Passenger demographics			
Auto description, license number			
Number of Individuals stopped for routine traffic violations	-	-	-
Total number of data elements to be collected	10	6	8

[a] Data collection under Public Law 99-108 is to begin January 1, 2000.

Florida HB 177	Illinois HB 1503	Maryland SB 430	Massa-chusetts Sb 1854	North Carolina[b] S.L.1999-26	Ohio HB 363	Oklahoma SB 590	Pennsyl-vania HB 873	Rhode Island SB 131	South Carolina SB 778
-	-	-	-	-	-	-	-	-	-
-	-	-	-	-	-	-	-	-	-
		-		-	-	-	..	-	-
-	-	-	-	-	-	-	-	-	-
		-	-	-	-	-	-	-	-
-		-	-	-	-	-	-	-	-
-		-	-	-	-	-	-	-	-
-	-	-	-	-	-	-	-	-	-
-	-	-	-	-	-	-	-	-	-
-		-	-	-	-	-	-	-	-
-			-	-	-	-		-	-
				-					-
				-					-
				-					-
				-	-	-		-	-
				-					-
	-			-		-			
	-			-					
				-					
11	9	10	10	16	15	12	10	12	16

[b] Data collection under Session Law 1999-26 is to begin January 1, 2000.

[c] Including nature of offense for which arrest was made, whether felony or misdemeanor, and whether occupants checked for prior criminal record, outstanding warrants, or other criminal charges.

Source: Federal and State Proposals on Racial Profiling, Professor David Harris, University of Toledo College of Law; California State Legislature Web site.

APPENDIX VI :
SELECTED LOCAL LAW ENFORCEMENT INITIATIVES TO COLLECT MOTORIST STOP DATA

San Diego Police Department

The San Diego Police Department initiated its program to collect vehicle stop data as a result of concerns about police racial profiling that were expressed by community groups, such as the Urban League and the National Association for the Advancement of Colored People. Beginning January 1, 2000, San Diego's police force, with 1,300 patrol and 60 motor officers, is to begin using forms to manually collect stop data. Later, plans are to use laptop or hand-held computers to collect information that would be sent to a department database via a new wireless system.[1]

Initial officer concerns about the data collection effort were addressed through departmental assurances that data would be collected in the aggregate, keeping officers' and motorists' names anonymous. In addition, the new data collection system is to track when a stop was initiated for a special assignment, such as when targeting African American gang members. For each stop, officers are to capture the following information: motorist's race/ethnicity; motorist's age; motorist's gender; reason for the stop; whether a search was conducted and whom/what was searched; legal basis for the search; whether a consent form was obtained; whether an oral warning or citation was issued; whether an arrest was made; whether property was seized; whether contraband was found; and whether the officer was on special assignment.

San Diego police officials said that they plan to enlist the assistance of a statistical expert in analyzing the data. They hope to obtain an initial analysis after the first 6 months of data collection. The department is also working with community-based organizations to address questions they have about the project and how data will be interpreted. San Diego has no plans to validate data submitted by officers. However, officials noted that actions by officers could always be reviewed and scrutinized by their supervisors.

San Jose Police Department

The San Jose Police Department also began its program to collect traffic stop data in response to community concerns about racial profiling by police. According to police officials, the data collection will allow them to learn more about the types of stops being made and to demonstrate the department's commitment to working with all members of the community. In addition, if analysis of the data reveals a pattern suggesting that race was a factor in motorist stops, then additional training and supervision will be considered to ensure fair treatment for all.

San Jose began collecting motorist stop data on June 1, 1999, and plans to continue the effort until May 31, 2000. For each stop, officers are to capture the following information: motorist's race/ethnicity; motorist's age; motorist's gender; reason for the stop; and what action was taken during the stop, for example whether a citation was issued or whether an arrest was made. Identities of the officer and motorist involved in each stop will be kept anonymous and not included in any reports.

San Jose officers call in traffic stop information by police radio to a radio dispatcher or by keying the information into a mobile computer terminal located in patrol cars. Dispatchers enter the radioed information into the computer-aided dispatch (CAD) system, and information entered into the mobile terminal is automatically entered into the CAD system. Officers use single digit alpha codes to identify traffic stop data elements. San Jose's code system has been in place since the 1970s; however, what is new is the addition of three new data elements to the existing code system. In addition to gender and traffic stop disposition, San Jose now collects reason for stop, race, and age information. The hardware and software cost to implement the data collection system was less than $10,000. According to a police official, costs were minimal because the department was able to make modifications to its existing automated system, thereby avoiding the need to design a new, potentially costly, one.

The department's Crime Analysis Unit is to compile the statistics and prepare two formal reports; one summarizing results for the first 6 months of data collection, and the other summarizing results for the full year. An initial review of the data from July 1, 1999, to September 30, 1999, was released by the San Jose Police Department in December, 1999. Aggregate figures indicate that Hispanic citizens in particular were stopped at a rate above their representation in the population. A spokesman for the department stated that the results do not support this conclusion when the figures are disaggregated by police district, although population figures by police district are not available. The official explained that more officers are assigned to areas with higher calls for service, and thus more stops are made in these areas, which tend to have higher minority populations. More analysis will be forthcoming. If results suggest that race may be a factor in motorist stops, the department may decide to collect data beyond 1 year. San Jose does not plan to check the validity of the data being submitted by officers, except to see if officers have entered the correct number of codes. However, a police official told us that supervisors have access to data submitted by officers, and they can "stop-in" on an officer call at any time.

Alameda Police Department

According to Alameda Police Department officials, most of Alameda County's police departments began to voluntarily collect motorist stop data in anticipation of state and federal legislation requiring the collection of such data.[2] The Alameda Police began collecting motorist stop data on October 1, 1999.

Alameda police officials told us that stop data are recorded on written or automated citations, if issued. For all noncitation stops, such as warnings or arrests, officers use the CAD system to call in each of the required data elements. For each stop, officers are to capture the following information: motorist's race/ethnicity, motorist's age, motorist's gender, reason for the stop, who/what was searched, whether an oral warning was given, and whether an arrest was made.

Alameda police officials said that information patrol officers write on citations will be keyed into an automated citations database. In addition, motorcycle officers have hand-held computers that they use to input and store traffic stop information. These data will be printed out and keyed into the automated citations database as well. A separate database is to contain the CAD-collected data for noncitation stops.

Although officers' and motorists' information will be captured in the data system, the department has no plans to generate any reports from the data collected. According to Alameda police officials, the police department does not plan to analyze, validate, or publish its data. They said that the data would be made available to the public if requested.

Piedmont Police Department

The Piedmont Police Department, located in Alameda County, began voluntary collection of motorist stop data in anticipation of pending state and federal legislation. Piedmont began collecting motorist stop data on October 1, 1999.

According to a Piedmont police official, Piedmont is a small department with 21 officers who record motorist stop data manually. For each traffic stop, the officer is to fill out an index card that contains data fields for recording the motorist's race, sex, and age. At the bottom of the card, the officer is to record the reason for stop, whether the vehicle was searched, whether an oral warning or citation was issued, and whether an arrest was made. No officer or motorist names will be included on the cards. A department official indicated that she expects a volume of no more than 400 cards per month. Information from the cards is to be input into an Excel spreadsheet for analysis, and results are to be tallied on a monthly basis.

The department reportedly has no planned effort to validate the information that officers record on the cards. Piedmont police officials said that the watch commander can monitor the activity of officers by listening to interactions between the officers and motorists over the dispatch system. The watch commander can then compare the information overheard on the dispatch system with that recorded on the index cards submitted by the officers.

APPENDIX VII :
COMMENTS FROM U.S. DEPARTMENT OF JUSTICE

U.S. Department of Justice

Civil Rights Division

Office of the Assistant Attorney General   *Washington, D.C. 20035*

February 10, 2000

Laurie E. Ekstrand
Director, Administration
 of Justice Issues
United States General Accounting Office
Washington, D.C. 20548

Dear Ms. Ekstrand:

This is in response to your February 8, 2000 letter to the Attorney General inviting the Department of Justice to review and comment on the revised draft of the General Accounting Office's report entitled <u>Racial Profiling: Results From Data on Motorist Stops Inconclusive</u>. We appreciate the draft report's efforts to provide a nationwide overview of current efforts to evaluate and monitor the extent to which law enforcement officers may engage in discriminatory traffic stops. The subject of racial profiling in traffic stops is of paramount concern for our nation, its citizenry, and the law enforcement community.

We agree with the draft report's conclusion that "[g]iven the paucity of available data for assessing whether and to what extent racial profiling may exist, current efforts to collect information on who is stopped and why, are steps in the right direction." (Draft report, at 3.) Given the large number of traffic stops that occur, it is essential that law enforcement agencies collect traffic stop data so as to permit jurisdictions to identify and analyze the full nature and scope of traffic stops being conducted. For this reason, the Department of Justice has endorsed H.R. 1443 and S. 821, which would expand efforts to collect traffic stop data, and the Department has a number of initiatives to promote data collection by federal, state, and local agencies both on a voluntary basis and, where necessary, as a remedy for discrimination.

We also agree with the draft report that additional studies should be undertaken to assess from a variety of perspectives "the extent to which racial profiling of motorists may occur" on the nation's roads. We disagree with the draft report's apparent conclusion, however, that such studies can provide conclusive statistical data <u>only</u> if they undertake extensive assessments of both (1) whether different racial groups may drive differently in terms of the types and seriousness of their traffic violations, and (2) how any such differences may interact with any standards used by law enforcement officers to decide which driving behaviors should result in a stop. In short, we disagree with draft report's conclusion that the only "conclusive empirical data indicating" the presence of racial profiling would be data that proved the use of race to a scientific certainty.

Federal courts throughout the country have repeatedly examined the question of what empirical data are relevant to assessing allegations of discrimination under the Fifth and Fourteenth Amendments, as well as the numerous federal anti-discrimination statutes. Over the last three decades, the courts have adopted a balanced, practical approach. In the context of an employment discrimination claim, for example, the Supreme Court has emphasized that plaintiffs "need not prove discrimination with scientific certainty; rather, [their] burden is to prove discrimination by a preponderance of the evidence." Therefore, a statistical "analysis that includes less than `all measurable variables' may serve to prove a plaintiff's case." <u>Bazemore</u> v. <u>Friday</u>, 478 U.S. 385, 400 (1986).

We recognize that the draft report uses "social science research principles" (Draft report, at 6) and applies "government auditing standards" (Draft report, at 7) rather than using legal principles and standards to assess the few existing studies of racial profiling. While the very high (and potentially impossible to achieve) level of scientific certainty sought by the draft report may be required by "government auditing standards," we disagree that such a standard is mandated by "social science research principles." Indeed, it is quite common in both litigation and peer review journals for highly respected social scientists to disagree vehemently as to what level of certainty is required and how many variables must be analyzed in order to draw conclusions about the likelihood that, in any particular instance, defendants such as law enforcement officers were engaging in discriminatory conduct. The draft report fails to recognize or comment on the extensive scholarly debate on the subjects of the degree of statistical certainty, and the extent to which potential variables must be examined in order to demonstrate discrimination from a social science perspective.

We agree with the draft report and the numerous court decisions which identify that a critical component of statistical analysis of discrimination claims is the selection and use of the appropriate "pool" or "benchmark" of eligible persons against which to compare the racial breakdown of persons selected by defendants for a particular activity (whether it be hiring or traffic stops). We believe that the draft report correctly notes the limited utility of studies which do not undertake to identify any appropriate benchmark or make such a comparison. We disagree, however, with the report's conclusion that in developing a benchmark of who is eligible to be stopped, it is always necessary to "fully examine whether certain driving behaviors may have placed different groups at different levels of risk for being stopped." (Draft report, at 1.)

On this issue, the Department's experience is that a flexible and multi-dimensional approach is more appropriate. First, the available data do not indicate that white and minority persons exhibit different driving behaviors with regard to the types of behaviors that typically result in a traffic stop. In light of this, and the draft report's observation that "the driving behaviors of minorities would have to be substantially worse than those of whites to account for the disproportion in the reported levels at which minorities and whites are stopped on the roadways," (Draft report, at 2), we must disagree with the report's criticism of the particular studies that have been relied upon by courts based on the fact that the studies did not differentiate among speeding drivers to determine who was most "at risk" of being stopped by the police patrolling the subject roadways.

Second, a flexible approach is necessary because, based on the Department's investigations, it appears that in many jurisdictions stops often are based on relatively minor traffic violations, such that the question of who is committing the most serious violations is not a significant factor. As the report notes, the Supreme Court recently held that, absent discrimination, "pretext" stops based on minor traffic violations (but for the real purpose of detecting contraband) are constitutional. Thus, we suggest that the draft report makes an unwarranted assumption that severe traffic violations account for such a large proportion of traffic stops that they have a significant effect on the data.

Third, contrary to the report's implication that a statistical analysis of traffic stops necessarily must involve a study of who was eligible to be stopped on a particular roadway, the Department's work in this area indicates that it may be appropriate to examine benchmark data relating to drivers who reside in a particular jurisdiction where, for example, discrimination claims relate to stops made on all the streets in that local area. Finally, a multi-dimensional approach to the benchmark is warranted because our experience demonstrates that it is often useful to examine benchmarks that are internal to the traffic stop data, such as by examining comparative data on different units of the same law enforcement agency, or different officers, who are enforcing the traffic laws on the same roadways.

We hope that these comments will be beneficial in completing
the final report. We appreciate the opportunity to provide
written comments, as well as the opportunity you provided for us
to provide oral comments on a previous draft of this report. If
you do not incorporate these comments in the final report, we ask
that you print the text of this letter in the "Agency Comments"
section of the final report. If you have any questions
concerning the Department's comments, you may contact Vickie
Sloan of the Department's Audit Liaison Office, at 514-0469.

Sincerely,

Bill Lann Lee
Acting Assistant
  Attorney General
Civil Rights Division

APPENDIX VIII:
GAO CONTACTS AND STAFF ACKNOWLEDGMENTS

GAO Contacts

Laurie E. Ekstrand (202-512-8777)
Evi. L. Rezmovic (202-512-8777)

Acknowledgements

In addition to those named above, David P. Alexander, Carla D. Brown, Ann H. Finley, Monica Kelly, Anne K. Rhodes-Kline, Jan B. Montgomery, and Douglas M. Sloane made key contributions to this report.

ENDNOTES

[1] As used in this report, traffic violations that can legitimately put motorists at risk of being stopped include actions by drivers and characteristics of motor vehicles that constitute traffic/vehicle code infractions. These could include, for example, speeding, tailgating, failing to signal a lane change, driving an unregistered vehicle, driving with license plates not clearly visible, failing to dim the vehicle's high beams when there is oncoming traffic, and equipment violations.

[2] 42 U.S.C. 2000d.

[3] 42 U.S.C. 3789d(c).

[4] 42 U.S.C. 14141.

[5] Whren v. U.S., 116 S. Ct. 1769 (1996).

[6] "Driving While Black: Racial Profiling On Our Nation's Highways." American Civil Liberties Union, June, 1999.

[7] Whitfield v. Board of County Commissioners of Eagle County, 837 F. Supp. 338 (D. Colo.1993).

[8] Both cases are described in David A. Harris, "Driving While Black" and All Other Traffic Offenses: The Supreme Court and Pretextual Traffic Stops." Journal of Criminal Law and Criminology, Vol. 87, No. 2 (1997), pp. 544-582.

[9] New Jersey v. Soto, 734 A.2d 350 (N.J. Super. Ct. Law Div. (1996)). The court therefore granted motions to suppress evidence of criminal activity by motorists that was obtained in these stops.

[10] In 1997, the National Highway Traffic Safety Administration (NHTSA) conducted a large-scale nationally representative telephone survey of drivers 16 and older to learn about the public's experiences and beliefs concerning speeding, and unsafe driving. Among other questions in a lengthy interview, respondents were asked whether they had committed a series of specific unsafe actions while driving. Demographic data, including race and ethnicity, were obtained on each respondent. Although answers to the unsafe or aggressive driving behavior questions were analyzed by some demographic characteristics, no analyses by race or ethnicity of driver were conducted. National

Survey of Speeding and Other Unsafe Driving Actions, U.S. Department of Transportation, National Highway Traffic Safety Administration, September 15, 1998.

[11] Lamberth, J.L. (1994, unpublished). Revised Statistical Analysis of the Incidence of Police Stops and Arrests of Black Drivers/Travelers On the New Jersey Turnpike Between Exits Or Interchanges 1 and 3 From the Years 1988 Through 1991.

[12] The race of the driver was not available in two-thirds of the cases.

[13] Report of John Lamberth, Ph.D. from ACLU Freedom Network, http://www.aclu.org/court/Lamberth.html

[14] Lamberth told us that his study noted four other types of traffic violations in addition to speeding.

The other violations consisted of no signal for a lane change, unsafe lane change, weaving, and tailgating.

[15] Does not sum to 100 percent due to rounding.

[16] David A. Harris, "Driving While Black and All Other Traffic Offenses: The Supreme Court and Pretextual Traffic Stops." The Journal of Criminal Law and Criminology, Vol. 87, No. 2 (1997), pp. 544-582.

[17] Plaintiffs' Fourth Monitoring Report: Pedestrian and Car Stop Audit, Philadelphia Office of the American Civil Liberties Union, July 1998.

[18] Interim Report of the State Police Review Team Regarding Allegations of Racial Profiling, New Jersey Attorney General's Office, April 20, 1999.

[19] Bills to provide for the collection of data on traffic stops were introduced in the House and Senate on April 15, 1999. These bills, H.R. 1443 and S. 821, called for the Justice Department to study racial profiling by acquiring data on motorist stops from law enforcement agencies. Neither bill had passed as of March 1, 2000.

[20] Vehicle Stop Demographic Study, San Jose, California Police Department, December 17, 1999. For each group, the percent of San Jose residents and the percent of motorist stops reported were as follows: Hispanics were 31 percent of residents and 43 percent of stops; African Americans were 4.5 percent of residents and 7 percent of stops; whites were 43 percent of residents and 29 percent of stops; and Asian Americans were 21 percent of residents and 16 percent of stops.

APPENDIX I

[1] The analysis was not included in Lamberth's unpublished report but was cited in the judge's decision in the related court case (New Jersey v. Soto, 734 A.2d 350 (N.J. Super. Ct. Law Div. (1996)).

[2] These calculations were performed by two statisticians, and the Justice Department provided us a report of their findings.

[3] Arrests generally include arrests for more serious offenses, including all drug-related arrests, but exclude arrests for drunk driving.

APPENDIX II

[1] See appendix I.

APPENDIX IV

[1] Operation Jetway is a drug interdiction program.

APPENDIX VI

[1] The department's move to a wireless system is part of an overall updating of technology for the agency. As of January, 2000, some technical flaws in the system were still unresolved.

[2] As noted in table 1 of our report, the governor of California vetoed legislation proposing the collection of motorist stop data. A federal bill (H.R. 118) requiring that the Department of Justice conduct a study of racial profiling was referred to the Senate, but no action has been taken.

INDEX

A

academics, 38
acceptance, 33, 34
access, 5, 38, 89, 100, 146
accumulation, 116
accuracy, 15, 68, 77, 84, 93, 97, 98, 121, 132
administrators, 5, 90
adults, 37, 61, 94
affect, ix, 3, 5, 48, 57, 77, 95, 123, 132
African Americans, 66, 72, 73, 114, 115, 121, 125, 126, 127, 128, 129, 152
age, 17, 37, 43, 50, 69, 73, 79, 81, 94, 100, 108, 112, 114, 115, 118, 120, 128, 131, 144, 145, 146
agent, 14, 17, 52
alcohol, 10, 11, 39
alternative, 22, 72, 93, 123
anger, 35
appendix, 114, 118, 121, 122, 124, 141, 153
argument, 6, 7, 9, 36
arrest, 5, 7, 15, 16, 27, 28, 34, 35, 38, 39, 45, 53, 63, 64, 66, 67, 69, 70, 75, 83, 89, 94, 102, 104, 118, 120, 125, 143, 144, 145, 146
Asian Americans, 152
assault, 44, 52, 69
assessment, 123
assignment, 120, 144
assumptions, viii, 27, 41, 47, 51, 123
attacks, 2, 6, 8, 42, 45, 54
attention, vii, 1, 12, 29, 31, 36, 46, 55, 94, 104, 132
attitudes, ix, 36, 57
Attorney General, vii, ix, 2, 12, 13, 14, 15, 16, 17, 18, 35, 41, 42, 47, 58, 64, 82, 85, 86, 93, 101, 106, 111, 122
auditing, 83, 84, 91, 98, 113
authority, ix, 39, 58, 111
automobiles, 129
awareness, 18

B

baggage, 33
barriers, 89
beams, 151
behavior, vii, 1, 2, 7, 19, 60, 66, 73, 80, 84, 94, 98, 101, 111, 151
benchmarks, 17, 78, 99, 100, 101, 123, 129, 130
bias, 12, 35, 82, 86, 112, 117, 127
birth, 83, 94, 142
bleeding, 86
blocks, 124
body, 20, 63
bonds, 19, 74
border crossing, 118, 142
breakdown, 99
Britain, 90

C

carbon, 87
Caribbean, 88
cast, 123
catalyst, 28, 59
categorization, 96
Census, 26
channels, 70
citizenship, 17
civil liberties, 60
civil rights, ix, 3, 7, 18, 57, 58, 82
classification, 48, 51
cocaine, 82
colleges, 98
commitment, 4, 80, 145
communication, 83, 92

D

E

S

T

U

V

W

Y